Schriften zum Internationalen
und Europäischen Strafrecht

Edited by

Volume 83

Claudia Cárdenas Aravena | Kai Cornelius
Milan Kuhli | Juan Pablo Mañalich Raffo [eds.]

Enforced Disappearances

Current Debates in Comparative and International Law

DIKE

Nomos

Onlineversion
Inlibra

The Deutsche Nationalbibliothek lists this publication in the Deutsche Nationalbibliografie; detailed bibliographic data are available on the Internet at http://dnb.d-nb.de

ISBN (Print) 978-3-7560-0131-6 (Nomos Verlagsgesellschaft mbH & Co. KG, Baden-Baden)

ISBN (ePDF) 978-3-7489-4738-7 (Nomos Verlagsgesellschaft mbH & Co. KG, Baden-Baden)

ISBN (Print) 978-3-03891-896-7 (Dike Verlag, Zürich/St. Gallen)

1st Edition 2026

Preface

This volume addresses the phenomenon of systematic disappearance of human beings committed as a means of violent rule by government authorities, or at least with their approval, to deal with internal and external conflicts. The issue led the editors to convene experts to make contributions to this collective volume, which deals with relevant cases and cross-cutting topics. The contributors include scholars and legal experts with a background in transitional justice and international and comparative criminal law. They represent different legal systems and traditions including those of Argentina, Brazil, Chile, Germany, Mexico, South Africa, Türkiye, and Ukraine. Drafts of the chapters were presented at a conference in June 2024. The conference was hosted by Universität Hamburg and it was convened by the editors.

We are indebted to Andrea Hearst, who provided invaluable support by language editing the volume. We are also grateful to our colleague Prof. Dr. Markus Kotzur for chairing a conference panel. Dilyara Adil, Dinah Cassebaum, and Charlotte Viktoria Kallien helped with the management of the conference and the copyediting of the manuscripts. We are also grateful to Universität Hamburg and to Universidad de Chile (Santiago de Chile) for providing funding for both the originating conference and this volume. Furthermore, we would like to thank the Nomos-Verlag for publishing this volume. Anke Tröltzsch did an excellent job throughout the production process.

Santiago and Hamburg
July 2025
Claudia Cárdenas, Kai Cornelius,
Milan Kuhli, and Juan Pablo Mañalich R.

Contents

List of Abbreviations

Abl. / KR Dtl. – Amtsblatt des Kontrollrates in Deutschland / Official Gazette of the Control Council in Germany

AC – Appeal Cases

ACHR – American Convention on Human Rights

ADPCP – Anuario de Derecho Penal y Ciencias Penales

Advoc Q – The Advocates' Quarterly

AFIS – Automated Fingerprint Identification System

AJIL – American Journal of International Law

Ala – Alabama Reports

Alberta L Rev – Alberta Law Review

All ER – All England Law Reports

ALR – Administrative Law Review

ALR – American Law Reports

Alternative L J – Alternative Law Journal

AMLO – Andrés Manuel López Obrador

ANC – African National Congress

ARSP – Archiv für Rechts- und Sozialphilosophie

Art. – Artikel / article

BeckRS – Beck-Rechtsprechung

BeZG – Bezirksgericht / District Court

BGBl. – Bundesgesetzblatt / Federal Law Gazette

BGH – Bundesgerichtshof / German Federal Court of Justice

BGH GS – Großer Senat des Bundesgerichtshof / Joint Senate of the German Federal Court of Justice

BGHSt – Entscheidungen des Bundesgerichtshofes in Strafsachen / Criminal Cases of the German Federal Court of Justice

BJCLCJ – Bergen Journal of Criminal Law & Criminal Justice

BT – Besonderer Teil

BT-Drs. – Bundestagdrucksachen; Documents of the German Bundestag

BVerfG – Bundesverfassungsgericht; German Federal Constitutional Court

Case W Rsrv L Rev – Case Western Reserve Law Review

Case W. Res. J. Int'l L. – Case Western Reserve Journal of International Law

Cato J – Cato Journal

CCL – Control Council Law
CCP – Code of Criminal Procedure
CDU / CSU – Christian Democratic Union of Germany / Christian Social Union in Bavaria
CED – Committee on Enforced Disappearance
Cf. – compare
Chs. – chapters
CIE - Centro de Inteligência do Exército / Army Intelligence Center
CNB – National Search Commission
CNDH – National Human Rights Commission
CNI – Central Nacional de Informaciones / National Information Centre
CNPPT – Comisión Nacional sobre Prisión Política y Tortura / National Commission on Political Imprisonment and Torture
CNV - Comissão Nacional da Verdade / National Truth Commission
CNVR – Comisión Nacional de Verdad y Reconciliación / Chilean National Truth and Reconciliation Commission
Colum. L. Rev. – Columbia Law Review
CONADEP – Comisión Nacional sobre la Desaparición de Personas
Cons – consideration
CSCL – Corte Suprema de Justicia de Chile

DINA – Dirección de Inteligencia Nacional / National Intelligence Directorate
DJZ – Deutsche Juristen-Zeitung
DOI-CODI – Information Operation Detachment – Internal Defence Operations Centre
Dops – Political and Social Order Departments
DPF - Departamento de Polícia Federal / Federal Police Department
DtZ – Deutsch-Deutsche Rechts-Zeitschrift
Duke L J – Duke Law Journal

EAC – European Advisory Commission
ECCC – Extraordinary Chambers in the Courts of Cambodia
ECHR – European Convention on Human Rights
EcommHR – European Commission of Human Rights
ECtHR – European Court of Human Rights
EEAF – Argentine Forensic Anthropology Team
EGStGB – Einführungsgesetz zum Strafgesetzbuch / Introductory Act to the German Criminal Code
EJIL – European Journal of International Law
ELR – Erasmus Law Review

ESG – Escola Superior de Guerra
EU – European Union

F2d – Federal Reporter, Second Series
FAFG – Guatemalan Forensic Anthropology Foundation
FRJ – Fraudulent res judicata

GA – Goltdammer's Archiv für Strafrecht
GDR – German Democratic Republic
GG – Grundgesetz / German Constitution
GLJ – German Law Journal
GULAG – Glavnoe Upravlenie Lagerei (System of forced labor camps in the Soviet Union)
GVG – Gerichtsverfassungsgesetz

Harv L Rev – Harvard Law Review
HCA – High Court of Australia
HHRJ – Harvard Human Rights Journal

IACtHR – Inter-American Court of Human Rights
Ibid – ibidem
ICC – International Criminal Court
ICCPR – International Covenant on Civil and Political Rights
ICL – International Criminal Law
ICMP – International Commission on Missing Persons
ICRC – International Committee of the Red Cross
ICTR – International Criminal Tribunal for Rwanda
ICTY – International Criminal Tribunal for the former Yugoslavia
IJTJ – The International Journal of Transitional Justice
IDH – Human Identification Programme
IFP – Inkatha Freedom Party
IGPM – General Inspectorate of Military Police
ILC – International Law Commission
IMT – International Military Tribunal
IMTFE – International Military Tribunal for the Far East
InDret – Indret: Revista para el Análisis del Derecho
INE – National Voter Registry / National Electoral Institute
IP – Ius et Praxis

JA – Juristische Arbeitsblätter
JCLC – Journal of Criminal Law and Criminology
JCS – Revista de Derecho y Jurisprudencia y Ciencias Sociales.
JICJ – Journal of International Criminal Justice JIPIT – Journal of International Political Theory
JOB – Judicial Officers Bulletin
JuS Juristische Schulung
JZ – JuristenZeitung

KJ – Kritische Justiz
KPD – Kommunistische Partei Deutschlands / Communist Party of Germany
KritV – Kritische Vierteljahresschrift für Gesetzgebung und Rechtswissenschaft

L&S – Langage et Société
LALS – Latin American Legal Studies
LaP – Law and Philosophy
Law of the German Federal Court of Justice in Criminal Law
Law Soc Rev – Law and Society Review
LG – Landgericht / District Court
LJIL – Leiden Journal of International Law
LRTWC – Law Reports of Trials of War Criminals
LSI – Law & Social Inquiry

MEIF – Extraordinary Forensic Identification Mechanism
MIR – Movimiento de Izquierda Revolucionaria / Revolutionary Left Movement
MLR – Missouri Law Review
Mod. L. Rev. – The Modern Law Review
MPTT – Missing Persons Task Team

Neb – Nebraska Reports
New Zealand L Rev – New Zealand Law Review
NJ – Neue Justiz
NJLP – Netherlands Journal of Legal Philosophy
NJW – Neue Juristische Wochenschrift
NKVD – Soviet People's Commissariat for Internal Affairs
NN – Nacht und Nebel / Night and Fog
NPA – National Prosecuting Authority
NStZ – Neue Zeitschrift für Strafrecht
NStZ-RR – Neue Zeitschrift für Strafrecht-Rechtsprechungs-Report
NSWLR – New South Wales Law Reports
NWU L Rev – Northwestern University Law Review

NYU L Rev – New York University Law Review
NZLR – New Zealand Law Reports

OAS – Organization of American States
OGHSt – Amtliche Sammlung der Entscheidungen des Obersten Gerichtshofes für die Britische Zone / Official collection of the judgments and decisions of the Supreme Court of the British zone
OHCHR – Office of the United Nations High Commissioner for Human Rights
OKW – Oberkommando der Wehrmacht
OTP – Office of the Prosecutor (at the International Criminal Court)
Oxf J Leg Stud – Oxford Journal of Legal Studies

PAC – Pan Africanist Congress of Azania
PFnR - unclaimed deceased person
PFsI – unidentified deceased person
PKK – Kurdish Workers Party
Polit. crim. – Politica Criminal
Punishm Soc – Punishment & Society

QB – Queens Bench
QBD – Queens Bench Division

RChD – Revista Chilena de Derecho
REJ – Revista de Estudios de la Justicia
Rev. derecho (Valdivia) – Revista de Derecho (Valdivia)
Rev. derecho penal criminol. – Revista Derecho Penal y Criminología
Rev. mex. cienc. polít. soc. – Revista mexicana de ciencias políticas y sociales
RGBl. – Reichsgesetzblatt / Imperial Law Gazette
RIAS – Radio in the American Sector
RIDPP – Rivista Italiana di Diritto e Procedura Penale
RIS – Revista Internacional de Sociología
RNPDNO – National Registry of Missing and Unlocated Persons
RStGB – Reichsstrafgesetzbuch / Criminal Code of the German Empire
RW – Rechtswissenschaft – Zeitschrift für rechtswissenschaftliche Forschung

S Carolina L Rev – South Carolina Law Review
San Diego L Rev – San Diego Law Review
SBZ – Sowjetische Besatzungszone / Soviet zone of occupation
SCOTUS – Supreme Court of the United States
SCSL – Special Court for Sierra Leone
SED – Sozialistische Einheitspartei Deutschlands / Socialist Unity Party of Germany

SINPEF – National Information System of Missing and Deceased Persons
SJZ – Süddeutsche Juristen-Zeitung
SMT – Soviet military tribunal
SMU L Rev – Southern Methodist University Law Review
SNI – National Information Service
SPD – Sozialdemokratische Partei Deutschlands / Social Democratic Party of Germany
StA – Staatsanwaltschaft / German public prosecution
State Ct J – State Court Journal
StGB – Strafgesetzbuch / German Criminal Code
StPO – Strafprozessordnung / German Code of Criminal Procedure

TCC – Turkish Criminal Code
Temp L Rev – Temple Law Review
Touro L Rev – Touro Law Review
TRC - (Southafrican) Truth and Reconciliation Commission

U Balt L Rev – University of Baltimore Law Review
UK – United Kingdom
UN – United Nations
UNB L J – University of New Brunswick Law Journal
UNFPA – United Nations Population Fund
Univ. Chic. Law Rev. – University of Chicago Law Review
UNWCC – UN War Crime Commission
UNWGEID – Working Group on Enforced or Involuntary Disappearance
US – United States (of America)

Va L Rev – Virginia Law Review
Vanderbilt j. transnatl. Law – Vanderbilt Journal of Transnational Law
VIZ – Zeitschrift für Vermögens- und Immobilienrecht
VStGB – German Code of Crimes Against International Law

ZaöRV – Zeitschrift für ausländisches öffentliches Recht und Völkerrecht
ZAP-Ost – Zeitschrift für die Anwaltspraxis-Ost
ZIS – Zeitschrift für internationale Strafrechtsdogmatik
ZJS – Zeitschrift für das juristische Studium
ZStW – Zeitschrift für die gesamte Strafrechtswissenschaft

Introduction

Milan Kuhli

1. The Schubart Case - a Historical Example

The phenomenon of systematic disappearances of human beings has been and continues to be used as a means of violent rule by government authorities, or at least with their approval, to deal with internal and external conflicts. Sad to say, we can find examples of this phenomenon in various parts of the world and at many different times of history.

At this point, we might have a look at a special case from German history which took place 250 years ago: the case of Christian Friedrich Daniel Schubart,[1] a political journalist. He lived in the south of Germany in the late 18th century, where, in 1774, he began to publish the journal, 'Deutsche Chronik' (*German Chronicle*). Before long, Schubart behaved in a way which likely did not amuse Carl Eugen, the Duke of Württemberg. In addition to critique of princes, which was disguised in the form of animal fables, Schubart's explicit denunciation of the feudal trade in soldiers was also apparent. Furthermore, he reviled Franziska von Hohenheim, the Duke's mistress. The Duke thus pursued a plan to keep Schubart quiet. However, the problem was that Schubart was not in the territory of Württemberg at this time. So, the Duke made use of a trick: he invited the journalist to Württemberg in 1777 and ordered Schubart's arrest after the journalist had crossed the border. Schubart was then taken to a fortress without any information regarding the reason for or the duration of his detention. It was only many years later that the prisoner was allowed to receive a visit from his family.

Schubart was first released in 1787, more than ten years after his imprisonment. In all this time, no legal proceedings were ever conducted. In the late 18th century, many German emperors claimed the power to imprison

1 The following explanation of the Schubart case is based on Kuhli 2024, 37 et seqq.; see also Warneken 2020, 31, 33–4; Myers 2007, 602 et seqq.; Streitberger 2001, 76, 82, 95; Ollinger 1997, 309, 315 et seq., 331; Walter 1987, 309–11.

their subjects.[2] Efforts to secure the release of detainees were therefore largely outside the existing legal sphere. Far-reaching legal regulation of arrests was yet to come in Germany.

2. Characteristics and Challenges of Enforced Disappearances

The Schubart case shows many aspects that are still important today for a scientific examination of the issue of enforced disappearances. In particular, this applies to the methods of secrecy and denial, which are significant in various respects: not only are people deliberately abducted and detained, often without any form of trial or official charge, but methods of secrecy and denial are also used to conceal responsibility. External third parties remain in the dark about the whereabouts of the abducted persons, which leads to fear and insecurity, especially among close relatives. This climate of fear thus created in a society is often aimed at suppressing dissidence and eliminating opposition. These dimensions, which make various people victims of enforced disappearance, are described by Julia Geneuss and Florian Jeßberger in this anthology as follows:

> The victim of enforced disappearance is, first and foremost, the individual who disappears. However, their family and relatives as well as the social environment often endure years, or even decades, of uncertainty and distress following the disappearance. Moreover, trust in state institutions can erode, either because the authorities themselves are involved in the disappearance or because they are unable to ascertain the whereabouts or fate of the disappeared person.[3]

As Rocío Lorca points out in this anthology, 'enforced disappearance is a 'concentric' type of crime, in the sense that its target is not only the person who is disappeared by state agents, but also his or her family and the public at large, who are diminished, intimidated and demobilised by this event.'[4] Considering these dimensions from a legal perspective, it is challenging to adequately capture the full scope of the legal interest violated by enforced disappearances and the offence of enforced disappearances. On

2 In addition, Ollinger points out that arrests and deprivations of liberty without justification and without any review of legality were perceived as unlawful and arbitrary (Ollinger 1997, 334).

3 Geneuss/Jeßberger in this anthology, 186.

4 Lorca in this anthology, 247 et seq.

a broader level, the large number of affected dimensions poses a challenge for the question of whether and to what extent it is possible to respond appropriately to the phenomenon of enforced disappearances.

3. *On the Contributions in the Anthology*

This anthology consists of thirteen contributions, which are dedicated to country reports and experiences respective to cross-cutting topics in regards to enforced disappearances.

3.1 Country Reports and Experiences

Several of the contributions of this anthology are dedicated to the historical developments as well as the respective methods and practices of systematic enforced disappearances. These country reports focus – from the early 20th century to the present day – on Latin America, Europe and selected examples in Asia and Africa. The contributions both contain an empirical overview and provide country-specific answers to the question of whether one or more distinguishable legal models have been or are being used to deal with the phenomenon of systematic disappearances. In detail, the articles deal with the following countries, which are listed here in alphabetical order:

- *Argentina:* Leandro Dias points out in his contribution that enforced disappearance was the main tool used by the military government that held *de facto* power in Argentina between 1976 and 1983. According to Dias, it is 'not surprising that the crime of enforced disappearance is currently regulated in considerable detail in Argentine criminal law.'[5] Specifically, Argentina has followed a path of double criminalisation: on the one hand, this country has criminalised the practice of enforced disappearance as a crime against humanity. On the other hand, the Argentine legislature has criminalised cases of 'isolated' enforced disappearance since 2011 as a separate domestic offence that can be committed even in democratic regimes that broadly respect human rights.[6]

5 Dias in this anthology, 26.
6 Dias in this anthology, 36.

- *Brazil:* Antonio Martins' article presents an overview of the political context that served as a backdrop for cases of enforced disappearance during the Brazilian civil-military dictatorship and the main characteristics of transitional justice in Brazil. In this regard, Martins emphasises the efforts to both identify (e.g., the recognition of the death of all those accused of participating in political activities between 1961 and 1988 and who had disappeared) and remedy enforced disappearances. Although Brazil was ordered by the Inter-American Court of Human Rights to make enforced disappearance an autonomous offense, this criminalization in domestic criminal law has not yet been achieved.[7]
- *Chile:* Javier Contesse's report traces the problem of enforced disappearances back to the phenomenon of disappeared detainees (*detenidos desaparecidos*) during the civil-military dictatorship of Augusto Pinochet, placing the problem in a broader historical context. Uncertainty about the whereabouts of the disappeared became the background of the systematic violations of human rights until the end of this dictatorship. According to Contesse, it 'is therefore no coincidence that one of the first measures adopted by the first democratic government after the end of the dictatorial regime in March 1990, under the presidency of Patricio Aylwin, was the creation of a commission to establish the truth about the crimes committed by Pinochet's regime.'[8] In terms of criminal law, enforced disappearance in Chile is currently only a crime against humanity.[9] However, there is a draft bill under discussion in the Chilean Congress which argues for the criminalization of enforced disappearance as an 'ordinary' offence. Juan Pablo Mañalich assesses this draft bill in detail in this anthology.[10]
- *German* history provides various examples of enforced disappearances. In this anthology, Kai Cornelius examines the mass phenomenon in 20th century Germany beginning with the Nazi regime's 'Night and Fog Decree' and its processing in the Nuremberg Trials through the Allied internment camps to the special camps in the Soviet Occupation Zone. Particular attention is paid to the impact of these events on the constitutionally guaranteed obligation to notify in cases of deprivation of liberty,

7 Martins in this anthology, 48 et seqq.
8 Contesse in this anthology, 68.
9 Contesse in this anthology, 71.
10 Mañalich in this anthology, 175 et seqq.

especially within the context of pretrial detention.[11] In terms of substantial criminal law, in 2024 a new offense of 'enforced disappearance of persons' was added to the German Criminal Code, which is assessed in detail in Julia Geneuss' and Florian Jeßberger's contribution to this anthology.[12]

- *Mexico:* Rocío Yoguez & Maximilian Murck provide a comprehensive analysis of the situation of disappearances and unidentified deceased individuals in Mexico, focusing on the technological advancements and international cooperation efforts for human identification. With this regard, the authors emphasize the crucial role of fingerprint analysis in Mexico as a key strategy in this endeavour.[13]
- *South Africa:* As Gerhard Kemp points out, enforced disappearance was a key feature of the State's efforts to suppress resistance during apartheid in South Africa. It remains part of the unfinished business of dealing with the past in post-apartheid South Africa. The country's ratification of both the Apartheid Convention and the Enforced Disappearance Convention that took place in 2024 points to renewed efforts to align South African law and policy with the international legal frameworks aimed at combating systemic crimes including enforced disappearance.[14]
- *Türkiye:* In her article, Burcu Yaşar addresses the movement of the so-called 'Saturday Mothers' (also referred to as 'Saturday People') that began their weekly sit-ins in Galatasaray Square in Istanbul in 1995 to demand the investigation of the fate and whereabouts of people who were forcibly disappeared after the military coup in the 1980s and the state of emergency of the 1990s. Yaşar focuses on the case law of the European Court of Human Rights that became the first judicial forum to uncover the enforced disappearances in Türkiye in the 1990s. Turkish law has undergone profound changes since the beginning of the century, providing a strengthened legal framework for the prevention and punishment of enforced disappearances. In terms of substantial law, the most notable development has been the enactment of international crimes despite some discrepancies with the international framework. In practice, however, the new crimes found no application in cases of enforced disappearances or any other past crime cases. Furthermore, the non-criminali-

11 Cornelius in this anthology, 81.
12 Geneuss and Jeßberger in this anthology, 185.
13 Yoguez and Murck in this anthology, 101 et seqq.
14 Kemp in this anthology, 119 et seqq.

sation of enforced disappearance as a distinct crime remains a significant obstacle to accountability for enforced disappearances.[15]

- *Ukraine:* As Denys Shylin points out, the problem of enforced disappearances has acquired a new meaning for Ukraine due to the ongoing armed conflict in its territory. Since 2014, following the occupation of the Crimean Peninsula and the armed confrontation within certain districts in the Donetsk and Luhansk regions, law enforcement agencies of Ukraine have recorded cases of disappearances and detentions of persons in the territory controlled by the Russian Federation. However, at the same time, there is also the risk that enforced disappearances can be committed by the Ukrainian authorities. Against this background, Shylin analyses the historical genesis of the recognition of enforced disappearance as a crime against humanity.[16]

3.2 Legal and Extra-Legal Response Possibilities

One of the anthology's purposes is to assess how the phenomenon of enforced disappearances is, and ought to be, responded to - this is a question which is addressed in most of the above-mentioned country reports. The assessment concerns legal approaches[17] and instruments but it should also shed light on the broader level of extra-legal response possibilities including the involvement of civil societies.

As we can see in the country reports, conceivable legal models include especially repressive approaches (such as substantive criminal law solutions[18]), but also preventive approaches (such as procedural solutions in the form of strict judicial reservations and notification obligations[19]). In terms of criminal law approaches, a basic distinction can be made between three offences - crimes against humanity under international or under domestic law and stand-alone crimes under domestic law. However, as can be shown

15 Yaşar in this anthology, 135 et seqq.

16 Shylin in this anthology, 159 et seqq.

17 E.g., Mañalich in this anthology, 175 et seqq.; Geneuss and Jeßberger in this anthology, 185 et seqq.

18 E.g., in corresponding reform proposals in Chile (see Mañalich in this anthology, 175 et seqq.) or in the UN Convention against Enforced Disappearances or in the form of the offense of crimes against humanity under international criminal law in accordance with Art. 7 para. 1 lit. i ICC Statute

19 E.g., currently in Germany as a safeguard against state violence; see Cornelius in this anthology, 81 et seqq.

in the country-reports, not every domestic law criminalises enforced disappearances as a stand-alone crime.

Even if a state criminalises enforced disappearances, it seems evident that the various legal approaches reach their limits within the given state due to their dependence on a functioning judicial system based on the rule of law. In countries where systematic enforced disappearances occur frequently there is often a lack of such a system. This makes the international legal dimension and extra-legal approaches all the more important, which is why attention should also be paid to them. With regard to the international criminal law perspective, Aziz Epik takes a look at the crime of enforced disappearances as crime against humanity under the ICC Statute.[20] Furthermore, Claudia Cárdenas addresses human rights questions: since enforced disappearance encompasses both a crime and a violation of human rights, due to the involvement of the state power, international legal instruments on the matter often address both criminal and human rights issues. With regard to the latter, Cárdenas takes a look at 'two robust regional tribunals', the Inter-American Court of Human Rights and the European Court of Human Rights.[21]

On a broader level, Rocío Lorca addresses the harm and the political significance of enforced disappearances.

> She argues 'that the harms of enforced disappearance can only be adequately understood by focusing both on what the practice destroys, i.e. identities, and on what the practice seeks to create, i.e. a new kind of political agency. The destructive dimension of these crimes provides grounds for recognising the relatives of the disappeared as direct victims and the denial of information as a way of perpetuating the crime. The constitutive dimension of the crime helps to understand why the public search for the disappeared is such a crucial condition for a genuine recovery of our democracies.'[22]

It should be obvious that both the political and legal responses to enforced disappearances are facing significant challenges. In terms of legal responses, this concerns the question of which specific types of behaviour should

20 Article 7 (1) (i) ICC Statute; Epik in this anthology, 227 et seqq.; see also Shylin in this anthology, 159 et seqq. with regard to the Ukraine.

21 Cárdenas in this anthology, 209 et seqq.; see also Yaşar, 135 et seqq. with regard to Türkiye.

22 Lorca in this anthology, 241.

be punishable. In this respect, Dias addresses the issue of initially lawful detentions that become unlawful over time.[23] A further challenge arises from the prohibition of retroactivity under criminal law - an issue that is addressed by several contributions in the anthology[24] and that often arises when a society is criminally charged with past unjust regimes. However, it should be obvious that dealing with the past is not only a criminal law issue. It is a multi-dimensional task that requires a willingness to search. Again, from Lorca:

> The relevant search is not primarily or exclusively the search for the body. We will probably never find most of them, but we must still search and try to reconstruct the history of the person after his or her abduction. By searching and trying to know more, the state redefines itself and restores the democratic political relationship [...].[25]

Bibliography

Kuhli, Milan. 2024. 'Schubart und Wekhrlin in Haft. Zur Rechtsgeschichte landesherrlicher Verhaftungen im späten 18. Jahrhundert'. In Bickhoff, Nicole, Mährle, Wolfgang, and Potthast, Barbara (eds.). *Die Geburt des modernen Journalismus: Christian Friedrich Daniel Schubart und Wilhelm Ludwig Wekhrlin*. Stuttgart: Anton Hiersemann Verlag. 37–48.

Myers, Michael. 2007. 'Schubart, Christian'. *Neue Deutsche Biographie (Onlinefassung)*. 23. 602–3. URL: https://www.deutsche-biographie.de/pnd118610953.html (accessed 17 October 2022).

Ollinger, Thomas. 1997. *Die Entwicklung des Richtervorbehalts im Verhaftungsrecht von den Anfängen bis zur Paulskirchenverfassung*. Berlin: Duncker & Humblot.

Streitberger, Fritz. 2001. *Der Freiheit eine Gasse. Die Lebensgeschichte des Christian Friedrich Daniel Schubart*. Bietigheim: Salzer.

Walter, Jürgen. 1987. *Carl Eugen von Württemberg. Ein Herzog und seine Untertanen. Biographie*. Irdning/Steiermark: Stieglitz.

Warneken, Bernd Jürgen. 2020. 'Ein Kritiker feudaler Willkür. Christian Friedrich Schubart'. In Haller, Michael and Hömberg, Walter (eds.). *»Ich lass mir den Mund nicht verbieten!« Journalisten als Wegbereiter der Pressefreiheit und Demokratie*. Stuttgart: Reclam. 31–5.

---

23 Dias in this anthology, 25 et seqq.; see also Epik in this anthology, 227 et seqq.

24 E.g., Kemp in this anthology, 119 et seqq.; Yaşar in this anthology, 135 et seqq.; Contesse in this anthology, 65 et seqq.

25 Lorca in this anthology, 254 et seq.

Part 1:
Country Reports and Experiences

The Criminalisation of Enforced Disappearances in Argentina

Leandro Dias[*]

Abstract: Regarding enforced disappearances, Argentina has followed a path of double criminalisation. On the one hand, Argentina has criminalised the practice of enforced disappearance as a crime against humanity under international customary law and under Article 7(1)(i) of the ICC Statute. On the other hand, the Argentine legislature has criminalised cases of 'isolated' enforced disappearance as a separate domestic offence that can be committed even in democratic regimes that broadly respect human rights. While this legislative move is not so novel today, as other countries, such as Germany, have done roughly the same thing, Argentina did this more than a decade ago. In this paper, I analyse the Argentinian experience to see if we can learn something useful for other countries. I highlight the problems that this kind of criminal policy create and show possible ways of dealing with them.

1. The Double Criminalisation of Enforced Disappearance in Argentina

The history of the offence of enforced disappearance of persons as a core crime is closely linked to Argentina. Defined as 'situations in which people take other people into their power and conceal, hide or disguise this fact, as well as the whereabouts and fate of these people, from third parties, even when asked,'[1] enforced disappearance was the main tool used by the military government that held de facto power in Argentina between 1976 and 1983.[2] Members of the military would kidnap a person suspected of

* I would like to thank Claudia Cárdenas, Alejandro Chehtman, Natalia Luterstein and Ana Clara Rivero for their valuable feedback on earlier drafts of this paper. I would also like to thank the conference participants at the University of Hamburg whose contributions made this book possible and provided valuable insights. Any omissions or mistakes are, of course, my responsibility.

1 Jeßberger/Geneuss 2024, 96 (translation made by the author) with further references.

2 See Hasan 2014, 153; Malarino 2009, 5; see also Weissbrodt/Bartolomei 1991, 1010: 'the most prevalent form of human rights abuse'.

being part of the ideological and political opposition, take them to a secret detention centre where they would be subjected to inhumane treatment that could lead to death and then not inform the relatives of the kidnapped person's fate.[3] This led to the famous report of the Inter-American Commission on Human Rights on the 'problem of the disappeared'[4] and Argentina's intensive participation in the subsequent development of enforced disappearance as an international crime.

It is therefore not surprising that Argentina is now a party to the three main international treaties on enforced disappearance: the Inter-American Convention on Enforced Disappearance,[5] the International Convention for the Protection of All Persons from Enforced Disappearance,[6] and the Rome Statute of the International Criminal Court.[7] In fact, Argentina was the driving force behind this entire regulatory movement, and one of its main protagonists.[8] It is also not surprising that the crime of enforced disappearance is currently regulated in considerable detail in Argentine criminal law. In fact, Argentina currently has a double criminalisation of the crime of enforced disappearance. On the one hand, this conduct has been criminalized as a 'classic'[9] core crime in Argentine domestic law since the ratification of the Rome Statute and the enactment of Act No. 26200 on the implementation of the Rome Statute on 13 December 2006. In other words, Argentine domestic international criminal law fully reflects the ICC Statute's regulation of enforced disappearance as a crime against humanity. This refers, of course, to Argentine (domestic) legislation on international criminal law. However, customary international law is also di-

3 See Chehtman 2024, 64; Malarino 2009, 6; for an overview of how this practice took place in most Latin America, see Dulitzky 2019, 432–39.

4 Inter-American Commission on Human Rights, Report on the Situation of Human Rights in Argentina, OEA/Ser.L/V/II.49, doc. 19, 11 April 1980.

5 Adopted by the OAS General Assembly on 9 July 1994, approved by Act No. 24556 and published in the Official Gazette on 11 October 1995 (entered into force internationally on 28 March 1996) with constitutional hierarchy from Act No. 24820 of May 29, 1997.

6 Adopted by the UN General Assembly on 20 December 2006, approved by Act No. 26298 and published in the Official Gazette on 30 November 2007 (entered into force internationally on 23 December 2010).

7 Adopted on 17 July 1998 during the United Nations Diplomatic Conference of Plenipotentiaries on the Establishment of an International Criminal Court (entered into force internationally on 1 July 2002), approved by Act No. 26200 and published in the Official Gazette on January 9, 2007.

8 For an overview, see Ambos/Böhm 2009, 218–19, especially fn. 74.

9 See Grammer 2005, 15.

rectly applicable law in Argentina through the interpretation of Articles 116, 117 and 118 of the Argentine Constitution.[10] If we consider the international rules that criminalise enforced disappearance as customary international law, then these customary rules can also be applied in court. Indeed, the Inter-American Court of Human Rights[11] has ruled that the prohibition of enforced disappearance and the obligation to investigate and punish it constitute a peremptory norm of customary law (jus cogens).[12] We will set this question aside because domestic legislation that criminalises enforced disappearance as a crime against humanity has the same content as the ICC Statute's provisions. This makes reference to customary law somewhat superfluous nowadays.[13] Of course, one cannot deny that there may be differences between the customary rules on enforced disappearance and the Argentine legislation on the same matter.

On the other hand, in 2011, the Argentine legislature criminalised enforced disappearance as a stand-alone crime under domestic law, through the enactment of Law No. 26679.[14] In a landmark legislative move, this crime can be committed even if the usual contextual elements of a crime against humanity are absent. To commit the crime of enforced disappearance in Argentina, it is not necessary to carry out a widespread or systematic attack against the civilian population. Indeed, this offence can be committed in isolation within a broadly legitimate democratic regime in Argentina. To put things in context, the German legislature did roughly the same thing in 2024, more than a decade later.[15]

The following sections will analyse this double criminalisation approach: both the criminalisation of enforced disappearance as a crime against humanity (section 2) and the criminalisation of enforced disappearance as a stand-alone domestic offence (section 3). I will then highlight some of the main problems posed by this double criminalisation and offer some

10 See Chehtman/Espósito 2023, section 2; Pinto/Maisley 2024 (119, 123–5).

11 See e.g. IACtHR, Caso Goiburú y otros vs. Paraguay. Fondo, Reparaciones y Costas, 22 September 2006, para. 84; Caso Masacres de Río Negro vs. Guatemala. Excepción Preliminar, Fondo, Reparaciones y Costas, 4 September 2012, para. 227.

12 See also Cançado Trindade 2012, 532–4.

13 Of course, it was not superfluous to apply international customary law when punishing crimes committed during Argentina's latest dictatorship. More on this later in the paper.

14 On this so-called 'sporadic' or 'isolated' commission of enforced disappearance see also Grammer, 2005, 16; Jeßberger/Geneuss 2024, 96; Raube 2024, 285.

15 For an overview, see Jeßberger/Geneuss 2024, 102–4.; Raube 2024, 285 et seq.

possible solutions (section 4). Finally, I will offer a very brief conclusion (section 5).

Before doing so, a clarification is in order. Since Germany has recently finished a criminalisation process that led to the creation of a new offence of enforced disappearance, I will also compare the Argentinian legal framework with the new German one. However, this comparison will not be merely anecdotal, as I will also explain how some of the problems of interpretation that arose in Argentina do not arise in Germany, while others do, and perhaps the German public, and anyone else interested in the double criminalisation of enforced disappearance, can learn from the Argentinean experience.

2. Enforced Disappearance as a Crime Against Humanity

Let us start with the criminalisation of enforced disappearance as a classic crime against humanity. Until the enactment of Act No. 26200 on the Implementation of the Rome Statute on 13 December 2006, the Argentine legal system did not have a crime of enforced disappearance.[16] From that date, however, all the crimes of the Rome Statute became applicable law in Argentina.[17] Specifically, Article 2, paragraph 2, of Act No. 26200 states: 'The acts described in Articles 6, 7, 8 and 70 of the Rome Statute, as well as all the crimes and offences that will henceforth fall within the jurisdiction of the International Criminal Court, shall be punishable in the Argentine Republic in the manner provided by this Act'.[18] This reference to the relevant provisions of the Rome Statute confirms that the crime of enforced disappearance as a crime against humanity defined in art. 7(1)(i) and 7(2)(i) is now an integral part of the Argentine legal system:[19]

> Art. 7(1)(i): 1. For the purpose of this Statute, 'crime against humanity' means any of the following acts when committed as part of a widespread or systematic attack directed against any civilian population, with knowledge of the attack: [...] (i) Enforced disappearance of persons.
> Art. 7(2)(i): 2. For the purpose of paragraph 1: [...] (i) 'Enforced disappearance of persons' means the arrest, detention or abduction of persons

16 De Langhe 2023, 30 et seq.; Malarino 2009, 7.
17 De Langhe 2025, 572; Malarino 2009, 5 et seq.
18 Translation by Leandro Dias.
19 See also De Langhe 2023, 30.

> by, or with the authorization, support or acquiescence of, a State or a political organization, followed by a refusal to acknowledge that deprivation of freedom or to give information on the fate or whereabouts of those persons, with the intention of removing them from the protection of the law for a prolonged period of time.

Due to this full incorporation of the provisions of the ICC Statute in Argentina, both the case law of the International Criminal Court on this core crime and the academic discussions on the interpretation of its various elements are, in principle, relevant to Argentine courts. The decision to fully incorporate Art. 7(2)(i), however, may not have been the best idea. While it is widely accepted in international criminal law that the crime against humanity of enforced disappearance can be committed alternatively by depriving the victim of her liberty *or* by refusing to acknowledge her whereabouts (the so-called 'dualistic' model),[20] the wording of the ICC Statute does not reflect this understanding. The relevant source here is not the Rome Statute, but rather Article 7(1)(i) of the Elements of Crimes, which was adopted by the Assembly of States Parties in 2002:[21]

> Article 7 (1) (i)
> Crime against humanity of enforced disappearance of persons[...]
> Elements
> 1. The perpetrator:
> (a) Arrested, detained(25),(26) or abducted one or more persons; or
> (b) Refused to acknowledge the arrest, detention or abduction, or to give information on the fate or whereabouts of such person or persons.
> 2. (a) Such arrest, detention or abduction was followed or accompanied by a refusal to acknowledge that deprivation of freedom or to give information on the fate or whereabouts of such person or persons; or
> (b) Such refusal was preceded or accompanied by that deprivation of freedom.
> Footnote 25: The word 'detained' would include a perpetrator who maintained an existing detention.
> Footnote 26: It is understood that under certain circumstances an arrest or detention may have been lawful.

---

20 See e.g. Werle/Jeßberger 2020, margin no. 1101 et seq.
21 See also Jeßberger/Geneuss 2024, 98.

Although it would be perfectly possible to invoke the Elements of Crimes in Argentina by invoking Article 21(1)(a) of the ICC Statute,[22] it would have been better, and not only for aesthetic reasons, to formulate the offence alternatively in Law No. 26200. Since Article 22(2) of the ICC Statute obliges the interpreter to 'strictly' interpret the definition of the crimes, it would not be far-fetched to argue that both forms of commission should be interpreted as necessarily *cumulative* acts.[23] For this reason, the Argentine legislator should perhaps have adopted the German dualistic approach and regulated the crime against humanity of enforced disappearance as an alternative offence, taking into account the developments offered by the Elements of Crimes. By way of comparison, the German legislator has regulated this crime in the Code of Crimes against International Law as follows:[24]

> Code of Crimes against International Law
> (1) Whoever, as part of a widespread or systematic attack directed against any civilian population,
> [...]
> 7. causes a person's enforced disappearance, with the intention of removing them from the protection of the law for more than just a brief period of time,
> (a) by abducting that person on behalf of or with the approval of a State or a political organisation, or by otherwise severely depriving them of their physical liberty, without immediately providing truthful information on that person's fate and whereabouts, or
> (b) by refusing, on behalf of a State or a political organisation or in contravention of a legal duty, to provide information immediately on the fate and whereabouts of the person deprived of their physical liberty under

22 'Article 21. Applicable law
1. The Court shall apply:
(a) In the first place, this Statute, Elements of Crimes and its Rules of Procedure and Evidence; [...].'

23 We will discuss this 'unified' model of criminalisation in more detail later in this paper.

24 I use the translation made by Brian Duffett (revised by Jan Christoph Nemitz/Steffen Wirth) that can be found in the website of the Federal Ministry of Justice, available at: https://www.gesetze-im-internet.de/englisch_vstgb/index.html (accessed 15 December 2024).

> the circumstances referred to under letter (a) above, or by providing false information,
> [...]
> incurs a penalty of imprisonment for life in the cases referred to under nos. 1 and 2, imprisonment for a term of at least five years in the cases referred to under nos. 3 to 7, and imprisonment for a term of at least three years in the cases referred to under nos. 8 to 10.

With regard to punishment and sentencing, Act No. 26200 establishes a penalty of 3 to 25 years' imprisonment for all cases of crimes against humanity. Only in the case of the death of the victim is the penalty life imprisonment. This may raise some problems of interpretation due to the interaction of these penalties with the higher penalties that the Argentine legislator has established for the crime of enforced disappearance as a crime under domestic law. We will return to this issue later in this paper.

It should be noted that these provisions have only been in force on Argentine territory since the enactment of Act No. 26200 of 13 December 2006, or at the earliest since the entry into force of the Rome Statute on 1 July 2002, given that Argentina ratified the treaty on 8 February 2001 and that international treaties are considered self-executing in Argentina without the need for an express act of transposition into domestic law.[25] As mentioned in the introduction, prior to the incorporation of the Rome Statute into Argentine law, acts of enforced disappearance were committed as crimes against humanity during the latest military dictatorship. Several of these acts have been prosecuted in Argentina in the last three decades, especially after the annulment of the amnesties and pardons granted to various military officials in the 1980s and 1990s.[26]

The key question in this regard is how these acts have been punished, given that enforced disappearance was not criminalised as a crime against humanity or as a crime under domestic law at the time it was committed. As Article 18 of the Argentinian Constitution explicitly prohibits punishment for conduct that was not prohibited by law before the act was committed, the courts have largely[27] ruled that the prohibition of enforced

25 Ambos/Böhm 2009, 201; Malarino 2009, 8. For a detailed analysis, see Pinto/Maisley 2024, 120–1, especially the analysis of the 1992 Supreme Court decision 'Ekmekdjian v Sofovich' (Fallos 315:1492).

26 See only Chehtman 2024, 64 and passim; Filippini 2011, 22–40; Islas Colín 2015, 254–7; Malarino 2009, 8–24.

27 For a description of other paths taken by the courts, see Malarino 2009, 32–5.

disappearance constitutes a crime against humanity under customary international law.[28] This customary law is said to have existed since at least the 1970s,[29] i.e. before the crimes were committed.[30] The courts then determined whether the contextual elements of a crime against humanity were met in order to trigger the main consequence that such crimes have in Argentine law: the inapplicability of the statute of limitations.[31] Having established that the crime was committed in the context of a widespread or systematic attack by the State against the civilian population, the courts then analysed whether the perpetrator's conduct constituted a domestic offence under the Argentine Criminal Code.[32] In the absence of a crime of enforced disappearance, the classic crimes in force at the time of commission, such as kidnapping and homicide, were used as a proxy.[33] The range of sentences was also determined according to the equivalent domestic offence in question.[34]

However, in recent rulings,[35] Argentinian courts have decided to use the new stand-alone domestic crime to sentence individuals for crimes against humanity committed during the military dictatorship. The courts reached this conclusion by accepting the argument that enforced disappearance is a

---

28 This argument draws on Article 118 of the Argentinian Constitution, which makes a general reference to crimes against international law. However, this kind of argument has been criticised because the 'principle of legality', typical of civil law jurisdictions, generally requires legislation to be in writing for a punishment to be lawful rather than based on customary law. For a detailed analysis, see Montiel 2012, 399–414.

29 For criticism, see Malarino 2011, 381 et seq.

30 See Supreme Court of Argentina, 'Simón, Julio Héctor', Fallos 328:2056 (2005), Separate Opinion of Judge Maqueda, 62. See also Malarino 2009, 26, with a critique at 29.

31 See Supreme Court of Argentina, 'Simón, Julio Héctor', Fallos 328:2056 (2005), Separate Opinion of Judge Highton de Nolasco, 31. See also Malarino 2009, 25.

32 Malarino 2009, 25.

33 See e.g. Supreme Court of Argentina, 'Simón, Julio Héctor', Fallos 328:2056 (2005), Separate Opinion of Judge Zaffaroni, 31; Cámara Federal de Casación Penal, Sala IV, 14 November 2018, 'MENÉNDEZ, Luciano Benjamín y otros s/recurso de casación'; Tribunal Oral Federal de Bahía Blanca, Sala IV, 15 May 2017, 'Boccalari, Gustavo Abel s/ inf. Art. 144 ter 1° párrafo – según ley 14.616; inf. Art. 144 bis inc. 1 y último párrafo – según ley 14.616 en función del art. 142 inc. 1 – ley 20.642; homicidio agravado con ensañamiento-alevosía'. See also Malarino 2009, 32.

34 Malarino 2009, 32.

35 See e.g. Tribunal Oral Federal de Mendoza, 1 February 2018, 'Menéndez Sánchez, Luciano Benjamín y otros s/ privación ilegitima de la libertad (art. 144 bis inc. 1) e imposición de tormentos (art. 144 ter cp)'.

'continuous' (or, better: permanent) crime,[36] meaning that it was still being committed at the time of the judgement. As the new offence of enforced disappearance, as defined in Article 142ter of the Penal Code, was in force at the time of the judgment, the courts decided to apply it.

3. Enforced Disappearance as a Stand-Alone Domestic Crime

The most interesting aspect of the criminalisation of enforced disappearance in Argentina is the not so recent decision of the legislature to include this crime in the Penal Code, but without the contextual requirements of a crime against humanity. On 14 April 2011,[37] the Argentine Parliament explicitly criminalised the crime of enforced disappearance as a domestic offence in Article 142ter of the Penal Code:

> Art. 142ter: A penalty of imprisonment from TEN (10) to TWENTY-FIVE (25) years and absolute and perpetual disqualification from the exercise of any public office and from the exercise of any private security activity shall be imposed on any public official or on any person or group of persons who, with the authorisation, support or acquiescence of the State, deprives in any manner whatsoever one or more persons of their liberty and subsequently refuses to acknowledge such deprivation of liberty or to provide information on the fate or whereabouts of such persons.
>
> The penalty shall be life imprisonment if death results or if the victim is a pregnant woman, a person under eighteen (18) years of age, a person over seventy (70) years of age or a disabled person. The same penalty is imposed if the victim is a person born during the enforced disappearance of her mother.
>
> The range of penalties provided for in this article may be reduced by one third of the maximum penalty and by one half of the minimum penalty in the case of perpetrators or accomplices who release the victim alive or provide information that allows the victim's actual appearance alive.[38]

---

36 See e.g. IACtHR, 23 September 2021, Caso Familia Julien Grisonas vs. Argentina, Excepciones Preliminares, Fondo, Reparaciones y Costas, para. 207; 26 August 2011, Caso Torres Millacura y otros vs. Argentina, Fondo, Reparaciones y Costas, para. 94, both with further references. See also Heredia/Heredia 2013, 17–8.

37 Act No. 26679, approval: 13 April 2011, publication in the Official Gazette: 9 May 2011.

38 Translation by Leandro Dias.

As can be seen, the first paragraph describes the crime of enforced disappearance with essentially four major differences from the crime in the Rome Statute. First, there is no longer a contextual element, precisely in order to punish acts of enforced disappearance that occur in isolation, even in democratic regimes that generally respect human rights.[39] Such cases have occurred in Argentina, and two of them have led to judgments against Argentina before the Inter-American Court of Human Rights, which partially explains the aim and scope of the crime against humanity of enforced disappearance as a stand-alone domestic offence.[40]

In the first case, 'Baigorria y Garrido vs. Argentina' (1998),[41] the Argentine State took responsibility for the enforced disappearance of two people (Adolfo Argentino Garrido Calderón and Raúl Baigorria Balmaceda), who were last seen on 28 April 1990, after being detained by the police.[42] Although the families of the victims wanted the federal government to create a separate crime of enforced disappearance as a form of reparation, the Court decided not to rule on this issue, since the state had already announced that it was working on a bill to address the issue.[43] However, in the second judgment, 'Torres Millacura and others vs. Argentina' (2011),[44] the Court took more drastic measures. This was another case of enforced disappearance in democratic times: on 2 October 2003, the police arrested Mr Iván Eladio Torres Millacura, who was then taken to the police station, where he was beaten and never seen again.[45] At the time of his arrest, Argentina did not have a stand-alone, domestic crime of enforced disappearance. While it is true that the Court did not find a violation of human rights in the failure

39 See Heredia/Heredia 2013, 13; Molina 2021, 415 et seq.; Parma/Gorra 2024, 340.

40 There is a third case (IACtHR, 23 September 2021, Caso Familia Julien Grisonas vs. Argentina, Excepciones Preliminares, Fondo, Reparaciones y Costas), but the judgment was issued after the legislation criminalising the stand-alone crime of enforced disappearance of persons was enacted. See the following footnotes for more on this judgment.

41 IACtHR, 27 August 1998, Caso Garrido y Baigorria vs. Argentina, Reparaciones y Costas.

42 IACtHR, 27 August 1998, Caso Garrido y Baigorria vs. Argentina, Reparaciones y Costas, para. 3.

43 IACtHR, 27 August 1998, Caso Garrido y Baigorria vs. Argentina, Reparaciones y Costas, para. 66.

44 IACtHR, 26 August 2011, Caso Torres Millacura y otros vs. Argentina, Fondo, Reparaciones y Costas.

45 IACtHR, 26 August 2011, Caso Torres Millacura y otros vs. Argentina, Fondo, Reparaciones y Costas, paras. 63–5.

to criminalise enforced disappearance, since this omission was not part of the facts analysed in the judgment,[46] it did state that Argentina was obliged to expressly criminalise such acts as of 28 February 1996, the date on which Argentina deposited its instrument of ratification of the Inter-American Convention against Enforced Disappearance with the Secretariat of the Organisation of American States.[47]

Although the 'Torres Millacura' ruling came a few months after the actual criminalisation of enforced disappearance as a separate offence, these two cases against Argentina played a decisive role in the decision to create article 142ter of the Penal Code.[48] In fact, the actual crime is seen in the literature as a way of implementing articles 1 to 3 of the Inter-American Convention on Enforced Disappearance,[49] which reads as follows:

> Article I
> The States Parties to this Convention undertake:
> [...]
> b. To punish within their jurisdictions, those persons who commit or attempt to commit the crime of forced disappearance of persons and their accomplices and accessories;
> [...]
> d. To take legislative, administrative, judicial, and any other measures necessary to comply with the commitments undertaken in this Convention.
> Article II
> For the purposes of this Convention, forced disappearance is considered to be the act of depriving a person or persons of his or their freedom, in whatever way, perpetrated by agents of the state or by persons or groups of persons acting with the authorization, support, or acquiescence of the state, followed by an absence of information or a refusal to acknowledge that deprivation of freedom or to give information on the whereabouts of that person, thereby impeding his or her recourse to the applicable legal remedies and procedural guarantees.

---

46 IACtHR, 26 August 2011, Caso Torres Millacura y otros vs. Argentina, Fondo, Reparaciones y Costas, para. 149.

47 IACtHR, 26 August 2011, Caso Torres Millacura y otros vs. Argentina, Fondo, Reparaciones y Costas, para. 149.

48 For a detailed analysis, see De Langhe 2023, 55–8.

49 Conti 2024, 148; Molina 2021, 413 et seq. See also Parma/Gorra, 2024, 340.

> Article III
> The States Parties undertake to adopt, in accordance with their constitutional procedures, the legislative measures that may be needed to define the forced disappearance of persons as an offense and to impose an appropriate punishment commensurate with its extreme gravity. This offense shall be deemed continuous or permanent as long as the fate or whereabouts of the victim has not been determined.
> The States Parties may establish mitigating circumstances for persons who have participated in acts constituting forced disappearance when they help to cause the victim to reappear alive or provide information that sheds light on the forced disappearance of a person.

Article I(b) establishes the obligation to punish enforced disappearance,[50] while Article III clarifies that 'punish' means proportional criminal punishment[51] under an offence that defines the crime of enforced disappearance (according to the standards set in Article II), established by statutory law.[52] The creation of a separate crime of 'isolated' enforced disappearance in Argentina then had nothing to do with the International Convention for the Protection of All Persons from Enforced Disappearance. This means that the process of criminalisation in Argentina began independently,[53] without the need for a critical review by the Committee on Enforced Disappearances, as was the case in Germany,[54] for example. Rather, it was a deliberate decision on the part of the Argentine State,[55] given its obligations

50 Molina 2021, 414.

51 On the so-called duty to punish in human rights law, see Ambos/Dias 2017, 175–7.

52 See also Article II(d): duty to take legislative measures to comply with the commitments of the Convention.

53 On the contrary, from the outset the Committee (Concluding observations on the report submitted by Argentina under article 29, paragraph 1, of the Convention, 13 December 2013, para. 12) expressly emphasized this positive feature of Argentine law: 'The Committee notes with satisfaction that the State party has made enforced disappearance an offence under the Criminal Code.' However, in the same paragraph, it also expressed its dissatisfaction with the fact that the 'application of the offence of enforced disappearance is somewhat problematic in practice.'

54 See e.g. Committee on Enforced Disappearances, Concluding observations on the additional information submitted by Germany under article 29 (4) of the Convention, 14 April 2023, paras. 9–11. For a critical analysis of the way in which the German Federal Government has dealt with this issue, see Jeßberger/Geneuss 2024, 99.

55 For a detailed analysis of the legislative debate on the bill, see Heredia/Heredia 2013, 12–4.

under the Inter-American Convention and the need to avoid international responsibility in cases before the Inter-American Court of Human Rights.[56]

The aim of this type of criminalisation is to comply with Argentina's international obligations and to fill a gap in the punishment of enforced disappearance: although it has been possible to punish at least some non-systematic or non-generalised practices of enforced disappearance in Argentina on the basis of classic domestic crimes, this has proved difficult and, moreover, has prevented a fair characterisation of the behaviour of the perpetrators.[57]

Second, the crime cannot simply be committed by regular non-state organisations: the perpetrator must be a public official or a person or group linked to the State.[58] Enforced disappearances committed by private groups with some territorial control, such as drug cartels, are excluded from the scope of the domestic crime if (and only if) they do not act with the support or acquiescence of the State. Of course, such cases may ultimately be considered crimes against humanity, provided that the 'political organisation' meets the requirements of Article 7(1)(i) of the ICC Statute. The question of whether this organization should be 'state-like'[59] or whether crimes against humanity can be committed in Argentina by any association of persons with an established structure[60] can be left aside here.

Third, the legislator decided to lower the subjective requirements of the offence by eliminating the intent to deprive the victim of the protection of the law for a prolonged period of time.[61] In Argentina, it is sufficient for criminal liability that the perpetrator commits any intentional crime with *dolus eventualis*, meaning they are aware that their actions pose a risk

---

56 However, in a recent ruling, the Inter-American Court of Human Rights (IACtHR, 23 September 2021, Caso Familia Julien Grisonas vs. Argentina, Excepciones Preliminares, Fondo, Reparaciones y Costas, para. 208) found that the Argentinian state had failed to comply with the obligation set out in Article 2 of the American Convention, in relation to Articles 8.1 and 25.1 of the same Convention, as well as the provisions of Article III of the Inter-American Convention on Forced Disappearance of Persons. According to the Court, the Argentinian state had delayed the criminalisation of enforced disappearance, hindering the investigation and prosecution of such crimes.

57 For a similar conclusion regarding the German stand-alone offence, see Jeßberger/Geneuss 2024, 99–101.

58 See Basílico 2024, 419; Parma/Gorra 2024, 340.

59 See e.g. Giorgou 2013, 1020.

60 See e.g. Stahn 2019, 67 with further references.

61 Molina 2021, 416.

of committing an offence and accept that risk.[62] However, if the legislator has decided to include a more specific subjective requirement, this takes precedence. As the Argentine legislator did not take his decision, then enforced disappearance as a domestic offence can be committed without any more specific intent,[63] so that the perpetrator need only be aware of the risk of committing an offence and to accept that risk.

And fourth, it appears that the offence can only be committed if three objective elements of the crime are present. This is known as the 'unified' offence of enforced disappearance, which is characteristic of how human rights law[64] addresses the issue:[65] crime consists of the victim being deprived of their liberty (1), the refusal to acknowledge this deprivation or provide information about the victim's whereabouts (2), and the state's assistance or acquiescence (3). This means that the deprivation of liberty *and* the failure to acknowledge the detention or to provide information on the whereabouts of the victim are not alternative criminal acts (the so-called 'dualistic' model), but cumulative.[66] This contrasts with the regulation of enforced disappearance as a crime against humanity in Argentina, which follows the 'dualistic' (or alternative) model of the crime, characteristic of international criminal law, especially the ICC Statute and the Elements of Crimes.[67] Such a decision of the Argentinian legislator is clearly different from that of the German legislator, since the new domestic crime of enforced disappearance (§ 234b StGB) was constructed according to the dualistic model:[68]

---

62 See Ferrante 2011, 25–7 with further references.

63 Some scholars argue for limiting the subjective elements of the crime by requiring direct intent ('willingly'). See e.g. Aboso 2011, 87–8; Amallo/Melconian 2023, 191; Basílico 2024, 149; Conti 2024, 148. However, they do not provide a justification for a limitation that would be contrary to the general system of the Argentine Criminal Code.

64 See Art. 2, International Convention for the Protection of All Persons from Enforced Disappearance: 'For the purposes of this Convention, 'enforced disappearance' is considered to be the arrest, detention, abduction or any other form of deprivation of liberty by agents of the State or by persons or groups of persons acting with the authorization, support or acquiescence of the State, followed by a refusal to acknowledge the deprivation of liberty or by concealment of the fate or whereabouts of the disappeared person, which place such a person outside the protection of the law.'

65 Jeßberger/Geneuss 2024, 97.

66 See e.g. Basílico 2024, 418–9; Molina 2021, 414.

67 Jeßberger/Geneuss 2024 97 et seq.

68 Jeßberger/Geneuss 2024, 102.

§ 234b. Enforced disappearance of persons
(1) Whoever as a public official on behalf of or with the approval of a State
1. abducts a person or otherwise deprives her of her physical liberty, and then refuses to provide information about his or her fate or whereabouts, or
2. conceals the fate or whereabouts of a person who has been abducted or otherwise deprived of her physical liberty by a public official or on behalf of or with the approval of a state, or refuses to provide information about this,
thereby depriving her of the protection of the law incurs a penalty of imprisonment of not less than one year.
(2) In less serious cases, the penalty is imprisonment for a term of between three months and five years.[69]

Going back to the Argentinian regulation, in the case of death of the victim, as well as in the case of the disappearance of particularly vulnerable persons (pregnant women, persons under eighteen years of age, persons over seventy years of age and children born during the deprivation of liberty of the mother), the penalty is increased from 10 to 25 years to life imprisonment.[70] With regard to mitigating circumstances, the penalty may be reduced by a third of the maximum penalty and by half of the minimum penalty if the perpetrator or an accomplice provides information that allows the missing person to be found alive.

This form of dual or double criminalisation of enforced disappearance is innovative, but it raises a number of problems that are difficult to resolve. Some of them are inherent to this type of double regulation, while others are due to the legislative technique used by the Argentine legislator. The following addresses some of these problems.

69 Translated by Leandro Dias.
70 See De Langhe 2023, 146–8.

4. Open Questions

4.1. Enforced Disappearance as an Isolated Act

The first problematic issue concerns the decision itself to engage in this kind of double criminalisation. While punishing enforced disappearance as a domestic offence, even in cases where no crime against humanity has been committed, seems to be an obligation under human rights law, it also contradicts a relatively common idea, at least in Argentina, about the rationale of the crime of enforced disappearance.[71] For example, some scholars argue that an essential part of the wrongfulness of this type of conduct lies precisely in the generalised or systematic nature of its execution, or at least its commission during a generalised or systematic attack against the civilian population.[72] According to this view, enforced disappearances have a social meaning that is at least partly linked to their widespread or systematic occurrence and which cannot be fully grasped if this contextual element is ignored.

This is not a trivial matter, and in fact, in the case of an activist who was last seen on 24 February 2019 and whose body has never been found, an Argentine court sought to supplement this domestic crime of enforced disappearance with the classic contextual element of crimes against humanity through interpretation.[73] Thus, according to the court,[74] the crime of enforced disappearance can only be committed if the contextual elements of a crime against humanity are present. If this interpretation were correct, the introduction of Article 142ter by the legislator would be just another way of criminalising enforced disappearances as crimes against humanity. This idea has not been accepted by the higher courts[75] or commentators,[76] mainly because it drastically contradicts both the intention of the legisla-

71 For a general description of this way of understanding the crime of enforced disappearance in Argentina, see De Langhe 2025, 573.

72 See e.g. Ambos/Böhm 2009, 227 et seq., 245.

73 A transcript of the relevant parts of the judgment can be found in De Langhe 2023, 111–3.

74 For a thorough analysis, see De Langhe 2023, 96–8.

75 See Cámara Federal de Casación Penal, Chamber 4, 'ECHAZÚ, Emmanuel s/recurso de casación', FCR 8232/2017/12/CFC, 12 December 2019, especially the separate opinion of Judge Hornos. But also see how the Court of Cassation of the City of Buenos Aires recently avoided the question: Cámara Nacional de Casación Penal, Chamber I, 'Karhanyan, Arshak. Incompetencia y denegatoria de ser tenido como parte querellante', CCC 15169/2019/CA2, 4 June 2021.

tor[77] and the wording of the law.[78] Moreover, the material wrongfulness of the crime, that is, the creation of a situation of uncertainty in which there is no trace of the person deprived of her liberty, is also present in cases of 'isolated' enforced disappearance, so no additional contextual element is needed.[79]

4.2. On the Removal from the Protection of the Law

At least at first glance, eliminating the specific intent to remove the victim from the protection of the law for an extended period of time in favour of a general requirement of *dolus eventualis* does not seem to adequately capture what is at stake in an enforced disappearance. Enforced disappearance would then only be a matter of taking the risk of not providing the necessary legal protection to the person deprived of his or her liberty, without wanting to contribute to the lack of protection of the victim for a long period of time.[80]

Consider the following case:

> *Reckless policeman:* Policeman arrests Victim, who was walking through a dangerous neighbourhood, mistaking her for a criminal who had recently robbed a shop. Policeman was aware of the risk of arresting the wrong person, but disregarded it. Victim was detained at the police station for approximately 8 hours until several of her family members arrived at the scene and asked Policeman if Victim was being held there.

---

76 De Langhe 2023, 157; Heredia/Heredia, 2013, 13; Molina 2021, 415 et seq.; Parma/Gorra 2024, 340.

77 The following paragraph from the rationale for Draft Bill S-933/10 (20 April 2010), drafted by Senators Escudero, Morandini, Juez and Bortolozzi, is particularly clear: 'Thus, the unlawful conduct of enforced disappearance of persons is incorporated into Argentine criminal law when it is not part of a widespread or systematic attack against a civilian population.' (page 13, translation by Leandro Dias).

78 See De Langhe 2025, 579 et seq.

79 Jeßberger/Geneuss 2024, 103. See also De Langhe 2023, 58.

80 One might think that it would not be possible to deprive someone of their liberty based on the assumption that they might not be adequately protected without also demonstrating a certain willingness to remove their legal protection. While most cases of *dolus eventualis* imply intent to remove the victim from legal protection for an extended period, I believe that in certain instances the perpetrator may act recklessly concerning the objective elements of the crime. While rare, these cases may pose problems for courts. I would like to thank Claudia Cárdenas for encouraging me to clarify this issue.

Policeman, realising her mistake, told the family members that Victim had never been arrested. Policeman released Victim a few hours later.

In such a case, Policeman may well be considered a perpetrator of the crime of enforced disappearance under Article 142ter of the Argentine Penal Code, since the latter does not require a specific intent to remove the victim from the protection of the law for a prolonged period of time, nor does it include any contextual element. However, most of us would find this counterintuitive. The case appears to be more akin to a typical instance of unlawful detention than to an enforced disappearance, since it lacks the 'indefiniteness' associated with removal from legal protection.[81] As Vermeulen puts it, the 'underlying presumption, then, is that there is a difference between, on the one hand, unacknowledged detention and incommunicado detention, and, on the other, enforced disappearance.'[82]

There are at least two possible solutions to this problem. The first would be to limit the scope of Art. 142ter of the Argentine Penal Code, by interpreting it to include the intention to remove the victim from the protection of the law for a prolonged period as an additional subjective requirement.[83] Of course, this solution would not be derived from the actual wording of the law, but since it would be an analogy made in favour of the accused, no problems of legality should arise. If this interpretation is correct, then there is no enforced disappearance in 'Reckless Policeman' because Policeman did not act with this specific intention.

A second way of solving this problem would be to limit the scope of the offence through interpretation without including an additional subjective requirement. As Jeßberger and Geneuss have recently suggested in relation to the German offence,[84] the element of deprivation of the protection of the law could well be interpreted as an objective crime result.[85] Since the victim in 'Reckless Policeman' was not actually deprived of the protection of the law for a sufficiently long period of time, it can be argued that no enforced disappearance took place. Of course, this does not mean that Policeman's actions were lawful, as other crimes may also be taken into account when analysing this behaviour. Which kind of restrictive interpretation of the

81 See Rodley/Pollard 2009, 332.
82 Vermeulen 2012, 172 (footnotes omitted).
83 De Langhe 2025, 585.
84 Jeßberger/Geneuss 2024, 103–5.
85 See also Rodley/Pollard 2009, 337.

offence should be preferred can be left aside here, as it deserves a more in-depth analysis.

4.3. The Problem of Lawful Deprivations of Liberty

Another problem that arises in the Argentine criminalisation of enforced disappearance as a separate crime is the issue of initially lawful detentions that become unlawful over time. While Article 7(1)(i) of the ICC Statute leaves this question open to interpretation, footnotes 25 and 26 of the Elements of Crimes make it clear that initially lawful arrests may also result in an enforced disappearance, provided that all other conditions are met.

Taking this into account, the Argentine legislator could have clarified this issue in the wording of art. 142ter of the Argentine Penal Code. However, it made no mention of the legality of the detention, leaving the matter open to interpretation. This is no strange thing, as the legislator is free to leave some things open for judges (and the scientific community) to decide and this is exactly what the German legislator also did with the new offence of sporadic enforced disappearance (§ 234b StGB).[86] What about the actual interpretation of the law by Argentinean courts and scholars? While there's no definitive answer in the case law, some commentators seem to support the view that initially lawful detentions can also constitute the crime of enforced disappearance in Argentina.[87] This interpretation is to be welcomed, since the material wrongfulness of the crime, the aforementioned creation of a situation in which there is no trace of the person deprived of their liberty, is also present in these cases.[88]

4.4. Problems of Ordinal Proportionality

Finally, the Argentine regulation of enforced disappearance presents some problems of ordinal proportionality. We have a problem of cardinal disproportionality when the punishment deviates from some kind of (mostly

86 Jeßberger/Geneuss 2024, 103 et seq.

87 See e.g. De Langhe 2025, 582; Molina 2021, 414.

88 For the same conclusion, but in relation to the German offense, see Jeßberger/Geneuss 2024, 103.

desert-based) criterion that is external to the legal system.[89] For example, if the punishment for theft were life imprisonment, this would lead to cardinal disproportionality, even if all crimes in that legal system were punishable by life imprisonment. Ordinal disproportionality occurs when an instance of punishment is inconsistent with other instances in the same legal system.[90] If the penalty for rape is 10 years' imprisonment, and the legislature has determined that the penalty for theft is 20 years' imprisonment, then we have a problem of ordinal disproportionality.

Remember that the range of punishment chosen by the Argentine legislator for the crime of enforced disappearance, as an autonomous domestic crime, is 10 to 25 years' imprisonment, which can be increased to life imprisonment in several cases: if the victim dies and also if the victim was particularly vulnerable. Meanwhile, the penalty for the crime against humanity of enforced disappearance, according to Act No. 26200, is 3 to 25 years' imprisonment, and a life sentence can only be imposed if the victim dies. This means that the crime against humanity of enforced disappearance, which has very strict requirements (contextual and additional subjective elements), leads to a lower penalty than the 'isolated' crime of enforced disappearance: the minimum penalty is lower (3 years versus 10 years) and, in addition, life imprisonment can only be imposed in one scenario, but not in many (death of the victim versus death of the victim and cases of special vulnerability).

The Argentine legislature provided a solution to the problem of ordinal proportionality by establishing, in Article 12 of Law No. 26200, that the penalty applicable to crimes against humanity shall in no case be less than that which would be applicable in the event of a conviction under the provisions of the domestic Penal Code. Thus, in the case of the crime of enforced disappearance, the general range of penalties for crimes against humanity was de facto modified by the more severe penalty established by the Argentine legislator for the stand-alone domestic offence of Art. 142ter of the Argentine Penal Code. However, this obviously does not fully resolve the problem of ordinal proportionality, since it only places the crime against humanity on the same level as the domestic crime, although the former is more serious than the latter.

89 See von Hirsch 1992, 77–9. For a detailed analysis, see Chiao 2022, 200–3.
90 von Hirsch 1992, 76–7. See also Chiao 2022, 195–200.

5. Conclusion

Argentina played a pivotal role in establishing enforced disappearance as both an international crime and a standard offence under domestic law. This resulted in a process of double criminalisation within the country. The first form began with the prohibition of enforced disappearances as a crime against humanity under customary international law — namely, acts committed in the context of a widespread or systematic attack against the civilian population by the state or a similar entity — which enabled the prosecution of enforced disappearances committed during Argentina's last military dictatorship. This ultimately led to the implementation of the Rome Statute. The second form of criminalisation focused on isolated cases of enforced disappearance, creating interpretative problems. Any states wishing to follow Argentina's example should pay attention to these issues and, if necessary, seek to improve this type of criminalisation.

Bibliography

Aboso, Gustavo. 2011. 'Aspectos sustanciales del nuevo delito de desaparición forzada de personas'. *Revista de Derecho Penal y Criminología*. 1. 71–88.

Amallo, María Laura and Melconian, Julieta. 2023. 'Delitos contra la libertad'. In Ramírez, Nicolás (ed.). *Curso de Derecho Penal. Parte Especial*. Buenos Aires: B de F. 183–228.

Ambos, Kai and Böhm, María Laura. 2009. 'Desaparición forzada de personas como tipo penal autónomo. Análisis comparativo-internacional y propuesta legislativa'. In Ambos, Kai (ed.). *Desaparición forzada de personas. Análisis comparado e internacional*. Bogotá: Deutsche Gesellschaft für Technische Zusammenarbeit. 195–255.

Ambos, Kai and Dias, Leandro. 2017. '¿Un derecho humano a la pena? Reflexiones sobre los alcances del llamado derecho a la justicia'. In Ambos, Kai, Malarino, Ezequiel and Pastor, Daniel (eds.). *Prevención e imputación*. Buenos Aires: Hammurabi. 173–93.

Basílico, Lourdes. 2024. 'Art. 142 ter'. In Basílico, Ricardo and Villada, Jorge (eds.). *Código Penal de la Nación Argentina. Comentado. Anotado. Concordado*. 4th edition. Buenos Aires: Hammurabi. 418–21.

Cançado Trindade, Antônio Augusto. 2012. 'Enforced Disappearances of Persons as a Violation of Jus Cogens: The Contribution of the Jurisprudence of the Inter-American Court of Human Rights'. *Nordic Journal of International Law*. 81. 507–36.

Chehtman, Alejandro and Espósito, Carlos. 2023. 'Argentina'. In Obregón Tarazona, Liliana, Betancur-Restrepo, Laura and Amaya Castro, Juan Manuel (eds.). *The Oxford Handbook of International Law and the Americas*. Oxford: University Press. Work in Progress URL: https://academic.oup.com/edited-volume/45649/chapter-abstract/454437597?redirectedFrom=fulltext (accessed 15 December 2024).

Chehtman, Alejandro. 2024. 'Re-Constructing Criminal Accountability for Human Rights Abuses: Argentina 1990-2024'. *Modern Criminal Law Review*. 1.1. 64–94.

Chiao, Vincent. 2022. 'Proportionality and its Discontents'. *Law and Philosophy*. 41. 193–217.

Conti, Nestor Jesús. 2024. 'Delitos contra la libertad'. In Simaz, Leonel (ed.), *Manual de Derecho Penal. Parte Especial, Segunda Edición Actualizada*. Buenos Aires: Erreius. 131–202.

De Langhe, Marcela. 2023. *Desaparición forzada de personas*. Buenos Aires: Hammurabi.

De Langhe, Marcela. 2025. 'Art. 142 ter'. In De Langhe, Marcela (ed.). *Código Penal de la Nación Argentina. Análisis doctrinal y jurisprudencial*. Buenos Aires: Hammurabi. 572–96.

Dulitzky, Ariel. 1999. 'The Latin-American Flavor of Enforced Disappearances'. *Chicago Journal of International Law*. 19.2. 423–89.

Ferrante, Marcelo. 2011. 'Argentina'. In Heller, Kevin Jon and Dubber, Markus D. (eds.). *The Handbook of Comparative Criminal Law*. Oxford: University Press. 12–48.

Filippini, Leonardo. 2011. 'La persecución penal en la búsqueda de justicia'. In Centro de Estudios Legales y Sociales (ed.). *Hacer Justicia. Nuevos debates sobre el juzgamiento de crímenes de lesa humanidad en la Argentina*. Buenos Aires: Siglo XXI. 19–47.

Giorgou, Irena. 2013. 'State Involvement in the Perpetration of Enforced Disappearance and the Rome Statute'. *Journal of International Criminal Justice*. 11.5. 1001–21.

Grammer, Christoph. 2005. *Der Tatbestand des Verschwindenlassens einer Person. Transposition einer völkerrechtlichen Figur ins Strafrecht*. Berlin: Duncker & Humblot.

Heredia, José Raúl and Heredia, Verónica. 2013. 'El Delito de Desaparición Forzada de Personas'. In Asociación Pensamiento Penal (ed.). *Código Penal Comentado de Acceso Libre*. Buenos Aires: Asociación Pensamiento Penal. URL: https://www.pensamientopenal.com.ar/cpcomentado/37756-art-142-ter-desaparicion-forzada-personas (accessed 15 December 2024).

Hazan, Luciano. 2014. 'La desaparición forzada de niños en Argentina a través de la sustitución de su identidad'. In Casado, María and López Ortega, Juan José (eds.). *Desapariciones forzadas de niños en Europa y Latinoamérica del convenio de la ONU a las búsquedas a través del ADN*. Barcelona: Universidad de Barcelona. 153–170.

Islas Colín, Alfredo. 2015. 'Desaparición forzada de personas y las sentencias de tribunales de América Latina'. In Carbonell Sánchez, Miguel and Cruz Barney, Óscar (eds.). *Historia y Constitución. Homenaje a José Luis Soberanes Fernández, Tomo II*. México, D. F.: Universidad Nacional Autónoma de México. 251–85.

Jeßberger, Florian and Geneuss, Julia. 2024. 'Ein Tatbestand des Verschwindenlassens im deutschen Strafrecht. Völkerrechtliche, straftatsystematische und kriminalpolitische Prolegomena zur Einführung des § 234b StGB-E'. *Kriminalpolitische Zeitschrift*. 2. 95–105.

Malarino, Ezequiel. 2009. 'Argentina'. In Ambos, Kai (ed.). *Desaparición forzada de personas. Análisis comparado e internacional.* Bogotá: Deutsche Gesellschaft für Technische Zusammenarbeit. 5–37.

Malarino, Ezequiel. 2011. 'La cara represiva de la reciente jurisprudencia argentina sobre graves violaciones de los derechos humanos'. In Maier, Julio, Sancinetti, Marcelo and Schöne, Wolfgang (ed.). *Dogmática penal entre naturalismo y normativismo.* Buenos Aires: Ad-Hoc. 381–442.

Molina, Gonzalo. 2021. *Manual de Derecho Penal. Parte Especial.* Chaco: ConTexto.

Montiel, Juan Pablo. 2012. 'La "mala costumbre" de vulnerar derechos humanos: análisis y pronóstico de la costumbre como fuente del derecho penal internacional'. In Montiel, Juan Pablo (eds.). *La crisis del principio de legalidad en el nuevo Derecho penal ¿decadencia o evolución?.* Madrid: Marcial Pons. 399–434.

Parma, Carlos and Gorra, Daniel. 2024. *Código Penal. Analizado. Concordado. Anotado con referencias jurisprudenciales. Cuarta Edición.* Buenos Aires: Hammurabi.

Pinto, Mónica and Maisley, Nahuel. 2024. 'Engagement of Argentina's Supreme Court with International Law'. In Nollkaemper, André, Shany, Yuval and Tzanakopoulos, Antonios (eds.). *The Engagement of Domestic Courts with International Law: Comparative Perspectives.* Oxford: University Press. 117–41.

Raube, Svenja. 2024. 'Das Gesetz zur Fortentwicklung des Völkerstrafrechts. Zu den jüngsten Arbeiten am Bau für deutsche Weltrechtspflege'. *Kriminalpolitische Zeitschrift.* 4. 278–97.

Rodley, Nigel and Pollard, Matt. 2009. *The Treatment of Prisoners Under International Law.* Oxford: University Press.

Stahn, Carsten. 2019. *A Critical Introduction to International Criminal Law.* Cambridge: University Press.

Vermeulen, Marthe Lot. 2012. *Enforced Disappearance. Determining State Responsibility under the International Convention for the Protection of All Persons from Enforced Disappearance.* Utrecht: University School of Law.

Von Hirsch, Andrew. 1992. 'Proportionality in the Philosophy of Punishment'. *Crime and Justice.* 16. 55–98.

Weissbrodt, David and Bartolomei, Maria Luisa. 1991. 'The Effectiveness of International Human Rights Pressures: The Case of Argentina, 1976-1983'. *Minnesota Law Review.* 75. 1009–35.

Werle, Gerhard and Jeßberger, Florian. 2020. *Völkerstrafrecht.* 5th edition. Tübingen: Mohr Siebeck.

Enforced Disappearances: the Brazilian Case

Antonio Martins

Abstract: The chapter deals with the problem of enforced disappearances, presenting an overview of the political context that served as a backdrop for cases of enforced disappearance during the civil-military dictatorship and the main characteristics of transitional justice in Brazil. The difficulties and successive efforts to identify and make reparation for enforced disappearances are also discussed. A central aspect of the text is Brazil's condemnation by the Inter-American Court of Human Rights in the Gomes Lund case and the obligation to criminalize enforced disappearance as an autonomous offense. In this sense, the criminalization proposal outlined in Bill 4.038/2008 is discussed in the light of international rules and comparative law. Finally, a reflection is presented on the historical continuity of the repressive violence exercised by the Brazilian State.

1. The historical context: the civil-military dictatorship from 1964 to 1985

On 31 March 1964, following a trend that would be confirmed in other countries within the continent, the democratically elected president João Goulart was deposed by force and a military government was established. The pretext, also continental in scope, was the reaction to the communist danger,[1] expressed in proposals for basic reforms,[2] including agrarian reform, and, a particularly recurring element in Brazilian political history, the fight against corruption.[3] The coup had international support, especially from the United States,[4] and was celebrated by various sectors of civil society[5] including the press,[6] which referred, contradictorily and cynically,

1 Motta 2021, 19.
2 On the defeat of a project for a Republic that meant the military coup, see Aarão Reis 2014, 11.
3 See Martins 2022, 5.
4 Motta 2021, 73.
5 Motta 2021, 126.
6 Motta 2021, 133.

to safeguarding democracy. Civil society's expectation seemed to be of a short-lived military regime, followed by a return to democratic normality. This expectation did not materialise and what followed were successive moments of increased authoritarianism, with the issuing of successive 'institutional acts', legislative decrees that suppressed political guarantees and rights (in particular Institutional Act 5 of 1968[7]) and an increase in the repressive force of the state, which ended up stifling civil society movements that opposed the regime and decimating armed opposition groups.[8] The harshest period of political repression was during the government of General Emílio Garrastazu Médici, from 1969 to 1974.

The internal tension between military wings[9] that recommended a return to democracy and radical wings that wanted to maintain dictatorial rule lasted with the latter clearly winning for at least ten years, until the process of a 'slow, gradual and safe' reopening advocated by the fourth military president, Ernesto Geisel, began.[10]

There was yet another presidential term for João Figueiredo from 1979 until the end of the dictatorial regime in 1985. As part of the process of reopening, the Amnesty Law was passed in 1979, which, on the one hand, allowed the release and return from exile of various political leaders and opponents of the military regime. On the other hand, understood as a historic social pact, the law effectively guaranteed impunity for crimes committed by the state's repression of the political opposition.

Contrary to a broad civil society movement calling for direct presidential elections, known as the 'Diretas Já' (Direct Elections Now) movement, the option for an indirect election for president prevailed in Congress. Tancredo Neves won, but he died before taking office in 1985, and his vice-president, José Sarney, who belonged to the conservative Arena party, which was linked to the government throughout the dictatorship, took over. Only in 1989 were direct elections held for the presidency of the Republic.

---

7 Cf. Motta 2018, 195, available at: https://www.scielo.br/j/rbh/a/jZh4sttTXLWN5KJMWXJNQzt/?format=pdf&lang=pt (accessed 6 July 2025).

8 On the left-wing opposition to the dictatorship, see Aarão Reis 2014, 32; on the parliamentary opposition, ibid, 34.

9 See Figueiredo 2015, 15.

10 For a correct analysis of the context of the decision to open up and the role of General Geisel, see Pedretti 2024, 71.

2. Violent political repression

2.1 The beginning and intensification of violent political repression

As Patto Sá Motta notes, from 1967 onwards there was a significant increase in opposition to the military regime, represented above all by the student movement, parliamentary action, workers' strikes and the start of the armed struggle.[11] After a famous and provocative speech by Congressman Moreira Alves, who accused the army of harbouring torturers, and the maintenance of his parliamentary immunity by Congress, the government issued the aforementioned Institutional Act 5, a break with the legality imposed by the regime itself.[12] This is how historian Patto Sá Motta describes it:

> Institutional Act 5 gave the President of the Republic practically unlimited powers. Although the first article affirmed the maintenance of the 1967 Constitution, in the following articles it became clear that the Charter was becoming subject to the will of the executive branch. The president could close parliamentary houses, revoke citizens' mandates and political rights, confiscate property accumulated in the exercise of public office, censor the press and decree a state of siege. In addition, the guarantee of habeas corpus for political offences, offences against national security, the economic and social order and the popular economy was suspended. To resume the purge of the civil service that had begun in 1964, once again the guarantees of life tenure, irremovability and stability were suspended. The government could dismiss, remove or retire any civil servant, without the need for a regular process or enquiry.[13]

This concentration of power paved the way for an increase in the repressive force of the state.[14] Supported by the idea that the armed struggle promoted by left-wing groups against the authoritarian government justified a practice of internal warfare,[15] the military dictatorship began to intensify its

---

11 Motta 2018, 199.

12 Aarão Reis 2014, 36.

13 Motta 2018, 202.

14 Motta 2021, 183.

15 This idea is still defended today, in the sense of a necessary reaction to the armed movements opposing the regime. On the 'dirty war' thesis, in the sense that acts of terrorism provoked a harsh reaction from the state, see Teles 2009, 119, 125. On the other hand, this does not mean that the victims of the regime who took part in

repressive methods. The intellectual context for the development of this repressive ideology predates the dictatorship, especially the influence of the US-influenced doctrine of national security and the French-influenced doctrine of revolutionary war within the Escola Superior de Guerra (ESG), permeated in any case by the strong sense of anti-communism typical of the Cold War.[16] The emergence of the armed struggle at the end of the 1960s brought the doctrine of revolutionary war back onto the agenda.[17]

Although repression of the regime's opponents had already existed since the 1964 coup and the National Information Service (SNI) was created by the first military president, Castello Branco, in June 1964 there was a substantial increase in the repressive apparatus with the articulation of opposition movements to the dictatorship. In addition to the Political and Social Order Departments (Dops), which were subordinate to the state governments and had been carrying out political police work since the 1920s, the military government began to rely on intelligence services linked to the Armed Forces (the Army created the CIE in 1967 and the Air Force the Cisa in 1968 – both were preceded by the Marina's Cenimar, created in the 1950s). In 1967, the DPF was created, a nationwide police force commanded by the Army, and the General Inspectorate of Military Police (IGPM). In 1970 the Information Operations Detachment - Internal Defence Operations Centre (DOI-CODI) was created, also commanded by the Army, which took part in the violent repression of armed groups and became veritable torture centres for political enemies.[18]

2.2 Systematic human rights violations

In the wake of the intensification of repression, a systematic practice of human rights violations was established. Between 1969 and 1976, the number

---

radical left-wing organisations presented themselves as mere resistance to military authoritarianism and did not have revolutionary ideals of deposing the government and establishing a communist regime based on the dictatorship of the proletariat. On these displacements of historical meaning carried out a posteriori, especially in the context of the amnesty, see Aarão Reis 2001.

16 Martins Filho 2009, 179.

17 Martins Filho 2009, 187.

18 For a retrospective of the creation of repressive organisations, see Motta 2021, 179. For an analysis of the repressive apparatus and its methods, see Joffily 2014, 158. On the ideological influence of French military doctrine on the creation and functioning of these bodies, see Martins Filho 2009, 161.

of dead and missing reached 340. Clandestine torture centres were set up, such as the infamous 'House of Death' in Petrópolis, in the mountainous region of the state of Rio de Janeiro. Torture was followed by death and the disappearance of bodies, allegedly as part of the psychological warfare waged against the regime's opponents.[19]

It is true that this military regime generated significantly fewer victims of homicide and enforced disappearances than other countries in the region, however it also sought to cloak its exceptional measures in a semblance of formal legitimacy, leading to a model known as 'legalistic authoritarianism'.[20] This legalism of exceptional measures is a defining feature of the Brazilian military dictatorship.[21]

This doesn't mean, however, that talk about the systematic practice of human rights violations and, in particular, enforced disappearances is off the table; nor does it mean that one should refute the classification of this criminalisation as state criminality, as some authors claim,[22] which ends up removing what is most specific about this constellation of cases: the subversion of the state apparatus to create a system of lawlessness, where the systematic practice of crimes becomes the *de facto* rule.

Beyond the crimes themselves, the lack of state prosecution and historical clarification regarding the whereabouts of the victims, as well as the state's silence and refusal to open the state archives, have prevented the recovery of memory of the victims, hindered the experience of mourning and contributed to a lack of definition of responsibility for the disappearances. In other words, the terror intentionally instigated through the forced disappearance of people remained, despite serious efforts to overcome it, a state policy after re-democratisation and allowed the rise to power of conservative forces that relativised the crimes committed by the military dictatorship, or openly justified and supported them.[23] This scenario was due to the *unique* context of the transition from authoritarian to democratic rule, compared to other countries in the region. It is this context that we will investigate next.

---

19 Motta 2021, 185.

20 Abrão 2011, 28.

21 Figueiredo 2015, 129.

22 Swensson Junior 2009, 65.

23 On the case of former president Jair Bolsonaro and his political group, see Motta 2021,174.

3. Transitional justice in Brazil

Transitional justice in Brazil stood out in the regional context for two key factors: the first was the enactment of an amnesty law (Law 6.683/1979) which has never been repealed, contrary to the case law of the Inter-American Court of Human Rights.[24] There are many factors that lead to the conclusion that the amnesty law is illegitimate, from reasons of material justice, which prevent those in power from absolving themselves in advance for the crimes committed, to the establishment of a normative support point to lay the foundations for a new democratic regime that condemns human rights violations. It is also important to emphasise the lack of bilateralism, since the amnesty for those persecuted by the regime was partial and restricted, with those who committed crimes of terrorism, robbery and kidnapping being excluded from the scope of the law, while agents of the state enjoyed a broad amnesty.[25]

The validity of this law was ratified, however, by the Federal Supreme Court,[26] in a decision that oscillated between an openly positivist argument that ignores the complexity of the case and the international discussion regarding the prosecution of serious human rights violations in the face of self-amnesties, on the one hand, and political arguments for the need for reconciliation between divided sectors of society and the historical significance of the amnesty for the process that culminated in the end of the dictatorial regime.[27]

The second factor concerns the hesitancy of interest in investigating the historical truth, in a rare combination of state efforts to hide and not open archives[28] and a lack of political will to confront the dictatorship's violent

24 See IACtHR 2001, Barrios Altos v. Peru, Serie C, N. 75, available at: https://www.corteidh.or.cr/docs/casos/articulos/seriec_75_esp.pdf (accessed 6 July 2025).
Also, IACtHR 2006, Almonacid Arellano y otros v. Chile. Serie C N. 154, available at: https://www.corteidh.or.cr/docs/casos/articulos/seriec_154_esp.pdf (accessed 6 July 2025).
To analyse these decisions and criticise the Brazilian case, see Piovesan 2009, 204.

25 See Weichert 2009, 164.

26 Federal Supreme Court 2010, ADPF 153. I critically analysed this decision in Martins 2012, 202. See also Matos 2012, 136.

27 Similar arguments have been used in defence of amnesty laws by other governments and in other contexts. For the cases of Argentina, El Salvador, Peru and Uruguay, see Canton, Santiago. Amnesty Laws, in: Reátegui 2011, 245, 268.

28 Figueiredo 2015, passim. This effort has continued since the end of the regime. Cf. Teles 2009, 126.

past. This hesitancy and lack of will are often translated into fear of a political reaction from the Armed Forces, corroborating the insubordination of military power to civilian power.[29]

On the other hand, we must also recognise the role of sectors of civil society, especially relatives of the disappeared, in efforts to demand that the state investigate and clarify cases of forced disappearance. Of particular note here is the Commission of Families of the Politically Disappeared in Brazil, whose national meeting in 1993 and the proposal of a bill culminated in the first legislative document to deal with the state's obligation to recognise and compensate the victims of enforced disappearances by the Brazilian state.[30]

4. *Efforts to identify and remedy enforced disappearances*

4.1 Law on the Recognition of Political Deaths and Disappearances (Law 9.140/1995)

In fact, it wasn't until 1995 that the process of holding the state accountable for the forced disappearances that took place during the military regime effectively began. This was when the Special Commission for the Recognition of Political Deaths and Disappearances was created.[31] An important reparation measure was the recognition of the death of all those accused of participating in political activities between 2 September 1961 and 5 October 1988 and who had disappeared.[32] This measure opened the way for the payment of compensation to the relatives of the disappeared.[33] This Commission was revoked at the end of Jair Bolsonaro's government and was only reinstalled on August 30 2024 by the Lula da Silva government, under the Ministry of Human Rights and Citizenship.[34]

---

29 Figueiredo 2015, 131, writes about a silent pact between the military and civilians to conceal the serious human rights violations perpetrated during the dictatorship.

30 Gallo 2014, 56.

31 On the work of this Commission, see Soares/Prado 2009, 353, 365.

32 See Teles 2009, 128.

33 See Ramos Tavares/Moura Agra 2009, 69, 84.

34 See https://www.gov.br/mdh/pt-br/assuntos/noticias/2024/agosto/retomada-historica-da-comissao-sobre-mortos-e-desaparecidos-politicos-e-classificada-como-201cmomento-de-cura201d-para-o-brasil (accessed 6 July 2025) and https://agenciabrasil.ebc.com.br/direitos-humanos/noticia/2024-07/lula-reinstala-comissao-sobre-mortos-e-desaparecidos-politicos (accessed 6 July 2025).

4.2 The National Truth Commission

Of great importance in the process of recovering the memory of the disappeared was the institution, by Law 12.528/2011, of the National Truth Commission, whose stated scope, in its Article 1, is to

> examine and clarify the serious human rights violations committed during the period established in Article 8 of the Transitional Constitutional Provisions Act, in order to fulfil the right to memory and historical truth and promote national reconciliation.

The Commission's Final Report sets parameters for recognising enforced disappearances and presents relevant information and historical reconstructions of these events. After presenting the definitions of enforced disappearances from the 1994 Inter-American Convention on Forced Disappearance of Persons and the 2006 UN International Convention for the Protection of All Persons from Enforced Disappearance, the Commission's Final Report establishes that:

> the CNV considered enforced disappearance to be any deprivation of liberty perpetrated by agents of the state – or by persons or groups of persons acting with the authorisation, support or consent of the state – followed by a refusal to admit the deprivation of liberty or to inform about the fate or whereabouts of the person, preventing the exercise of the relevant procedural guarantees.[35]

For enforced disappearance to be characterised, according to the Commission, the following elements must be present: the deprivation of the victim's liberty in any form; the direct intervention of state agents or third parties acting with state authorisation, support or consent; and the state's refusal to acknowledge the detention or reveal the fate or whereabouts of the person.[36] Enforced disappearance is defined as a multiple and multi-offensive or complex violation, violating several rights recognised by international standards such as the right to liberty, physical integrity, life, judicial protection and recognition of personality.[37] It is also characterised by being

35 National Truth Commission, Final Report, vol. 1, Brasilia 2014, 291, available at: https://www.gov.br/memoriasreveladas/pt-br/assuntos/comissoes-da-verdade/volume_1_digital.pdf (accessed 6 July 2025).

36 Ibid.

37 National Truth Commission, Final Report, vol. 1, 292.

an autonomous and permanent violation. As such, it is consummated the moment the victim's liberty is deprived, with the state denying information of their whereabouts, until the person is found and identified.[38] This creates an obligation for the state to act and investigate the disappearance for as long as there is uncertainty about the person's whereabouts. In line with this understanding,

> For the purposes of the CNV's work, the following were classified as enforced disappearances, considering the refinement of the logic of this disappearance in accordance with the state's standards of conduct: a) cases arising from detentions that were not officially recognised, followed by the denial of information about the victim's whereabouts: this is the model of disappearance that became standard between 1973 and 1974, in which militants were captured by the organs of repression in a context of intelligence operations around the organisations and intense monitoring of militants, often underground; b) cases arising from officially recognised arrests, followed by denial of information about the victim's whereabouts: although rare and sparse, such cases occurred in relation to militants who were not living underground and whose death, apparently unplanned, could leave no trace; and c) officially recognised deaths, with the absence of full identification of the remains: this is a pattern intended to exonerate the responsibility of the repression agency, with the assembly of false official versions for deaths caused by torture.[39]

Thus, as the Commission notes in its report, the official recognition of the death by the state does not imply the end of the enforced disappearance.

Enforced disappearance is therefore recognised by the Truth Commission as a strategy for concealing state crimes perpetrated during the military dictatorship in Brazil, whose primary victims were members of a series of resistance organisations.[40] The concealment of information about the whereabouts of the victims systematically colluded with various state bodies, including the connivance of the judiciary.[41] The refusal to provide information on missing persons was therefore institutionalised and included methods such as concealing corpses, burying people with false identities

38 National Truth Commission, Final Report, vol. 1, 293.
39 National Truth Commission, Final Report, vol. 1, 294.
40 Listed in National Truth Commission, Final Report, vol. 1, 501.
41 National Truth Commission, Final Report, vol. 1, 502.

and using clandestine cemeteries and graves,[42] dumping bodies in the sea or rivers,[43] incineration[44] and the dismemberment of bodies.[45]

The Commission's report also identifies the organisations responsible for enforced disappearances and the places where political prisoners were systematically taken.

In all, the National Truth Commission identified 243 cases of enforced disappearance between 1964 and 1980.[46]

5. Conviction by the Inter-American Court of Human Rights and Criminalization of Enforced Disappearance

In 2010, in the Gomes Lund case, Brazil was ordered by the Inter-American Court of Human Rights to take a series of measures, which included continuing to investigate cases of enforced disappearance and making enforced disappearance an autonomous offense.[47]

There are many international precedents in this context. Enforced disappearance is defined as a crime against humanity in Article 7 (2) (i) of the Statute of the International Criminal Court, in the United Nations Declaration on the Protection of All Persons from Enforced Disappearance (1992), in the Inter-American Convention against Enforced Disappearance (1994) and in the International Convention for the Protection of All Persons from Enforced Disappearance (2005).[48] To date, however, this autonomous criminalization in domestic criminal law has not been achieved, despite the efforts to do so established by the National Truth Commission.

---

42 Evidence was found, for example, in the Dom Bosco Cemetery in Perus, São Paulo, with the discovery of a clandestine grave; and in the Ricardo Albuquerque cemetery in Rio de Janeiro. For the forensic archaeology work carried out in this cemetery, see Vieira de Carvalho 2009, 341, 352.

43 National Truth Commission, Final Report, vol. 1, 518 et seq.

44 National Truth Commission, Final Report, vol. 1, 520.

45 National Truth Commission, Final Report, vol. 1, 522.

46 National Truth Commission, Final Report, vol. 1, 576. The victims are listed from page 577 onwards.

47 See n. 284, 285, 287 of the judgment, available at: https://www.corteidh.or.cr/docs/casos/articulos/seriec_219por.pdf (accessed 6 July 2025).

48 See Japiassú 2022, 154.

Congress is currently considering Bill 4.038/2008, which

> provides for the crime of genocide, defines crimes against humanity, war crimes and crimes against the administration of justice of the International Criminal Court, establishes specific procedural rules, provides for cooperation with the International Criminal Court, and makes other provisions.[49]

Article 33 of the bill defines enforced disappearance, imposing a penalty of 5 to 15 years in prison for the conduct of

> apprehending, detaining, kidnapping or otherwise depriving someone of their liberty, even legally, on behalf of the state or a political organization, or with their authorization, support or acquiescence, concealing or denying the deprivation of liberty or information about their fate or whereabouts to anyone who has the right to know, leaving the detainee without legal protection for more than forty-eight hours.

§ 1 establishes that those who order the act or keep the person under guard, custody or surveillance incur the same penalty and § 2 that 'the crime lasts as long as the fate or whereabouts of the detained person is not clarified, even if their death occurred at an earlier date.' Finally, § 3 defines the qualified form, with a penalty of 10 to 30 years in prison if the disappearance lasts more than 30 days.

It is clear that the legal definition does not link the punishable conduct exclusively to state actors; what is required is that the perpetrator acts on behalf of or with the authorization, support or acquiescence of the state or political organizations.[50] The concept of political organizations is limited to those whose duty it is to provide information about people's whereabouts.[51] It should be noted that the conduct linked to the deprivation of liberty and the denial of information about whereabouts are not alternatives, but must be concurrently present.[52] The mere concealment or disguise of infor-

---

49 Available at: https://www.planalto.gov.br/ccivil_03/projetos/PL/2008/msg700-080917.htm (accessed 6 July 2025).

50 Other legal systems rule differently this subject. For example, the German Penal Code, in its recent inclusion of the crime of enforced disappearance in § 234b, limits the list of active subjects to officials or people acting on behalf of the state or with its consent. See Valerius 2024, n. 6–8.

51 See Werle/Jeßberger 2022, n. 96.

52 Unlike, for example, the aforementioned § 234b of the German Penal Code. See Valerius 2024, n. 9–17, in which there is the variant of hiding or concealing information

mation cannot be grounds for participation by complicity, but it can give rise to a crime of improper omission if it involves a state agent with specific duties related to clarifying the fact. Keeping the person outside legal protection for more than forty-eight hours is a prerequisite for prosecution, unlike the rule in the Rome Statute, which is content with denying the person the protection of the law for a prolonged period of time.[53]

The offense requires intent – *dolus eventualis* would only be imaginable in the event of the concealment or concealment of information about the whereabouts of the person as autonomous variants, which is not the case in the proposed definition. Intent must also extend to the concealment or dissimulation of information on the part of the direct perpetrator; the same goes for the instigator and the accomplice, in other words: they must be aware that the direct perpetrator will refuse or refuses to provide truthful information about the victim's whereabouts.

The establishment of the penalty for the person who ordered the crime in § 1 raises the question of whether the instigator or the person who has command responsibility would be punished independently if the theory of control over the act by organized power apparatuses were adopted. Strictly speaking, the determination for the act presupposes its effective practice, and without explicit provision, it is not advisable to break with the structure of the concurrence of agents in criminal law. As such, the article is undoubtedly dogmatically innocuous as regards the first part of the heading – the act of kidnapping and deprivation of liberty itself: the one who ordered the crime would already be included in the list of participants in the crime. What about the need for information on the victim's whereabouts?

It should be considered that the final formula for concealing or denying the whereabouts of the person and keeping the person outside legal protection for more than forty-eight hours is what effectively characterizes the device.[54] Otherwise, the criminalization of legal kidnapping or deprivation of liberty, as provided for in the legal definition of the offense, would

---

about whereabouts. It should be noted, however, that refusing to provide information about the victim's whereabouts is also a constituent element of the first variant linked to deprivation of liberty.

53 It is also one of the elements that distinguishes the new rule of § 234b of the German Criminal Code from § 7, n. 7, of its International Criminal Code, which was content, like the Rome Statute, with the intention of keeping the person outside legal protection.

54 Regarding the concealment of information about a person's whereabouts as a fundamental characteristic of enforced disappearance, see Japiassú 2022, 154.

not make sense. Therefore, the commanders (and obviously the agents maintaining the deprivation of liberty) are also subject to the combination of kidnapping and hiding the whereabouts of the victims in order to fulfill the offense.

It should also be pointed out that, despite the provision about the possibility of 'competition with other crimes' in the sanctioning rule of art. 33 of Bill 4.038/2008, the conduct provided for in art. 148 of the Penal Code (kidnapping and private imprisonment) is necessarily excluded, under penalty of an obvious *bis in idem.*

6. Historical continuity of repressive violence: the unfinished re-democratisation

The longstanding absence of state recognition of enforced disappearances and the impunity imposed by the recognition of the validity of the amnesty law had the effect of not only hindering the memory of the victims of the authoritarian regime and the experience of mourning by their families,[55] but also perpetuated the practice of violence as an operational strategy of the Brazilian state.[56] It's as if this violence were de facto legitimised as a war strategy.

Militarisation continues to be one of the institutional characteristics of how public security is handled in Brazil.[57] Recent cases show that, although sometimes disconnected from a defined command centre, a common practice of the police continues to be to force the disappearance of people in order to conceal crimes committed within their scope of action.[58] The logic of eliminating political enemies and disregarding human rights, present in the public discourse on public security after re-democratisation, was only transferred to the ordinary criminal justice system, if it wasn't there all along, naturalising the acceptance of authoritarian practices by broad sectors of civil society during the period of exception.

In this sense, identifying cases of systematic disappearance of enemies of the state cannot be seen as a strategy to make the historical continuity of state violence in Brazil invisible; on the contrary, it is a provocation to think

55 See Teles 2009, 151; Soares/Prado 2009, 317.

56 See Pedretti 2024.

57 See Soares 2019.

58 The case of Amarildo de Souza, who was taken to a hearing by the Pacifying Police Unit and has since disappeared, has gained notoriety in the media and civil society.

about the historical continuity of this violence as a past that has not been overcome, which is always present, painfully present.

Bibliography

Aarão Reis, Daniel. 2001. 'A anistia recíproca ou a arte de reconstruir a História'. In Teles, Janaína (ed.). *Mortos e desaparecidos políticos: reparação ou impunidade?*. 2nd edition. São Paulo: Humanitas. 131–7.

Aarão Reis, Daniel. 2014. 'A ditadura faz cinquenta anos: história e cultura política nacional-estatista'. In Aarão Reis, Daniel, Ridenti, Marcelo and Motta, Rodrigo Patto Sá (eds.). *A ditadura que mudou o Brasil.* Rio de Janeiro: Zahar. 11–29.

Abrão, Paulo and Torelly, Marcelo. 2011. 'Democratization and Human Rights: Sharing the Latin American Experience'. In Reátegui, Félix (ed.). *Transitional Justice. Handbook for Latin America.* Brasília: Brazilian Amnesty Commission, Ministry of Justice. New York: International Center for Transitional Justice. 23–30.

Dorneck, Carina. 2024. 'Das Gesetz zur Fortentwicklung des Völkerstrafrechts'. *Neue Juristische Wochenschrift.* 43. 3102–7.

Figueiredo, Lucas. 2015. *Lugar nenhum. Militares e civis na ocultação dos documentos da ditadura.* São Paulo: Companhia das Letras.

Gallo, Carlos Artur. 2014. *Para que não se esqueça, para que nunca mais aconteça. Um estudo sobre o Trabalho da Comissão de Familiares de Mortos e Desaparecidos Políticos no Brasil.* Jundiaí: Paco Editorial.

Japiassú, Carlos Eduardo. 2022. *Direito Penal Internacional.* 2nd edition. São Paulo: Tirant lo Blanch.

Joffily, Mariana. 'O aparato repressivo: da arquitetura ao desmantelamento'. In Aarão Reis, Daniel, Ridenti, Marcelo and Motta, Rodrigo Patto Sá (eds.). *A ditadura que mudou o Brasil.* Rio de Janeiro: Zahar. 158–71.

Martins Filho, João Roberto. 2009. 'Tortura e ideologia: os militares brasileiros e a doutrina da guerre révolutionnaire (1959-1974)'. In Macdowell Santos, Cecília, Teles, Edson and Teles, Janaína de Almeida (eds.). *Desarquivando a ditadura. Memória e justiça no Brasil.* São Paulo: Hucitec. 179–202.

Martins, Antonio. 2012. 'A legalidade e a proibição de retroatividade das leis no direito penal e no direito penal internacional e o tratamento dos crimes estatais praticados durante o regime militar no Brasil'. *Revista Anistia Política e Justiça de Transição.* Brasília: Ministério da Justiça. 7. 202–30.

Martins, Antonio. 2022. 'Korruption – Demokratie – Strafrecht. Eine deutsch-brasilianische Betrachtung'. In Jeßberger, Florian and Kuhli, Milan (eds.). *Korruption – Demokratie – Strafrecht.* Tübingen: Mohr Siebeck. 5–22.

Motta, Rodrigo Patto Sá. 2018. 'Sobre as origens e motivações do Ato Institucional 5'. *Revista Brasileira de História.* 38.79. 195–216.

Motta, Rodrigo Patto Sá. 2021. *Passados presentes.* Rio de Janeiro: Zahar.

Pedretti, Lucas. 2024. *A transição inacabada. Violência e direitos humanos na redemocratização.* São Paulo: Companhia das Letras.

Piovesan, Flávia. 2009. 'Direito internacional dos direitos humanos e lei de anistia: o caso brasileiro'. In Soares, Inês Virgínia Prado and Kishi, Sandra Akemi Shimada (eds.). *Memória e verdade: a justiça de transição no Estado Democrático brasileiro.* Belo Horizonte: Fórum. 197–211.

Ramos Tavares, Andre and Moura Agra, Walber. 2009. 'Justiça reparadora no Brasil'. In Soares, Inês Virgínia Prado and Kishi, Sandra Akemi Shimada (eds.). *Memória e verdade: a justiça de transição no Estado Democrático brasileiro.* Belo Horizonte: Fórum. 69–91.

Soares, Inês Virgínia Prado. 2009. 'Memória democrática e desaparecidos políticos'. In Soares, Inês Virgínia Prado and Kishi, Sandra Akemi Shimada (eds.). *Memória e verdade: a justiça de transição no Estado Democrático brasileiro.* Belo Horizonte: Fórum. 317–40.

Soares, Luiz Eduardo. 2019. *Desmilitarizar: segurança pública e direitos humanos.* São Paulo: Boitempo.

Soares, Samuel Alves and Prado, Larissa Brisola Brito. 2009. 'O processo político da anistia e os espaços da autonomia militar'. In Macdowell Santos, Cecília, Teles, Edson and Teles, Janaína de Almeida (eds.). *Desarquivando a ditadura. Memória e justiça no Brasil.* São Paulo: Hucitec. 353–71.

Swensson Junior, Lauro. 2009. *Anistia penal. Problemas de validade da lei de anistia brasileira.* Curitiba: Juruá.

Teles, Edson. 'Brasil e África do Sul: rupturas e continuidades nas transições políticas'. 2009. In Soares, Inês Virgínia Prado and Kishi, Sandra Akemi Shimada (eds.). *Memória e verdade: a justiça de transição no Estado Democrático brasileiro.* Belo Horizonte: Fórum. 119–31.

Teles, Janaína de Almeida. 2009. 'Entre o luto e a melancolia: a luta dos familiares de mortos e desaparecidos políticos no Brasil'. In Macdowell Santos, Cecília, Teles, Edson and Teles, Janaína de Almeida (eds.). *Desarquivando a ditadura. Memória e justiça no Brasil.* São Paulo: Hucitec. 151–76.

Valerius, Brian. 2024. '§ 234b'. In von Heintschel-Heinegg, Bernd and Kudlich, Hans (eds.). *Beck Online Kommentar.* 63rd edition. München: Beck.

Weichert, Marlon Alberto. 'Responsabilidade internacional do Estado brasileiro na promoção da justiça transicional'. In Soares, Inês Virgínia Prado and Kishi, Sandra Akemi Shimada (ed.). *Memória e verdade: a justiça de transição no Estado Democrático brasileiro.* Belo Horizonte: Fórum. 153–68.

Werle, Gerhard and Jeßberger, Florian. 2022. 'VStGB § 7'. *Münchener Kommentar zum Strafgesetzbuch.* 4th edition. München: Beck.

Report on the Situation of Enforced Disappearance in Chile

Javier Contesse

Abstract: The report provides an overview of the main issues to be considered when analysing the situation of enforced disappearance in Chile. To this end, it traces the problem of enforced disappearances back to the phenomenon of disappeared detainees (*detenidos desaparecidos*) during the civil-military dictatorship of Augusto Pinochet, placing the problem in a broader historical context. It then examines the different ways in which the problem has been addressed during the democratic governments that followed the dictatorship, distinguishing between political-administrative, judicial, and political-legislative strategies. The central thesis in this regard is that an important part of Chile's difficulties in dealing with the issue of enforced disappearances can be explained by the overemphasis on both the political-administrative and the judicial strategies. Finally, it analyses some features of the progressive legislative recognition of enforced disappearance not only as an international crime, but also as a (possible) ordinary offence punishable under Chilean criminal law.

Introduction

The purpose of this report is to provide a descriptive overview of the main aspects to be considered when it comes to analysing the situation of enforced disappearance in Chile. This means taking into account both the specific features of the phenomenon, particularly its historical roots, and the way in which it has been dealt with institutionally. To this end, the report is divided into three parts. The first one looks at enforced disappearance in Chile as a phenomenon that can be traced essentially to the policy of systematic repression and extermination pursued by the Augusto Pinochet dictatorship between 1973 and 1990. The second part analyses the two main institutional ways in which this problem was addressed during the subsequent democratic governments, highlighting their inherent limitations. Finally, the third part examines some features of the process of gradual legislative recognition of enforced disappearance not only as an international crime but also as an ordinary offence punishable under domestic criminal law.

1. The phenomenon of enforced disappearance in Chile: a retrospective view

One of the most distinctive features of state terrorism in the Latin American dictatorships of the second half of the 20th century was the implementation of a policy of enforced disappearance directed against their political opponents or anyone who was perceived as a hindrance to the model of society to be imposed. Broadly speaking, enforced disappearance can be understood as the deprivation of liberty of a person, perpetrated by an agent of the State or a person acting at its behest or with its authorization, followed by a refusal to provide information about the fate or whereabouts of the victim.[1] From the very first day of Augusto Pinochet's *coup* on September 11 1973, the repression policy of the Chilean civil-military dictatorship involved the mass disappearance of political opponents throughout the country and even abroad.

The most intense repression took place between 1973 and 1976. During that period the arrests and subsequent disappearances were carried out by agents of the State, mostly members of the armed forces and the intelligence agencies (mainly the so-called *Dirección de Inteligencia Nacional* or DINA). The detainees were usually taken to secret detention centres (regiments, barracks, private homes, sports facilities, etc.), where they were tortured and, in many cases, killed. Some of them were held for several months before being released or killed, others died a few days or hours after being detained, either as a result of torture or summary executions. The mortal remains were usually buried in mass graves. Although there is no consensus on the matter, the number of people who disappeared during the civil-military dictatorship is estimated at 1092, of whom only 307 have been located and identified.[2]

1 This is a conveniently broad definition of enforced disappearance, aimed simply at allowing to explain the *phenomenon* of enforced disappearance. For an instructive overview of the various definitions available in the literature and in international law, Sferrazza 2019, 131–94.

2 Information available at: https://www.plannacionaldebusqueda.cl. Slightly different figures can be found in Sferrazza/Bustos 2022, 171; Collins 2018, 23–4; Guzmán 2009, 55. According to the National Plan for the Search of Truth and Justice (*Plan Nacional de Búsqueda de Verdad y Justicia*), the number of victims of enforced disappearance

After the first weeks of the regime's installation, the relatives of those who were already then known as *detenidos desaparecidos* (disappeared detainees) began to gather and found shelter in various civil society organizations that were mainly church-based.[3] As a result of this joint work, in 1975 the so-called *Agrupación de Familiares de Detenidos Desaparecidos* (Association of Relatives of Disappeared Detainees) was founded. Its first task was to raise the problem of the disappeared detainees in the (extremely intimidated) Chilean public opinion through various forms of peaceful demonstration.[4] The regime's reaction, though, was to continue denying the existence of disappeared detainees and to explain the disappearances as the result of internal purges of the leftist organizations.

However, the situation began to change in 1978. In November of that year, human remains were found in the furnaces of an old mine in Lonquén, a rural town near Santiago, which were believed to belong to disappeared detainees. The discovery had a huge impact on public opinion and forced the Supreme Court to launch an investigation. The investigation determined that the remains belonged to fifteen people who had disappeared in October 1973, after being detained by police officers. The Lonquén furnaces discovery posed then a major setback for the Pinochet regime's strategy of denial. The existence of the disappeared detainees became undeniable, to some extent ironically, as a result of their appearance, or more precisely, the appearance of their mortal remains.[5]

The discovery of Lonquén furnaces led to a radicalization of the policy of enforced disappearance. The regime decided to deploy a nationwide operation to exhumate the remains of the detainees that had been killed and make them disappear *definitively* by burning them or throwing them into the sea. The so-called *Operación Retiro de Televisores* (Operation to remove televisions) took the policy of disappearance and extermination to a crueller level: it was no longer enough to detain, murder and deny information to the relatives of the victims, but to destroy all traces of these crimes.[6]

---

is 1469. However, 377 of these correspond to executed persons whose bodies have not been located and 307 to persons whose remains have already been returned to their families. The number of strictly disappeared persons is 1092.

3 Between 1973 and the end of 1975, the main organization was the *Comité Pro-Paz* (Pro Peace Committee), which was replaced in early 1976 by the *Vicaría de la solidaridad* (Vicariate of Solidarity).

4 More information, available at: https://afdd.cl (accessed 30 December 2024).

5 Escalante et al. 2013, 357.

6 Escalante et al. 2013, 357–73.

This systematic strategy of concealment revealed a distinctive, though not necessarily exclusive, feature of the practice of enforced disappearance in Chilean history: the phenomenon went beyond what is understood by the most established conventions to be the enforced disappearance of persons. For the use of state terror was not limited to the abduction of persons and their subsequent removal from the protection of the law, but also included the destruction of their remains in order to remove the *perpetrators* from the *realm* of the law. As we shall see, this mechanism of self-exoneration would critically condition the fate of truth-processes after the return to democracy.

2. *Institutional approaches to the issue of detenidos desaparecidos in Chile*

2.1 The political-administrative approach: truth or reconciliation?

Uncertainty about the whereabouts of the disappeared continued to be the background of the systematic violations of human rights even after the end of the dictatorship. The Association of Relatives of Disappeared Detainees, together with other civil society groups, continued to work tirelessly to find their relatives during the whole period, but as long as Pinochet remained in power and the entire institutional system, including the judiciary, remained under his control, their efforts were unlikely to succeed.

It is therefore no coincidence that one of the first measures adopted by the first democratic government after the end of the dictatorial regime in March 1990, under the presidency of Patricio Aylwin, was the creation of a commission to establish the truth about the crimes committed by Pinochet's regime. The so-called *Comisión Nacional de Verdad y Reconciliación* (National Commission of Truth and Reconciliation), also known as *Comisión Rettig* (Rettig Commission), was created on April 25 1990, and met continuously for nine months, receiving more than 3400 testimonies from victims and their relatives.[7] In February 1991, it issued its report, known as the 'Rettig Report', in which it established the number of (di-

7 Comisión Nacional de Verdad y Reconciliación 1991, 5, available at: https://www.memoriachilena.gob.cl/602/w3-article-85803.html (accessed 30 December 2024).

rect) victims of state terrorism at 2298, of whom 979 were disappeared detainees.[8]

The work of the Rettig Commission not only marked a milestone in the process of reconstructing the dictatorial past, but also set a precedent for the way in which governments during the transition to democracy would address the problem of human rights violations, particularly enforced disappearances. The task would be carried out mainly by political-administrative means, through the creation of *ad hoc* commissions promoted on the initiative of the current government and composed of both representatives of the political forces opposed to the Pinochet regime and representatives of the political sector that supported it. In the Rettig Commission, for instance, four of its eight members belonged to this political sector.

Of course, such a design was not random. It was the result of a far-reaching political decision made early on within the Aylwin government, that consisted in carrying out the task of establishing the truth in a way that it would not upset (too much) the fragile political balance of the nascent regime. It should be remembered that during the Aylwin government (1990-1994) and a large part of the Eduardo Frei government (1994-2000), Pinochet continued to occupy the position of Commander-in-Chief of the Army, which he only left in March 1998 to become a senator. So, instead of making the establishment of the historical truth the basis of the new political order, the Aylwin, Frei and, to a lesser extent, Lagos (2000-2006) governments chose to subordinate this end to the goal of achieving the country's longed-for 'reconciliation' as soon as possible. Consequently, a quite significant role in the reconstruction of the dictatorial past was given to those who politically supported the dictatorial regime in the past.[9]

A clear expression of this approach can be found in the most prominent measure adopted by the Frei government to address the problem of disappeared detainees. After Pinochet's arrest in London in October 1998, and in order to legitimize its strategy of preventing his extradition to Spain and bringing him back to Chile, the government invited members of both sides of the political spectrum, important figures of civil society and repre-

8 Corporación Nacional de Reparación y Reconciliación 1996, 535, *Informe sobre la calificación de víctimas de violaciones de derechos humanos y de la violencia política. Anexo Nº 1*, available at: https://pdh.minjusticia.gob.cl/wp-content/uploads/2015/12/Informe_CNRR.pdf (accessed 30 December 2024).

9 See Mañalich 2023, 31, who speaks in this regard of an authentic 'ideology of reconciliation'.

sentatives of the army to a space for institutional dialogue, with the aim of creating conditions for the army to provide information about the detainees whose whereabouts were still unknown. The result was the creation of the so-called *Mesa de Diálogo* (Table of Dialogue) in August 1999. The *Mesa de Diálogo* met for a year before issuing its final report in August 2000. The role played by members of the army in the *Mesa* was crucial, and to some extent defined the spirit in which the dialogue was to take place. As the army representative pointed out in his first speech: 'The search for absolute justice can threaten the happiness and peace of the Chilean people, values that must be placed above all others in the pursuit of the common good.'[10] Although the report had valuable information about the whereabouts of some of the disappeared, it was discovered years later that some of the information provided by the army was inaccurate and, in some cases, outright false.

Although not strictly concerned with enforced disappearances, in 2003 the government of President Lagos created a third truth commission, called *Comisión Nacional sobre Prisión Política y Tortura* (National Commission on Political Prisoners and Torture), also known as Valech Commission, which afterwards became two successive commissions (Valech Commission I and Valech Commission II). Both focused on clarifying the cases of torture suffered by those who were political prisoners of the regime, a dimension whose in-depth analysis had been deliberately overlooked in the two previous instances. The reports of both commissions, published in 2004 and 2010, respectively, identified 27255 victims of torture and political imprisonment.

The latest manifestation of the political-administrative strategy to address the problem of disappeared detainees is the so-called *Plan Nacional de Búsqueda de Verdad y Justicia* (National Plan for the Search of Truth and Justice), created by the government of President Gabriel Boric.[11] The aim of the plan is to comply with the commitments made by Chile when it ratified the International Convention for the Protection of All Persons from Enforced Disappearance in December 2010, and with the recommendations subsequently made by the United Nations Committee on Enforced Disap-

10 First intervention of General Juan Carlos Salgado, available at: http://www.archivochile.com/Derechos_humanos/M_Dialogo/interv/hhddinterv0026.pdf (accessed 30 December 2024).

11 Available at: https://www.derechoshumanos.gob.cl/wp-content/uploads/2023/12/Publicacion-PNB-diario-oficial.pdf (accessed 30 December 2024).

pearances (CED) in May 2019. Among other things, the recommendations seek to ensure that 'the State continues to intensify its efforts to find persons who were subjected to enforced disappearance, during or after the dictatorship.'[12] As the search plan began in September 2023, its results are still unknown.

2.2 The judicial approach: the so-called 'legal solution to the problem of human rights violations'

2.2.1 Amnesty and statutory limitations as institutional obstacles

Nevertheless, the history of the investigation of human rights violations in Chile, and in particular of cases of enforced disappearance, is not primarily a political one, but a judicial one.[13] Since the early 2000s, and in response to the complaints filed by the victims' relatives, it has been mainly the courts that have taken on the task of reconstructing in detail the events that took place between 1973 and 1990. This so-called 'legal solution to the problem of human rights violations' has been the key factor in the process of reworking the dictatorship's past in Chile.[14]

It should be noted from the outset, however, that the characterization of these events as 'events that occurred between 1973 and 1990' is anything but innocent. Indeed, one of the most controversial aspects of the judicial solution was, and has been, the question of the *end* of the perpetration of the acts that could be classified as enforced disappearances; not only as a problem of judicial determination of truth, but also (and mostly) as a problem of the determination of the applicable law. To understand why, it is necessary to take a look to two distinctive aspects of the Chilean experience of enforced disappearance.

First, at the time when the crimes began to be committed, already on September 11 1973, there was no legal provision for the crime of enforced disappearance (nor is there today, except as crime against humanity). The criminal rules applicable to cases of deprivation of liberty with disappear-

12 Committee on Enforced Disappearances 2019, 6, *Concluding observations on the report submitted by Chile under article 29, paragraph 1, of the Convention*, available at: https://digitallibrary.un.org/record/3861509?v=pdf (accessed 30 December 2024).

13 Sferrazza 2021, 84–90.

14 Mañalich 2010, 9.

ance of the victim were then those of ordinary kidnapping, whose most simple case was regulated in the first paragraph of article 141 of the Chilean Criminal Code, and whose qualified cases were regulated in the following paragraphs.[15] Thus, the penalties imposed for acts that could constitute enforced disappearance have been the penalties for the crime of ordinary kidnapping (simple or qualified). Second, the aforementioned strategy of the regime to conceal the crimes was not only applied at a *factual* level, but also at an *institutional* one by creating legal obstacles to future criminal prosecution. The most important of these was the enactment of the so-called Amnesty Statutory-Decree of April 18 1978 (*Decreto-ley de amnistía* or just DL 2191), whose retroactive temporal scope of application was extended to the events that occurred between September 11 1973 and March 10 1978.[16] Despite what is stated in its preamble, DL 2191 was intended to institutionally ensure the impunity of the regime, anticipating the judicial scenario that would be faced after the return to democracy. It was, in other words, an authentic *self-amnesty*, which has not yet been derogated or annulled.[17]

Against this background, it is not difficult to understand what the problem of the determination of the end of the crimes of enforced disappearance was. Since, according to article 93 No. 3 of the Chilean Criminal Code, the amnesty 'completely extinguishes the penalty and all its effects', the validity of DL 2191 should prevent the courts from determining the criminal responsibility of those who perpetrated the enforced disappearances during the period of its applicability. Even if they were found to be responsible for the crimes, the courts would have to apply the article 93 No. 3 as a circumstance of extinction of responsibility and acquit them of the corresponding charges.

---

15 The norm at that time was as follows:
'Art. 141. Whoever imprisons or detains another person without right, depriving him of his liberty, shall be punished by minor imprisonment or reclusion in any of its degrees.
The same penalty shall be imposed on the person who provides a place for the commission of the crime.
If the imprisonment or detention lasts longer than ninety days, or if it causes serious harm to the person or interests of the imprisoned or detained person, the penalty shall be major imprisonment in any of its degrees.'
The norm has been amended several times since then.

16 On the origins and the historical context of the enactment of DL 2191, Correa 2014, 14–7.

17 Mañalich 2004, 21–5; Mañalich 2010, 155–83.

Something similar happens with the second institutional obstacle linked to the passage of time: the statute of limitations. According to article 93 No. 6 of the same code, the statute of limitations of criminal prosecution is also a circumstance that extinguishes criminal responsibility. Consequently, even in the cases where the enforced disappearances were committed after the period of temporal applicability of DL 2191, their prosecution under the ordinary criminal law would be barred, because between the end of the perpetration of the crimes and the time of their judgment usually more than ten years have elapsed. The period of statutory limitation for this type of crime under the Chilean criminal code is precisely ten years.[18]

2.2.2 Enforced disappearance as 'permanent kidnapping'?

The history of judicial recognition of the enforced disappearances in Chile is the history of the courts' and the victims' efforts to circumvent both obstacles. This is quite clear in the case of the most controversial of these efforts: the so-called doctrine of 'permanent kidnapping'.[19]

The doctrine is as follows: since the judicial proceedings brought against the State agents could certify the beginning of the deprivation of liberty, but not its end (because the person was missing), it should be assumed at the time of the judgement that the victim was still deprived of liberty and that, henceforth, the crime was still being committed. This would make it possible to avoid the obstructive effect of DL 2191. For the decree would not be applicable to the entire period in which, according to this doctrine, the crime is still being committed after March 10th 1978. The same would apply to the statute of limitations. As long as the victim (or her remains) have not been found, it could be assumed that the crime would continue to be committed until the time of judgment and so the period of the statute of limitations would not yet have begun. The nature of the crime as a 'permanent kidnapping' would then make it possible to deal with both obstacles judicially, without the need for the legislator to derogate or annul DL 2191 or, as the case may be, to modify the periods of the statute of limitations.

18 For an overview of the debate on the effects of the statute of limitations, Mañalich 2010, 205–25; Parra 2019, 247–85.

19 See Bascuñán 2005, 372–7; Mañalich 2004, 12–9; in more detail Mañalich 2010, 162–70.

The main consequence of this doctrine is not difficult to envisage: to some extent, it transformed, *de facto*, the crime of (ordinary) kidnapping into the crime of enforced disappearance.[20] The reason is that prosecution was only possible on the (implicit) assumption that the fact that perpetrators of the kidnappings do not provide any information about the whereabouts of the victims made their reluctance punishable; of course, not in its own right, but as a continuation of the original kidnapping. On the other hand, though this is exactly what makes the strategy so problematic. Since the continuation of the deprivation of liberty is presumed by the courts, the possibility of the accused being acquitted of the charge of kidnapping depends on *him* proving that the victim is no longer deprived of her liberty (in practice, proving that she is dead). To this extent, and beyond the fact that the expression 'permanent kidnapping' constitutes a mere pleonasm (kidnapping is already a permanent crime), the strategy entails a reversal of the burden of proof and thus a violation of the presumption of innocence.[21]

This and other difficulties led to the gradual disregard of the doctrine of 'permanent kidnapping.' The courts were then compelled to develop alternative strategies to deal with the problem of amnesty and statutory limitations. The main one consisted in *directly* challenging the applicability of DL 2191 and the statute of limitations by considering the crimes in question to be crimes against humanity and therefore not subject to amnesty and statutory limitations in the first place.[22] The problem was that, since neither of these two characteristics could be directly based on domestic criminal law at the time, the ground for the strategy had to be found in a different place. The obvious solution was to look to international human rights law and international criminal law.

This judicial trend was inaugurated by an emblematic decision of the Chilean Supreme Court in 2004, where the Court sought to 'illustrate' the seriousness of the crimes that were judged by invoking the Inter-American Convention on Enforced Disappearance of Persons and the Rome Statute of the International Criminal Court,[23] even though at that time neither of these instruments had been ratified by Chile.[24] This judicial construction

20 Mañalich 2004, 18; Mañalich 2023, 41.

21 Bascuñán 2005, 375–7; Mañalich 2010, 165-6.

22 Mañalich 2010, 171.

23 Corte Suprema No. 517–2004 (c. 18); see in this regard Bascuñán 2005, 377–85; Mañalich 2004, 11–6.

24 The Inter-American Convention on Enforced Disappearance of Persons was ratified only on January 27, 2010.

was further developed through the application of international humanitarian law, in particular the Geneva Conventions (1949) and the Additional Protocols to the Geneva Conventions of 1977.[25] Here, the Court's reasoning was based on the premise that the context in which the crimes were committed corresponded to a situation of 'internal armed conflict.'[26] Later on, references to the prohibition of enforced disappearance as a peremptory norm of international law (*jus cogens*) were also to be found in several decisions.[27] This has led to the emergence of a judicial practice of recognizing the kidnappings committed during the civil-military dictatorship as a problem of international law, a practice that continues to this day.[28]

3. *Enforced disappearance in democracy: a prospective view*

3.1 Political-legislative developments and the attempt at constitutionalisation

Now, the above strategy has not been without its problems, as has been noted several times in the specialized discussion.[29] In a nutshell, the main difficulty consists in the fact that, in order to make international conventions applicable, the courts have had to disregard part of their wording (for example, when applying the Geneva Conventions, while there was no armed conflict as referred to in these conventions) or to transform duties to protect human rights into duties of strict penalisation (for example, when applying the American Convention on Human Rights).[30] However, it is not the legal interstices of the strategy that matter here, but the underlying phenomenon that explains its adoption by the judiciary.

Indeed, the efforts of the courts to avoid the effects of the amnesty and the statute of limitations are largely due to the inability – or more precisely, the unwillingness – of the legislative bodies to take on the task of dealing *politically* with the dictatorial past. In this regard, the judicial treatment of human rights violations can be seen as a kind of 'privatisation' of the

25 Corte Suprema No. 3125–2004; Corte Suprema No. 3452–06.

26 For a critical analysis of this premise, see Fuentes 2005, 1193–200; see also Díaz 2006, 305–27.

27 Corte Suprema No. 559–2004; Corte de Apelaciones de Valparaíso No. 96–2010.

28 See, for example, Corte Suprema No. 104.196–2020 of March 6, 2023.

29 Bascuñán 2005, 377–85; Fuentes 2005, 1193–8; Mañalich 2010, 171–83.

30 Bascuñán 2005, 377–85; Mañalich 2010, 171–83.

problem of human rights violations: as a legal issue, the problem tends to disappear from the political arena and be confined to the corridors of the courts and the claims of victims, leading to a process of 'trivialisation' (through 'juridification') of state terrorism.[31] One would have expected, on the contrary, that post-dictatorship democratic legislatures would have promoted the adoption of a political decision to remove the institutional obstacles to the prosecution of the crimes of the dictatorship. Maybe the clearest expression of this state of affairs is the persistence of DL 2191 as a law in force, even after Chile was condemned by the Inter-American Court of Human Rights in its ruling in the *Almonacid Arellano* case for, among other things, failing to derogate or annul the decree.[32] At no time in the more than thirty years since the return to democracy has there been sufficient political will to make this fundamental decision.[33]

In spite of this, some legislative progress has been made. Chile's gradual integration into the international community after the return to democracy has led also to a gradual acceptance of international human rights law and international criminal law obligations, including those related to the regulation of the enforced disappearance. In July 2009 Chile ratified the Statute of the International Criminal Court (Rome Statute), whose article 7 (i) considers enforced disappearance as a crime against humanity. Then, in January 2010, it ratified the Inter-American Convention on Enforced Disappearance of Persons, and in December of the same year, the International Convention for the Protection of All Persons from Enforced Disappearance. Additionally, reference should be made to the legal reform of 2010 that transferred jurisdiction over many crimes committed by officials from specialised military courts to civilian courts.

As a result, a mainly legal-repressive model to deal with systematic disappearances has been adopted. In fact, the State has committed itself,

31 See Mañalich 2010, 29–45; Mañalich 2023, 46–50.

32 IACtHR 2006, Almonacid Arellano et al. *v.* Chile, available at: https://www.corteidh.or.cr/docs/casos/articulos/seriec_154_esp.pdf (accessed 30 December 2024).

33 In a recent ruling, the IACtHR has once again condemned the Chilean State for (failing to remove) some of the institutional obstacles in the prosecution of crimes of enforced disappearance. This time, the problem was the application by the Supreme Court of the rule of gradual statute of limitations contained in Article 103 of the Chilean Criminal Code, despite the fact that the Court itself recognises that these crimes are not subject to any statute of limitations; see IACtHR 2024, Vega González et. al. *v.* Chile, available at: https://jurisprudencia.corteidh.or.cr/serie-c/sentencia/1039351567 (accessed 30 December 2024). On the problem of the applicability of this rule in general, Parra 2019, 277–78; Sferrazza/Fernández 2009, 183–92.

among other things, to making enforced disappearance an autonomous crime. This commitment, however, has only been partially fulfilled. Today enforced disappearance is penalised as a crime against humanity in Article 6 of the 2009 Act No. 20357, which implements the penalisation of the international crimes of the Rome Statute under the Chilean law. Enforced disappearance is thus an offence that is punishable under the condition that it belongs to a generalised or systematic attack against a civil population, whereas the attack must respond to a policy either of the State or its officials or of an organised group of some kind. However, there is no *ordinary* crime of enforced disappearance in Chile. Only a draft bill proposing the criminalisation of enforced disappearance as an ordinary crime is currently being discussed in Congress, whose fate, however, remains uncertain.[34]

Finally, the draft of the new Constitution of 2022, which included a rule declaring enforced disappearance as a crime against humanity and obliging the State to punish it (Art. 24), was rejected in the referendum of September 4 2022.[35] Other institutional preventive measures against enforced disappearance, such as special procedural mechanisms, are not envisaged.

3.2 Enforced disappearance under normal institutional conditions

Both the decision to include enforced disappearance in domestic legislation as a crime against humanity and the discussion whether to penalise it as an ordinary crime express a concern that goes beyond the problem of disappeared persons during the civil-military dictatorship. Since both decisions assume that enforced disappearances could be committed and prosecuted within a normative context grounded on the rule of law, the concern is about the possibility that enforced disappearances could also be perpetrated under 'normal' institutional conditions.

This concern is not unfounded. There is serious information about the existence of at least four cases of enforced disappearance that have occurred

34 Bulletin 9818-17 of December 17, 2014. The article 147 of the draft bill declares: 'Anyone who deprives one or more persons of their liberty and who refuses to report or acknowledge the deprivation of liberty or the whereabouts of the victim commits the crime of enforced disappearance of persons and shall be punished with imprisonment ranging from 3 years and one day to 15 years.'

35 On this effort of constitutionalisation, see Contesse 2023, 273 et seqq.; on constitutionalisation of enforced disappearance in general, Sferrazza/Bustos 2021–2022, 157–89.

since the return to democracy, one of which resulted in a criminal conviction for (simple) kidnapping against four police officers.[36] This is the case of José Vergara Espinoza, a young man suffering from schizophrenia, who was arrested in September 2015, in Alto Hospicio, a town located in the far north of the country, and then transferred to an isolated area in the desert, where he eventually disappeared. His whereabouts remain unknown to this day. The case was brought before the Inter-American Commission on Human Rights, which admitted it in September 2023.

However, the fact that this concern is factually founded does not mean that it is also normatively justified. The idea of criminalising the deprivation of liberty followed by the failure to report the victim's whereabouts – concretely, the failure to report the deprivation of liberty – as a crime distinct from kidnapping (or, for that matter, from unlawful detention) could be seen as problematic in contexts that do not lead to a situation of structural impunity generated by the State. What is consequently at stake is no more and no less than respect for such fundamental principles as the presumption of innocence and *nemo tenetur*.[37] This shows the importance of deciding whether, in cases of enforced disappearance, the deprivation of liberty itself should be a crime or not. The discussion of this problem, though, is beyond the scope of this report, as it concerns the analysis of the legal regulation of enforced disappearance in Chile, a problem that is addressed by other contributions to this volume.

Conclusion

The above considerations can be summarised as follows:

1. The phenomenon of enforced disappearance in Chile stems from the phenomenon of disappeared detainees during the civil-military dictatorship of Augusto Pinochet Ugarte between 1973 and 1990. The Pinochet regime pursued not only a systematic policy of disappearance and extermination of its political opponents, but also a factual and institutional strategy of obstructing the search for the truth, which would have important consequences after the return to democracy.

36 Sferrazza/Bustos 2021–2022, 172 et seq.; see also Instituto Nacional de Derechos Humanos, *Informe Complementario al Comité contra las Desapariciones Forzadas de Naciones Unidas*, 2, available at: https://bibliotecadigital.indh.cl/server/api/core/bitstreams/a3ffa4ec-3ec8-4f9f-a987-bd077c8c7594/content (accessed 29 September 2025).

37 Bascuñán 2007, 67 et seq.

2. During the democratic governments that followed the dictatorship, the problem of the disappeared detainees was basically tackled in two ways: a political-administrative one, consisting of the creation of truth commissions, and a judicial one, characterised by the efforts of the higher courts to circumvent the institutional obstacles contained in the current law, which is still a partial legacy of the dictatorship. No real political-legislative path has been taken to overcome these obstacles.
3. Beyond the issue of the disappeared during the dictatorship, efforts to criminalise enforced disappearance in Chile have been timid. At present, enforced disappearance in Chile is only a crime against humanity. There is still no ordinary crime of enforced disappearance, nor are there any institutional, preventive mechanisms that go beyond a legal-repressive model.

Bibliography

Bascuñán, Antonio. 2005. 'Ley penal'. *Revista de Derecho de la Universidad Adolfo Ibáñez.* 2. 361–85.

Bascuñán, Antonio. 2007. 'Derechos fundamentales y derecho penal'. *Revista de Estudios de la Justicia.* 9. 50–74

Collins, Cath. 2018. 'Transitional Justice »From Within«: Police, Forensic, and Legal Actors Searching for Chile's Disappeared'. *Journal of Human Rights Practice.* 10. 19–39.

Contesse, Javier. 2023. 'Bienes jurídicos, derechos fundamentales y Constitución'. In Ambos, Kai and Guzmán, José Luis (eds.). *Constitución y derecho penal en Chile.* Santiago de Chile: Der Ediciones. 243–83.

Correa, Cristián. 2005. 'El Decreto Ley de Amnistía: orígenes, aplicación y debate sobre su validez'. In Veloso, Paulina (ed.). *Justicia, Derechos Humanos y el Decreto Ley de Amnistía.* Santiago: Lom Ediciones. 13–68.

Díaz, Regina. 2006. 'Aplicación de los convenios de Ginebra por los tribunales de justicia chilenos'. *Revista Chilena de Derecho.* 33.2. 305–27.

Escalante, Jorge et al. (eds.). 2013. *Los crímenes que estremecieron a Chile. Las memorias de La Nación para no olvidar.* Santiago de Chile: Ceibo Ed.

Fuentes, Ximena. 2005. 'Derecho internacional público'. *Revista de Derecho de la Universidad Adolfo Ibáñez.* 2. 1193–220.

Guzmán, José Luis. 2009. 'Chile'. In Ambos, Kai (ed.). *Desaparición forzada de personas.* Bogotá: Temis. 55–75.

Mañalich, Juan Pablo. 2004. 'El secuestro como delito permanente frente al DL de amnistía'. *Revista de Estudios de la Justicia.* 5. 11–33.

Mañalich, Juan Pablo. 2010. *Terror, pena y amnistía.* Santiago: Flandes Indiano.

Mañalich, Juan Pablo. 2023. *Derechos penal y terrorismo de Estado.* Santiago: Roneo.

Parra, Francisco. 2019. 'Los efectos de la media prescripción penal'. *Revista de Derecho*. 246. 247–85.

Sferrazza, Pietro and Fernández, Karinna (eds.). 2009. 'La aplicación de la prescripción gradual del delito en las causas sobre violaciones de derechos humanos'. *Anuario de Derechos Humanos*. 5. 183–92.

Sferrazza, Pietro. 2019. 'La definición de la desaparición forzada en el derecho internacional'. *Ius et Praxis*. 25.1. 131–94.

Sferrazza, Pietro. 2021. 'La búsqueda de personas desaparecidas en Chile: ¿necesidad de un complemento humanitario?'. *Revista Mexicana de Ciencias Políticas y Sociales*. 243. 79–108.

Sferrazza, Pietro and Bustos, Francisco. 2021–2022. 'La constitucionalización del derecho a toda persona a no ser sometida a desaparición forzada'. *Estudios Constitucionales*. Especial Issue. 157–89.

Enforced Disappearance in Nazi and Post-War Germany

Kai Cornelius

Abstract: The following article focuses on the criminal procedural safeguards against enforced disappearance that have existed within the German criminal procedure for decades. The analysis traces a historical trajectory beginning with the Nazi regime's Night and Fog Decree (and its processing in the Nuremberg Trials) through the Allied internment camps to the special camps in the Soviet Occupation Zone (SBZ), thereby also addressing the Soviet methods of domination and practices of Stalin's GULAG. Particular attention is paid to the impact of these events on the constitutionally guaranteed obligation to notify in cases of deprivation of liberty, especially within the context of pre-trial detention. The contribution also considers how these issues were received and reflected in post-war German legal public discourse and among legal scholars.

1. Introduction

The following analysis examines 'enforced disappearance' as a mass phenomenon in 20th-century Germany. The analysis is based on a two-part offence, consisting, on the one hand, of deprivation of liberty against the will of the victim with the involvement of state authorities, and, on the other hand, of the concealment or denial of this fact to the outside world.

In this context, reference should be made to the introduction of Section 234b of the German Criminal Code (StGB), which provides for the substantive criminal prosecution of enforced disappearances.[1] This provision complements existing protections under international criminal law[2]

1 Cf. the contribution by Geneuss/Jessberger, in this volume p. 185.

2 See also the international criminal law standardization as a crime against humanity in Art. 7 para. 1 lit. i. of the Rome Statute and in section 7 para. 1 no. 7 German Code of Crimes against International Law (VStGB) as well as the International Convention for the Protection of All Persons from Enforced Disappearance ratified by Germany, UN Resolution 61/177.

by establishing a national legal framework against the secret abduction of individuals by state authorities.

2. Nazi State

2.1 'Protective and preventive custody'

When Hitler came to power on 30 January 1933, the Weimar Republic was almost immediately transformed into a dictatorship. This led to an unleashing of police power, which significantly restricted the functional range of the criminal justice system. From the very beginning concentration camps were employed – among other things – to detain political opponents of the regime. Formal judicial detention law was increasingly displaced by informal police power, exercised under the concepts of so-called protective and preventive custody. However, it was not the initial intent of the National Socialist rulers to systematically deny those arrested contact with the outside world or cause them to disappear. The concentration camps used for protective and preventive custody were not hermetically sealed off from the outside world.

Conversely, the fact that contact with the outside world was not intended to be entirely prohibited from the outset can also be seen from the 'Disciplinary and Penal Regulations,' which initially only applied to the Dachau concentration camp and were issued on 1 October 1933. These regulations included, among other things, a postal ban as a disciplinary measure – something that presupposes the general possibility of postal communication. These disciplinary and penal regulations were also gradually introduced in other concentration camps.[3] Similarly, the civil status provisions regarding the regulations on the reporting and registration of deaths applied to the administration of the concentration camps. This included the obligation under Section 159 of the Code of Criminal Procedure (StPO) requiring police and municipal authorities to report all cases of non-natural death to the public prosecutor's office or the district judge.[4]

Whereas detainees taken in police custody were practically without rights, those arrested within the framework of criminal proceedings still retained certain rights. Prisoners on remand were subject to the provisions

3 Gruchmann 2002, 646; cf. Suhr 1985, 71.
4 Gruchmann 2002, 633.

of the Code of Criminal Procedure (StPO), including the right to notification under (at that time) Section 114a StPO.[5] Disregarding this right to notification can only be documented for detainees who were subject to the Night and Fog Decree, which is why this is examined in more detail below.

2.2 Night and Fog Decree

2.2.1 Contents

With the start of the Russian campaign in 1941, resistance activities also increased in the western occupied territories and in Norway. Seemingly in response to a major case of espionage and resistance (the Porto case) in occupied France,[6] Hitler commuted the death sentence of a French woman convicted of participating in resistance activities to imprisonment, with the simultaneous provision that she be secretly taken to Germany and kept completely isolated from the outside world. Hitler pursued two goals with this course of action: on the one hand, it was intended to prevent the woman from becoming a martyr by carrying out the death sentence, and on the other hand, her disappearance without a trace was intended to act as a deterrent to the population and dissuade potential copycats from carrying out their plans.[7]As resistance activities intensified, in September 1941 Hitler decided to systematically use enforced disappearances by secretly deporting perpetrators and suspects of such actions to Germany, under the utmost secrecy and complete exclusion of the public – except in cases where an

---

5 Section 114a RStPO in the version valid from 13 January, 1927 – 1 October, 1950 read: 'Dem Verhafteten ist Gelegenheit zu geben, Angehörige und, soweit er daran ein wesentliches Interesse hat, andere Personen von der Verhaftung zu benachrichtigen, sofern der Zweck der Untersuchung nicht gefährdet wird; auf Verlangen des Verhafteten ist die Benachrichtigung von Amts wegen zu bewirken.' ('The arrested person shall be given the opportunity to inform relatives and, if he has a substantial interest in doing so, other persons of the arrest, provided that the purpose of the investigation is not jeopardized; at the request of the arrested person, notification shall be effected ex officio.')

6 Wagner 2011, 416, 432.

7 Gruchmann 1981, 342 with reference to the genesis of the 'Nacht - und Nebel - Erlass' in fn. 2.

immediate execution of a death sentence by the military courts was anticipated.[8]

This ultimately served as the foundational idea for the drafting of the Night and Fog Decree, during which informal discussions between Ministerial Director Lehmann, head of the legal department in the OKW, and Freisler resulted in the involvement of the 'civil' judiciary in the process; the Wehrmacht judiciary was to conduct prosecutions only under certain conditions.[9] The Night and Fog Decree and its implementing regulations applied in Norway, the Netherlands, Belgium, and occupied France.[10]

To ensure that the objective of enforced disappearance without a trace was met, it was ordered that the court hearing in Germany be held in strictest secrecy.[11] In order to ensure the secrecy regarding the prisoners' fate, questions from foreign and German authorities were to be answered by stating that the prisoner had been arrested and that the status of the proceedings did not permit any further communication.[12] This regulation is interesting in that it shows that German authorities did not intend to conceal the mere fact of the arrest. The relatives were therefore not to be left in complete uncertainty; their uncertainty was to be confined solely to what happened to the prisoner after his arrest.[13]

A second implementing regulation contained detailed instructions that served to maintain the secrecy of the proceedings. It again specified that inquiries were to be answered solely by confirming the arrest.[14] For the first time, an explicit order was issued to completely prohibit the prisoner's

8 Cf. Keitel's statement on the origin of the Nacht und Nebel decree before the International Military Tribunal, International Military Tribunal (ed.), Trial of the Major War Criminals, vol. 10, 609 et seqq.

9 Wagner 2011, 418.

10 Compare the Secret Directive of the High Command of the Wehrmacht, Amt Ausland/Abwehr, of 2 February, 1942, reprinted in Cornelius 2006, 419 et seq. and no. XIV para. 1 of the second decree on the implementation of the directives of the Führer and Supreme Commander of the Wehrmacht for the prosecution of crimes against the Reich or the occupying power in the occupied territories, reprinted in Cornelius 2006, 421–3.

11 No. 5 of the implementing decree of December 7, 1941, reprinted in Cornelius 2006, 414–6.

12 No. 3 of the decree of December 7, 1941, reprinted in Cornelius 2006, 413 et seq.

13 See also the description in Wagner 2011, 416 et seq.

14 Item IX para. 1 of the second decree on the implementation of the directives of the Führer and Supreme Commander of the Wehrmacht for the prosecution of offences against the Reich or the occupying power in the occupied territories, reprinted in Cornelius 2006, 421–3.

communication with the outside world. The prisoner was explicitly forbidden from writing, sending or receiving letters, parcels or visitors.[15] Even the defence lawyers were prohibited from contacting foreign or German offices and individuals regarding a prisoner brought to Germany.[16]

Even in the case of NN deaths, the relatives were not notified. The body was buried at the place of death and this place of burial was not disclosed.[17] For deaths in NN cases that occurred in the prisons under the jurisdiction of the Ministry of Justice, the secret circular decree of 6 March 1943 ordered that the legally prescribed notification to the registrar was to be made in all cases. A restriction notice, agreed with the Reich Ministry of the Interior, was to be included in the report, which declared that the inspection and issuing of information, certified copies and death certificates was only permitted with the consent of the Reich Minister of Justice.[18]

When the judiciary could no longer keep up with the processing of the trials, it was decided as a measure of relief that the defendants who were not charged or acquitted due to lack of guilt or minor guilt would no longer be held in custody by the judicial authorities. These defendants were to be handed over to the Gestapo. The Gestapo was to detain them for the duration of the war.[19] Since this agreement at the latest, it was irrelevant

15 No. IX para. 4 of the second decree on the implementation of the directives of the Führer and Supreme Commander of the Wehrmacht for the prosecution of offences against the Reich or the occupying power in the occupied territories, reprinted in Cornelius 2006, 421.

16 No. X of the second decree on the implementation of the directives of the Führer and Supreme Commander of the Wehrmacht for the prosecution of offences against the Reich or the occupying power in the occupied territories, reprinted in Cornelius 2006, 421–3.

17 The letter from the Chief of the SiPo and the SD dated 24 June, 192 to the OKW states: 'It is the purpose of the Führer's directives ... to create uncertainty among relatives and acquaintances about the fate of the prisoners for reasons of deterrence. This objective would be broken if the relatives were notified in the event of death. Releasing the body for burial at home is inappropriate for the same reasons and also because the burial site can be misused for demonstration purposes. I :: -:: therefore propose :: -:: that the following regulation :: -:: be made for the treatment of deaths ::-::: a) the relatives are not notified, b) the body is buried at the place of death in the territory of the Reich, c) the place of burial is not disclosed for the time being.' International Military Tribunal (ed.), Trial of the Major War Criminals, vol. 26, 242 et seq. (Nuremberg Doc PS-668).

18 Peschel-Gutzeit 1996, 115; Wagner 2011, 425 et seq.

19 See instruction of the Reich Ministry of Justice regarding the treatment of NN prisoners dated January 21, 1944, reprinted in Cornelius 2006, 426; see also Steiniger/Lesczynski 1969, 56 (exhibit 318), 59 (exhibit 328); Wagner 2011, 424.

how the judiciary decided on the accused. In any case, the accused was handed over to the Gestapo at the end of the trial and execution and sent to a concentration camp by the Gestapo. The paradoxical situation arose that a defendant who was sentenced to prison was in a better position after serving his sentence than someone who was acquitted and then immediately sent to a concentration camp by the Gestapo.

In the concentration camps, care was taken to ensure that the 'NN' prisoners were housed separately from the other prisoners. In the Natzweiler concentration camp, for example, they were specially marked with yellow horizontal stripes on their clothing. They also wore the letters 'NN' on their backs and thighs.[20]

2.2.2 Analysis

It is not known how many people were deported to Germany in complete isolation from the outside world. According to the last available statistics from the Reich Ministry of Justice dated 30 April 1944, 6,639 defendants had been handed over to the judiciary by this date on the basis of the NN decree.[21] However, this does not take into account the arrivals until the NN proceedings were discontinued by the judiciary in August 1944, nor the people who were not handed over to the judiciary by the Gestapo but were deported and imprisoned in 'administrative proceedings', which is why research assumes, albeit tentatively, that there were 'perhaps 10,000' NN prisoners.[22]

Overall, it should be noted that the total number of NN prisoners among the millions of victims of National Socialism was only a very small group in quantitative terms.[23] However, the 'Nacht-und-Nebel' decree already described and intended essential elements that can be recognized today as enforced disappearances.

However, this did not necessarily mean particularly cruel treatment for the prisoners concerned as part of the overall Nazi terror system, and in some cases, they were even saved from extermination, as long as the judicial

20 Brunner 2000, 67.

21 Files of the RJM, BA Sign. R 22/20198, vol. 2; Steiniger/Lesczynski 1969, 61 (exhibit 333); the figure of 8639 in the Juristenurteil is obviously a typographical error; see Peschel-Gutzeit 1996, 119.

22 Huhle 2016, 10.

23 Huhle 2016, 10.

method of enforced disappearance by 'night and fog' was adhered to. The ultimate goal of the 'Nacht-und-Nebel-Aktionen' was not the physical extermination of the prisoners, but their isolation until after the war and the psychological terror effect on the relatives and the affected population by concealing the fate of these prisoners.[24]

The actual significance of the 'Nacht-und-Nebel' (Night and Fog) decree therefore lies not so much in the rather small circle of NN prisoners affected, if one considers the largely unregulated barbarity of the murder of millions of people in the concentration camps and extermination camps during the Third Reich, but rather in the extensive file material of the Nazis, which clearly documented both the origin and the implementation of the 'Nacht-und-Nebel' decree.[25] This may also be the reason why this decree is repeatedly mentioned as a historical starting point for the technique of 'enforced disappearance.'[26]

2.2.3 Legal Proceedings in Nuremberg

The issue of the disappearance without a trace of civilians from the occupied territories based on the Night and Fog Decree was legally dealt with both in the Nuremberg main war crimes trial[27] and in the follow-up trials against leading lawyers[28] (Case 3) and the OKW[29] (Case 12).[30]

This is because the terrorist intent so clearly stated within the 'Night and Fog' decree already attracted a great deal of attention in the main war crimes trial and was given particular weight in the indictment and verdict. Like the prosecution, the court took the view that enforced disappearances in the context of the 'cloak-and-dagger operations' were among the crimes

24 Huhle, 2016, 8, 11.
25 Huhle, 2016, 12.
26 Huhle 2016, 14 et seq.
27 International Military Tribunal (ed.), Prozess gegen die Hauptkriegsverbrecher, vol. 1, 327; vol. 2, 152 et seqq.; cf. the remark of Dr. Nelte at the trial before the International Military Tribunal: 'There is hardly an order which has impressed itself more strongly on the memory during the trial before this Tribunal than the 'Nacht-und-Nebel' order.' International Military Tribunal (ed.), Trial of the Major War Criminals, vol. 18, 27.
28 Peschel-Gutzeit 1996, 101–3.
29 Knieriem 1953. 440–2.
30 Cornelius 2006, 95.

that were already prohibited under Article 46[31] of the Hague Convention.[32] Article 6b of the IMT Statute, under which the defendant, Keitel, was convicted of war crimes, was therefore, according to the Court, 'merely a repetition of the existing law of war.'[33] Moreover, the Court continued, these rules of the law of war had already been recognized by all civilized nations at the beginning of the Second World War and had thus become customary international law.[34]

The crime so well documented by the 'Night and Fog Decree,' which we now call 'enforced disappearance,' was recognized in its essential features as a special form of psychological terror not only against the disappeared person themselves but also against their family and their entire environment, and was defined as an international crime in Nuremberg.[35]

3. *Post-War Germany*

3.1 Common foundations of the occupation policy

In order to develop a common occupation policy for the future, the Moscow Foreign Ministers' Conference of the Allies fighting against Germany had already decided in October 1943 to form a 'European Advisory Commission' (EAC) based in London.[36] In the 'Agreement on the Control Machinery in Germany' signed on 14 November 1944, it was stated that an Allied Control Council was to be formed for matters concerning Germany as a whole. At the same time, however, it was stipulated that 'supreme authority in Germany... would be exercised by the commanders-in-chief... each in his own occupation zone.'[37] This created the possibility that the actual treatment of German civilians would differ fundamentally in the respective occupation zones.[38]

31 This reads: 'The honor and rights of the family, the life of citizens and private property, as well as religious beliefs and acts of worship shall be respected.'
32 Steiniger 1957, 260.
33 Steiniger 1957, 260.
34 Steiniger 1957, 260.
35 Huhle 2016, 13.
36 Wettig 1967, 35 et seq.
37 Possekel 1998, 26 et seq.
38 Possekel 1998, 29.

In accordance with joint resolutions, the Allies set up many internment camps immediately after the occupation of Germany.[39] Former Nazi concentration camps were also used: in the British occupation zone, for example, Neuengamme, in the American, Dachau, in the Soviet, Buchenwald, Sachsenhausen and the former Jamlitz satellite camp.[40]

As the Allies initially operated the internment as a temporary security measure for the occupying troops, the detainees were to be completely isolated from the outside world; accordingly, the internees were initially denied any contact with the outside world.[41] It is worth noting that the relatives of internees who were isolated from the outside world were also threatened with severe punishment if they informed third parties about the internees by letter or telephone. The censorship regulations of the Military Government, Section I, 6g, stated that it was forbidden to communicate the names of persons who had been arrested, detained, interrogated or interned by the Allied Forces, as well as the location and description of internment sites.[42] This was primarily based on fears of an underground resistance movement operating in occupied Germany and the associated security considerations.

3.2 Occupation zones of the Western Allies

When these fears were not confirmed, the Western Allies loosened the contact ban from 1946 at the latest.[43] For example, internees in the American zone were allowed to send a postcard for the first time in the fall of 1945.[44] In the British zone, '25-word cards' were only permitted from the beginning of 1946, which could be written every two weeks.[45] Visiting opportunities were handled even more rigidly. With very few exceptions, prison leave was not possible.[46] Permission to write letters was not granted until November 1946. It was now permitted to write a letter of up to 250 words every

39 Niethammer/Mironenko 1998, 473.
40 Plato 1998, 32.
41 Niethammer/Mironenko 1998, 479; Friedrich 1995, 846 et seq.
42 Friedrich 1995, 847.
43 Cornelius 2006, 115.
44 Niethammer 1995, 455; Schick 2007, 306 et seq.; Horn 1992, 221; Wember 2007, 138.
45 Wember 2007, 138.
46 Wember 2007, 136, 140.

two weeks (from spring 1947, every week).[47] On 1 December 1947, the postal restrictions were considerably relaxed. From this date, internees were allowed to send three letters of 150 words per week.[48]

3.3 Special camps in the Soviet occupation zone

The Soviet Union itself had – contrary to the above-mentioned considerations on internment, which were only to take effect after Germany's capitulation – carried out summary arrests of Germans behind the frontline troops until mid-April 1945. These arrests initially served to secure the troops against German resistance and (once the territories of the German Reich were reached) to paralyze the German state and economic apparatus, but above all to recruit manpower.[49] This largely indiscriminate arrest practice changed when the territory of the future Soviet Occupation Zone (SBZ – i.e. the area that later became the German Democratic Republic – GDR) was reached, as more precise criteria for arrest and internment were issued for the first time and it was determined that 'the necessary number of prisons and camps should be set up.'[50]

This marked the inception of the Soviet special camps in Germany. The history of their development is closely linked to the German war of aggression and the occupation policy in the Soviet Union during the Second World War, the agreements of the anti-Hitler coalition and the Stalinist character of the Soviet actors and the 'Gulag Archipelago.'[51] The Stalinist camp system came to Germany with the Red Army. Although some of the special camps were set up in former National Socialist concentration camps, they were based on the legal understanding and methods that had been shaped by the experiences of the Soviet GULAG.[52] The term 'special camp' became synonymous with inhumane camp conditions, mass deaths and prolonged strict isolation of prisoners in the Soviet occupation zone.[53]

47 Wember 2007, 139.
48 Wember 2007, 140.
49 Cornelius 2006, 107–9.
50 Basic Decree of the People's Commissar for Internal Affairs of the USSR of April 18, 1945 (NKVD Order no. 00315), reprinted in German translation in Possekel 1998, 178 et seq.
51 Prieß 1997, 11 et seq.
52 Bonwetsch, 1999, 62; in detail Cornelius 2006, 116–8.
53 Prieß 1997, 9 et seq.

The disappearance of inmates without a trace also led to the alternative designation of the special camps as 'silence camps.'[54] This type of camp in particular pursued the isolation of prisoners.[55]

While the internments initially carried out immediately after the end of the war were based on common Allied law, internment policy in the Soviet Occupation Zone developed differently from that in Western occupation zones, not only because of the prolonged isolation of the camp inmates from the outside world, but also with regard to detention practice.[56]

Over time, instead of the original internees (i.e. prisoners without a sentence – a total of 122,671 Germans are said to have been directly affected),[57] more and more prisoners with the status of prisoners sentenced by a Soviet military tribunal (SMT) were held in the special camps.[58] In November 1946, just under 10% of the special camp prisoners were SMT convicts, while this proportion amounted to around 55% of the more than 30,000 prisoners still in the special camps at the end of 1949/beginning of 1950.[59] In total, around 35,000 people were sentenced for war crimes and crimes against humanity, but also for crimes against the occupying power and the GDR.[60]

There were several arrests in the special camps with a concrete connection to the power struggles between the SPD and the KPD/SED and to the disputes during the unification process between the two parties.[61] Increasingly, the suspicion of the formation of political opposition groups, 'espionage and agent activity,' in particular, contacts with the SPD's Eastern Office, the *Kampfgruppe gegen die Unmenschlichkeit* (Combat Group Against Inhumanity) or the Radio in the American Sector (RIAS), was a reason for arrests.[62]

In the special camps of the Soviet Occupation Zone, the total isolation of the camps and the ban on contact between prisoners and their relatives was maintained until the respective release campaigns in 1948 and 1950.[63]

54 Prieß 1997, 14; Cornelius 2022, 257.
55 Prieß 1997, 14.
56 Cornelius 2006, 126.
57 Prieß 1997, 9.
58 Jeske 1998, 477.
59 Oleschinski/Pampel 1997, 19; Kersebom/Niethammer 1998, 515.
60 Müller 2015, 21.
61 Erler/Friedrich 1995, 320; Prieß 1997, 19.
62 Erler 1999, 210.
63 Posseckel 1998, 87 et seq.

The prisoners here suffered particularly from the complete isolation from the outside world and the compulsion to inactivity, whereby they were forbidden any meaningful activity such as reading and writing.[64]

This mirrored the Stalinist purges in the USSR, which had already been used there to punish 'counter-revolutionary crimes' and determined the fate of millions of Soviet citizens.[65]

4. Reflection in German post-war society

4.1 'Night and Fog Decree' and Nuremberg trials

Although many Germans had had a positive attitude towards the Nazi regime, the Nuremberg trials were initially followed with interest and acceptance. As high-ranking representatives of the Third Reich sat in the dock at these trials, this attitude may also have been due to the exculpatory function the Nuremberg trials served for the 'average German.'[66] This attitude changed in the course of the progressive 'denazification,' which affected millions of Germans.[67] For this reason, the entire Nuremberg follow-up trials were met with predominantly decisive rejection by the political public.[68]

In German jurisprudence itself, there was little discussion of the NN issue in connection with the Nuremberg trials. At least the follow-up trial against the leading lawyers (Case 3) would have given sufficient cause for discussion. The 'Süddeutsche Juristenzeitung' reported on the start of the trial.[69] The few other articles in the specialist press about the outcome of the trial and the verdict were reported only in broad outline.[70] Only Gustav Radbruch's essay, entitled 'Des Reichsjustizministeriums Ruhm und Ende. Zum Nürnberger Juristenprozess,'[71] dealt with the trial and in particular with Schlegelberger's justification that he had chosen the lesser evil to prevent the greater evil.[72] There was therefore no real discussion of

64 Benz 1999, 369.
65 Cornelius 2006, 127–9.
66 Bästlein 1996, 27; see also Wrobel 1989, 188.
67 Cornelius 2006, 96.
68 Perels 1998, 96.
69 Radbruch 1948, 216.
70 Haensel 1948, 40 et seqq.; Behling, 1949, 502–4.
71 Radbruch 1948, 57 et seqq.
72 Kastner 2018, 63.

the lawyers' verdict in the specialist press during the immediate post-war period.[73] There was even less discussion of the OKW trial. Initially, only a book containing the defence speeches of lawyer Heinrich Latenser was published.[74]

4.2 Perception of internment

Similar to the initial acceptance of the Nuremberg Trials, the fact of denazification and internment itself was recognized and supported by many Germans immediately after the end of the war.[75] Due to the initially absolute isolation of the internment camps, only rumors about them circulated among the population, most of which related to the living conditions in the camps.[76] The more it became clear that almost the entire population was affected by the wave of denazification, the more attitudes towards denazification and internment changed. From 1947, the view spread among Germans that denazification should be ended and only those who had committed a criminal offence themselves should be charged.[77] This attitude can also be observed in the evaluation of the contemporary press.[78]

4.3 Perception of the special camps among the population of the SBZ / GDR

If family members are included, hundreds of thousands of people were in fact affected by the special camps in the Soviet Occupation Zone.[79] The arbitrary arrests and the disappearance without a trace of relatives, neighbours and colleagues created a climate of fear and uncertainty among the population.[80] In their despair over their uncertain fate, the relatives of those arrested repeatedly asked both the German and Soviet authorities for

73 Perels 1998, 94; Wrobel 1989, 188; Bästlein 1996, 23.
74 Laternser 1950.
75 Wember 2007, 224; see also Cornelius, 2006, 115 et seq.
76 Wember 2007, 225.
77 Wember 2007, 228.
78 Wember 2007, 228 et seq.; Meiser 1980, 199 et seq.
79 Ritscher 2020, 119.
80 Cornelius 2006, 144 et seq.

information or for the release of the internees.[81] The internees were sworn to secrecy if they survived and were released.[82] After the Waldheim trials in 1950, the subject of the special camps disappeared almost completely from the GDR media. A silence began that lasted for almost four decades. It was only with the political change in the GDR in the fall of 1989 that former camp inmates and their relatives began to come forward with their accounts.[83]

4.4 Special case Berlin

Berlin was the 'frontline city' of the Cold War. There the problems of the post-war period came to the fore with particular drama. On the one hand, the practices of the Soviet occupying power were applied in the eastern part of the city. On the other hand, relatively free reporting by the mass media was possible in the three western sectors of the city occupied by the Western Allies. The discussion about the disappearance of people was conducted with considerable intensity in the media as well as in the parties and municipal authorities of Berlin.[84] People disappeared not only from the eastern sectors of the city but in some cases from the western sectors as well.[85]

5. Reaction in the constitution-making process

5.1 Consultations on the Berlin post-war constitution

As in the newly formed states throughout post-war Germany, Berlin was also working on a new constitution. The highly topical and ever-present issue of disappearances played a prominent role in this process.[86] The intention to put a stop to state arbitrariness by introducing a duty of notification in the event of deprivation of liberty became clear. This is because only an *obligation* – as opposed to a waivable *right* to notification – can prevent

81 Ritscher 2020, 148.
82 Morré 1997, 62.
83 Ritscher 2020, 126; Cornelius 2006, 147.
84 Cornelius 2006, 199–201.
85 Ibid, 150.
86 Ibid, 221.

the authorities from simply claiming that it was the detainee's wish not to inform the outside world of the arrest.[87] The demand for a notification *obligation* can be traced for the first time during the consultations on the Berlin post-war constitution,[88] even if its representatives were unable to assert themselves.[89]

5.2 Constitutional Convention of Herrenchiemsee

The work on the state constitutions also had an impact on the deliberations of the constitutional convention at Herrenchiemsee for the forthcoming Constitution. In the process, Otto Suhr attempted – ultimately successfully – to strengthen the notification obligation, which ultimately failed in the Berlin Constitution, into an unconditional directive to the judge. In addition to the 'experiences from the Nazi era,' he was concerned with the 'events in the East.'[90] Suhr was particularly concerned with establishing a connection with the outside world 'under all circumstances.' This can only be achieved if third parties are always informed of all arrests.[91]

Why the then current 'events in the East' had such an influence on the Constitutional Convention becomes clear when looking at the overall situation. For the Convention participants, the quality of the constitution to be drafted was a contentious issue. This was also due to the unresolved question of how the states in the Soviet occupation zone and Berlin should be involved in the new state. It was unclear whether an overall state was to be established that already included the states in the Soviet occupation zone as components, or whether only a provisional arrangement was to be created; and the establishment of an overall state postponed to a later date.[92]

87 Ibid.
88 Ibid, 216.
89 Ibid, 216 et seqq.
90 For more details, see Cornelius 2006, 235–7.
91 Cornelius 2006, 228.
92 Bucher, Parliamentary Council, vol. 2, LXX. Cf. also Spitta's statement on this, Sten. Prot. of the second plenary session of the Constitutional Convention at Herrenchiemsee of 11.08.1948, repr. in Bucher, Parlamentarischer Rat, vol. 2, 94 et seq.

5.3 Notification obligation in Art. 104 para. 4 GG

Article 104 (4) of the Constitution, which then actually came into force, contains an unrestricted duty of *notification* in the event of deprivation of liberty – as does its statutory codification in Section 114 c (2) of the Code of Criminal Procedure. The courts are obliged to immediately inform a relative of the person concerned or a person they trust of the decision to deprive them of their liberty. This duty is to be fulfilled ex officio, i.e. it is not dependent on a corresponding application by the person concerned.[93]

It also contains a subjective *fundamental* right of the detained person to notify a relative or a trusted person of the deprivation of liberty, which is independently protected in relation to personal liberty.[94] The genesis of the provision shows,[95] that it is intended to prevent the disappearance without a trace of undesirable persons.[96] State-controlled disappearances of opponents of the regime without a trace create uncertainty for relatives and trusted persons, making legal and political action against arrests impossible:[97] by deliberately not providing any information regarding their whereabouts, detentions cannot be denounced legally, politically or by civil society.[98] Limiting the abuse of state power by preventing enforced disappearances is also in the public interest, as it ensures compliance with the procedural rules of the rule of law so that the notification requirement must be regarded as an inherent part of the principle of the rule of law.[99] It is therefore all the more important that the obligation to notify is also taken seriously by the specialist courts and handled in accordance with its significance. Recent decisions by the Federal Constitutional Court on this issue show that this is not always the case in Germany; it is therefore all the more important that the Federal Constitutional Court has taken corrective action here.[100]

93 BVerfGE 16, 119, 123 – 2 BvR 516/62; Schulze-Fielitz in: Dreier 2018, Art. 104 para. 56.
94 Rüping 2025, Art. 91; Mehde 2024, Art. 104 para. 175; Amelung 1981, 6.
95 Cornelius 2006, 224–6.
96 BVerfG, decision of 14.5.2020 - 2 BvR 2345/16, para. 43; Schulze-Fielitz, (fn. 93), para. 56; Radtke 2023, Art. 104 para. 17.
97 Brodowski 2012, 980 et seq. (984).
98 Cf. for example the case ECtHR 2002, Orhan v. Turkey, para. 328 et seq.
99 Grzeszick 2024, Art. 20 para. 27.
100 BVerfG, decision of 18.12.2023 - 2 BvR 656/20, 2 BvR 1816/22, and 2 BvR 1210/23.

5.4 Conclusion

The Night and Fog Decree on disappearances without a trace shows how the last constitutional procedural rights were dismantled with great (also bureaucratic) zeal. However, it is noteworthy that this decree only applied to the occupied western territories. Germany's own population was not affected by systematic, untraceable disappearances. The criminal procedure regulations still provided for the possibility of notification in the event of arrests. Even in the case of 'administrative' deprivations of liberty, which were carried out in the concentration camps, the prisoners did not disappear without a trace from their relatives. Contact with the outside world was not excluded from the outset in the concentration camps.

It was not until the end of the Second World War and the mass internment of Germans in the Allied camps that mass disappearances without a trace became apparent. This was facilitated by the absolute ban on contact between internees and their relatives, which applied to all Allied internment camps at least until the fall of 1945. However, it should be noted that in the immediate aftermath of the collapse of the Third Reich, with its vast numbers of displaced persons, which included prisoners of war, fallen soldiers and, ultimately, internees, many people were searching for their relatives for a variety of reasons. The missing persons in the internment camps were only one part of the search for relatives. In view of this fact and bearing in mind the fears and worries of people in the immediate post-war period, some of which threatened their very existence, it is not surprising that the internment camps were not given a prominent place in the German public eye with regard to the ban on contact between relatives and internees.

The Soviet occupying power brought its means and methods of dealing with political opponents to Germany. Even though the initial isolation of prisoners in the special camps of the Soviet Occupation Zone was carried out in accordance with the Western Allies, this development increasingly diverged from the internment practice in the Western zones. The occupying power gradually concentrated on political opponents. While internees in the Western Allies were able to communicate with the outside world from 1946 at the latest, this was not permitted for prisoners in the Soviet Occupied Zone until 1948 at the earliest, and in most cases not until 1949. People in the Soviet Occupation Zone had to live with the fact that they (or relatives, friends and colleagues) were arbitrarily arrested and never heard from again. This fact was known to the population in both the Soviet Occupation Zone and the Western zones. The mass media in the Western zones reported on the conditions in the Soviet Occupation Zone, no doubt because the fact that people disappeared without a trace also made excellent headlines during the Cold War.

This led to the standardisation of a notification obligation in Art. 104 para. 4 GG. This is intended to prevent the 'enforced disappearance' of unwelcome people, which is practised in particular by dictatorial-totalitarian apparatuses of power. This is because the state-organized disappearance without a trace of opponents of the regime leads to uncertainty for relatives and trusted persons, so that legal, political and civil society action against detentions is excluded or at least made considerably more difficult. However, recent decisions by the Federal Constitutional Court show that the specialized courts do not consistently implement the obligation to notify, which emphasizes the importance of the corrective intervention of the Federal Constitutional Court.

Bibliography

Amelung, Knut. 1981. *Die Einwilligung in die Beeinträchtigung eines Grundrechtsgutes.* Berlin: Duncker & Humblot.

Bästlein, Klaus. 1996. 'Das Nürnberger Juristenurteil und seine Rezeption in Deutschland.' In Peschel-Gutzeit, Lore Maria (ed.). *Das Nürnberger Juristen-Urteil von 1947: historischer Zusammenhang und aktuelle Bezüge.* Baden-Baden: Nomos. 9-35.

Behling, Kurt. 1949. *Nürnberger Lehren.* Berlin: De Gruyter.

Benz, Wolfgang. 1999. *Deutschland unter alliierter Besatzung 1945-1949/55.* Berlin: Akademie Verlag.

Bonwetsch, Bernd. 1999. *Der GULAG – das Vorbild für die Speziallager in der SBZ.* Berlin: Ch. Links.

Brunner, Bernhard. 2000. *Auf dem Weg zu einer Geschichte des Konzentrationslagers Natzweiler.* Baden-Württemberg: Landeszentrale für politische Bildung.

Brodowski, Dominik. 2012. 'Grundfälle zu den Justizgrundrechten'. *Juristische Schulung.* 52.10. 892–984.

Cornelius, Kai. 2006. *Vom spurlosen Verschwindenlassen zur Benachrichtigungspflicht bei Festnahmen.* Berlin: Berliner Wissenschaftsverlag.

Cornelius, Kai. 2022. 'Der Einfluss der Isolierung von Speziallagerhäftlingen auf die Rechtsentwicklung in Nachkriegsdeutschland.' In Heitzer, Enrico and Landau, Julia (eds.). *Zwischen Entnazifizierung und Besatzungspolitik, Sowjetische Speziallager im Kontext.* Göttingen: Wallstein Verlag. 257–66.

Dreier, Hans. 2018. *Grundgesetz Kommentar: GG.* 3rd edition. Tübingen: Mohr Siebeck Verlag.

Erler, Peter and Friedrich, Thomas. 1995. *Das sowjetische Speziallager Nr. 3.* Berlin: Biographische Forschungen und Sozialgeschichte e.V.

Erler, Peter. 1999. *Zur Tätigkeit sowjetischer Militärtribunale in Deutschland.* Berlin: De Gruyter.

Friedrich, Jörg. 1995. *Das Gesetz des Krieges.* München: Piper.

Grzeczik, Bernd. 2024. 'Art. 20'. In Dürig, Günter, Herzog, Roman and Scholz, Rupert (eds.). *Grundgesetz Kommentar.* 106th edition. München: C. H. Beck.

Gruchmann, Lothar. 1981. *Nacht- und Nebel-Justiz.* München: De Gruyter Oldenbourg.

Gruchmann, Lothar. 2002. *Justiz im Dritten Reich 1933-1940.* Berlin: De Gruyter.

Huhle, Rainer. 2016. *Nacht und Nebel: Mythos und Bedeutung.* Stiftung Topographie des Terrors: Gedenkstätten Rundbrief Nr. 184 12/2016.

Haensel, Carl. 1948. *Das Urteil im Nürnberger Juristenprozeß.* Tübingen: Mohr Siebeck Verlag.

Heitzer, Enrico and Landau, Julia. 2022. *Zwischen Entnazifizierung und Besatzungspolitik: Die sowjetischen Spezialleger 1945-1950.* Göttingen: Wallstein Verlag.

Horn, Christa. 1992. *Die Internierungs- und Arbeitslager in Bayern, 1945-1952.* München: Peter Lang GmbH.

Jeske, Natalja. 1998. *Kritische Bemerkungen zu den sowjetischen Speziallagerstatistiken.* Berlin: De Gruyter.

Kastner, Klaus. 2018. 'Der Dolch des Mörders war unter der Robe des Juristen verborgen' – Der Nürnberger Juristenprozess des Jahres 1947. *Recht und Politik.* 54.1. 53–69.

Kersebom, Heinz and Niethammer, Lutz. 1998. *"Kompromat" 1949: Eine statistische Annäherung an Internierte, SMT-Verurteilte, anitsowjetische Kämpfer und die Sowjetischen Militärtribunale.* Berlin: De Gruyter.

Laternser, Hans. 1950. *Verteidigung deutscher Soldaten.* Berlin: Giradet & Co.

Mehde, Veith. 2025. 'Art. 104'. In Dürig, Günter, Herzog, Roman and Scholz, Rupert (eds.). *Grundgesetz Kommentar.* 108th edition. München: C. H. Beck.

Meiser, Hans. 1980. *Der Nationalsozialismus: Gescheiterte Friedensinitiativen 1939-1945.* Berlin: De Gruyter.

Morré, Jörg. 1997. 'Mühlberg/Elbe - Speziallager Nr. 1.' In Morré, Jörg (ed.). *Speziallager des NKWD.* Brandenburg: Brandenburgische Landeszentrale für politische Bildung. 51–62.

Müller, Klaus-Dieter. 2015. 'Verbrechensahndung und Besatzungspolitik. Zur Rolle und Bedeutung der Todesurteile durch Sowjetische Militärtribunale.' In Weigelt, Andreas et al. *Todesurteile sowjetischer Militärtribunale gegen Deutsche (1944-1947).* Göttingen: Vandenhoeck & Ruprecht. 15–62.

Niethammer, Lutz. 1995. *Der "gesäuberte" Antifaschismus.* Berlin: De Gruyter.

Oleschinski, Brigitte and Pampel, Bert. 1997. *"Feindliche Elemente sind in Gewahrsam zu halten".* Berlin: Gustav Kiepenheuer.

Perels, Joachim. 1998. 'Der Nürnberger Juristenprozess'. *Kritische Justiz.* 31.1. 84–98.

Peschel-Gutzeit, Lore Maria. 1996. *Das Nürnberger Juristen-Urteil von 1947.* Baden-Baden: Nomos.

Possekel, Ralf. 1998. 'Sowjetische Lagerpolitik in Deutschland' In Mironenko, Sergej et al. 1998. *Sowjetische Speziallager in Deutschland 1945 bis 1950.* Band 2. Berlin: De Gruyter. 15–110.

Prieß, Lutz. 1997. 'Einleitung – Sowjetische Internierungslager in der SBZ.' In Morré, Jörg (ed.). *Speziallager des NKWD*. Brandenburg: Brandenburgische Landeszentrale für politische Bildung. 9–24.

Radbruch, Gustav. 1948. 'Des Reichsministeriums Ruhm und Ende. Zum Nürnberger Juristenprozeß'. *Süddeutsche Juristenzeitung*. 3.2. column. 57-64.

Radtke, Henning. 2023. 'Art. 104'. In Epping, Volker and Hillgruber, Christian (eds.). *BeckOK Grundgesetz*. 56th edition. München: C. H. Beck.

Ritscher, Bodo et al. 2020. *Das sowjetische Speziallager Nr. 2 1945-1950*. Göttingen: Wallstein Verlag.

Rüping, Hinrich. 2025. 'Art. 91'. In Kahl, Wolfgang, Waldhoff, Christian and Walter, Christian (eds.). *Bonner Kommentar zum Grundgesetz*. Heidelberg: C. F. Müller.

Schick, Christa. 2007. *Die Internierungslager*. Berlin: De Gruyter.

Steiniger, Peter Alfons. 1957. *Der Nürnberger Prozess in zwei Bänden: Band 1*. Frankfurt: Rütten & Loening.

Steiniger, Peter Alfons and Lesczynski, Kazimierz. 1969. *Das Urteil im Juristenprozess, gefällt am 4. Dez. 1947 vom Militärgerichtshof 3 der Vereinigten Staaten von Amerika*. Berlin: Deutscher Verlag der Wissenschaften.

Suhr, Elke. 1985. '*Konzentrationslager – Justizgefangenenlager – Kriegsgefangenenlager im Emsland 1933–1945.' In: Ludwig Eiber (ed.), Verfolgung, Ausbeutung, Vernichtung. Die Lebens- und Arbeitsbedingungen der Häftlinge in deutschen Konzentrationslagern 1933– 1945*. Hannover: Westerhahn Verlag. 66–89.

Von Knieriem, August. 1953. 'Nürnberg: Rechtliche und menschliche Probleme.' *International Affairs*. 30.2. 207–8.

Von Plato, Alexander. 1998. 'Zur Geschichte des sowjetischen Speziallagersystems in Deutschland. Einführung.' In Mironenko, Sergej et al. (eds.). *Sowjetische Speziallager in Deutschland 1945 bis 1950*. Band 1. Berlin: De Gruyter. 19–75.

Wagner, Walter. 2011. *Der Volksgerichtshof im nationalsozialistischen Staat*. München: Verlag Oldenbourg.

Wettig, Gerhard. 1967. *Entmilitarisierung und Wiederbewaffnung in Deutschland*. München: Verlag Oldenbourg.

Wember, Heiner. 2007. *Umerziehung im Lager*. Essen: Klartext Verlag.

Wrobel, Hans. 1989. *Verurteilt zur Demokratie*. Berlin: Decker & Müller.

Human Identification in Mexico: A Technological Approach to Identification and the Role of International Cooperation[1]

Rocío Yoguez and Maximilian Murck

Abstract: This article describes UNFPA's role in supporting Mexico's strategic and technical efforts on human identification, focusing on the role of international cooperation to implement recommendations from the UN Committee on Enforced Disappearances (CED). It highlights the Human Identification Program implemented by UNFPA Mexico with generous funding from the governments of Germany and Norway and in close cooperation with the Mexican government. The article emphasizes the crucial role of fingerprint matching with the National Electoral Institute (INE) as a key strategy to accelerate the identification process.

1. The Scale of Mexico's Forensic Challenges and CED Recommendations

Mexico officially reports over 130,000 missing persons to date. Families and relatives are searching for their loved ones across the country. These are countless stories of loss, desperation, anger and the relentless pursuit of truth and justice.

Contextually, forensic institutions across the country face a significant and growing backlog of identification cases. It is estimated that over 72,000 unidentified human remains are in the forensic morgues and public cemeteries across the country.[2] In addition, Mexico registers approximately 80

1 Disclaimer: The views expressed herein are those of the authors and do not reflect the views of UNFPA or the United Nations. Any information that may be contained in this chapter does not imply recognition by the United Nations of the validity of the views in question and is included without prejudice to the position of any Member State of the United Nations. The author's contributions are made in their personal capacity and do not reflect the view of UNFPA or the United Nations or their own institutions.

2 AMLO's six-year term ends with more than 72,100 unidentified bodies (2024), available at: https://quintoelab.org/project/sexenio-amlo-72-mil-cuerpos-crisis-forense (accessed 10 July 2025).

homicides per day.[3] According to the National Institute of Statistics and Geography of Mexico, in 2023, 9,134 unidentified bodies and 2,366 unidentified human remains were stored in forensic institutes, 90% of which were stored in forensic services institutions.[4]

Despite the sheer number of disappearances and unknown deaths, the Mexican government has shown significant commitment to addressing the issue. Since December 1, 2018, the federal administration has emphasized addressing the root causes of disappearances in Mexico and strengthening technical support for families and forensic institutions.

It is reasonable to assume that a significant number of persons reported as missing may be among the unidentified bodies stored in the Forensic Services Departments and their corresponding Medical Examiner's Offices across the 32 states. In the meantime, families and those searching for their loved ones are unable to find certainty about what has happened to them. This uncertainty and the inability to grieve impose enormous emotional pressure on these relatives.

In Mexico, the term NN individuals (unknown name) refer to individuals whose identities remain unknown after their examination in the forensic medical service. It is important to distinguish between unidentified individuals and unclaimed identified individuals. The latter refers to persons who have been identified after a legal medical necropsy but whose families have not requested the restitution. The National Information System of Missing and Deceased Persons (SINPEF, by its Spanish acronym) uses the terms 'unidentified deceased person' (PFsI) and 'unclaimed deceased person' (PFnR) to categorize these groups.

The classification of unidentified deceased persons (PFsI) pertains to those whose identities remain unknown due to a lack of evidence or accessible information, despite the forensic efforts made to identify them, such as DNA analysis, fingerprinting and comparisons with missing persons databases. On the other hand, unclaimed deceased persons (PFnR) are individuals whose identity has been established through forensic examination but whose families have not come forward to claim the remains. This can occur due to various reasons, such as the families being unaware of the

3 Crime incidence. Executive Secretariat of the National Public Security System (2025), available at: https://www.gob.mx/sesnsp/acciones-y-programas/incidencia-delictiva-299891?state=published (accessed 10 July 2025).

4 Forensic Services and Forensic Medical Service, National Institute of Statistics and Geography of Mexico (2024), available at: https://www.inegi.org.mx/contenidos/programas/cnge/2024/doc/resultados_serv_per.pdf (accessed 10 July 2025).

individual's death, family estrangement or the lack of resources to claim the body. These cases often lead to the remains being held in morgues or other facilities for extended periods, further complicating the burden on already overwhelmed forensic services.

One of the major challenges faced by the forensic system in Mexico is the increasing number of unidentified remains, especially in the context of violence related to organized crime and the disappearance of migrants. As mentioned, according to civil society organizations, there are over 72,000 unidentified bodies in morgues across Mexico. These are remains that entered Forensic Institutes between 2006 and 2023, whose identification processes remain ongoing.

Of these 72,000 bodies and human remains, 73 percent are men, and 8 percent are women. The sex of the remaining 19 percent is not reported. The majority of the bodies are concentrated in five states: Baja California, State of Mexico, Mexico City, Jalisco and Chihuahua, which together account for 6 out of every 10 bodies (Tzuc and Sánchez 2024).

Regarding the storage of these more than 72,000 bodies, over 67 percent are in common graves at cemeteries across the country, and it is believed that their use has increased since the beginning of the 'war on drugs', a strategy that led to a rise in homicide victims and resulted in the overcrowding of forensic services.

As part of the Mexican government's ongoing commitment to strengthening the national search and identification system, the National Search Commission (CNB) was formally strengthened and tasked with ensuring the establishment of 32 state search commissions across all Mexican federal states. Additionally, the CNB received a substantial public budget increase to strengthen forensic services. This includes funding for the construction of identification centers and cemeteries, the purchase of DNA databases and context analysis for criminal investigations and preventative measures.

This commitment marked an important step following the approval of the General Law on Disappearances in 2017 by the outgoing federal administration. The General Law is widely perceived as a result of the tireless advocacy of families and civil society. It comprehensively addresses the issue of disappearances and is generally considered a strong, broad, and helpful legal framework. However, there have been several delays in its implementation, such as that of the creation of a nationwide forensic database.

2. *Forensic challenges and Committee of Enforced Disappearances recommendations to Mexico*

The Committee on Enforced Disappearances (CED) report, following its November 2021 visit to Mexico, provided a critical assessment of the country's forensic challenges. While acknowledging regulatory and institutional advances like the General Act on Enforced Disappearance, the Committee expressed deep concern over the existing forensic challenges, noting over 52,000 unidentified deceased persons highlighting the need to further strengthen forensic services nationwide. These findings highlighted the urgent necessity for a cohesive national policy on human identification. Specifically, the CED recommendations called for strengthening forensic capacities and emphasized the crucial importance of standardized data management systems and fingerprint identification technologies, thereby setting the essential framework for the subsequent focus of the UNFPA Human Identification Program.

The CED states that '[f]orensic services are insufficient and, as will be explained below, several of the instruments provided for in the General Act have not yet been established and there is no public policy on human identification in relation to the disappearance of persons'.[5] In addition to these technical challenges, forensic services in many states are underfunded and understaffed, which further exacerbates the identification process. The disappearance of migrants from Central and South America presents an additional challenge, including the lack of accessible records in their countries of origin and the need for cross-border collaboration to facilitate timely and accurate identification efforts. Yet, there have been advances in this regard. For example, the ICRC recently signed a Cooperation Agreement with the National Registry of Persons of Honduras, which allows for the comparison of fingerprint data with that country.

The following examples illustrate the challenges that forensic services face:

- **Example 1: Jalisco 'Refrigerated Truck' Case of 2018:** In this incident, a refrigerated truck was used to store over 200 unidentified bodies due to the severe overcrowding of morgues in the state. The truck was moved across various locations in Guadalajara and surrounding areas. This case underscored the systemic failures of forensic and governmental institu-

---

5 United Nations (2022), CED/C/MEX/VR/1 Sec. III. C para. 29.

tions[6] to adequately respond to the escalating number of violent deaths and disappearances in the region. Many of the bodies remained unidentified due to significant delays in DNA testing, a shortage of trained forensic personnel, and poorly managed or disorganized databases.[7]

- **Example 2: Colinas de Santa Fe mass grave in Veracruz in 2016:** The Colectivo Solecito de Veracruz uncovered what is now considered the largest clandestine mass grave in the country. Located near the port of Veracruz, the site contained over 300 bodies and thousands of bone fragments. This discovery was largely the result of the tireless efforts of victims' families, who organized their own searches using rudimentary tools and information provided through anonymous tips (see also the documentary 'Persistencia').[8]
- **Example 3: Clandestine Graves of Jojutla, Morelos:** Jojutla is a town marked by violence stemming from drug trafficking and the ongoing conflict between drug cartels. Over the years, the southern region of Morelos has been a hotspot for clashes between criminal groups, resulting in a high number of victims. In May 2018, a joint operation between the Attorney General's Office of the State of Morelos and the National Human Rights Commission (CNDH)[9] led to the discovery of several clandestine graves in an area on the outskirts of Jojutla. In this location, the remains of at least 60 individuals were found, although some reports suggest there could have been more, as investigations continued for some time. Most of the bodies were unidentified and were buried in precarious conditions, making their analysis and identification difficult.

  The human remains in the Jojutla graves belonged to people who had disappeared in recent years. Authorities initially found bodies that had been buried in a disorganized manner, suggesting that, in many cases, the victims were executed by criminal groups and then buried

6 United Nations (2022), CED/C/MEX/VR/1 Sec. III. C paras. 29 et seq.

7 Semple 2018.

8 Documentary directed by Anne Huffschmid and Jan-Holger Hennies, which depicts the search for human remains in clandestine graves and the process of reconstruction and identification of bodies, focusing on the efforts of forensic anthropologists and families to identify the victims.Watch the documentary at the following link, available at: https://docs-enlinea.com/fichas/persistencia-2019 (accessed 10 July 2025).

9 Comisión Nacional de los Derechos Humanos, Desaparición forzada en México: Una mirada desde los derechos humanos, available at: https://www.cndh.org.mx/sites/default/files/documentos/2019-09/lib_DesaparicionForzadaMexicoUnaMirada.pdf (accessed 10 July 2025).

clandestinely. To this day, authorities have faced significant challenges in carrying out effective exhumations and forensic analysis. Many bodies were buried without any proper documentation, complicating their identification, and the forensic identification system remains therefore insufficient.[10]

Although forensic institutions eventually collaborated on these cases and with these families, the latter were often the driving force behind the search and recovery operations.[11] The case further exposed the limitations of Mexico's forensic institutions, which struggled to excavate and analyze the remains effectively due to insufficient resources, inadequate staffing, and the overwhelming scale of the task. This situation highlights the critical gaps in institutional capacity to address the challenges posed by large-scale disappearances and mass graves.

- **Example 4: Discovery of Concealed Bodies in a Crematorium in Ciudad Juárez, Chihuahua:** In July 2025, nearly 400 bodies were discovered in a crematorium located in Ciudad Juárez, Chihuahua, which had been subcontracted by several funeral homes. According to information from the State Prosecutor's Office, the bodies were found in an advanced state of decomposition, piled up and concealed within the premises; many are believed to have remained there since 2020. Based on the Prosecutor's hypothesis, most of the bodies had been transported to the crematorium for cremation and the subsequent delivery of ashes to their families. However, the case constituted a serious violation of the regulations governing the handling and preservation of human remains.

  Official reports indicated that the facility lacked refrigeration chambers and even the minimum conditions for proper storage. The accumulation of bodies resulted from the crematorium's limited processing capacity. The fact that numerous bodies remained unprocessed for years highlights a structural backlog in forensic services, the registration of deceased persons, and the chain of custody.

  In many Mexican states, forensic services are critically overstretched: morgues are overcrowded, and both staffing and resources are inade-

10 United Nations (2022), CED/C/MEX/VR/1 Sec. III. C para. 29: 'According to several experts interviewed during the visit, under the prevailing conditions, it would take 120 years to identify all such bodies, and that is without taking into account the new bodies that are being added to the total every day.'

11 Dittmar 2020.

quate.[12] This case revealed the extent of the backlog and saturation affecting the forensic system, underscoring the urgent need to strengthen coordination among private funeral homes, crematoria, state authorities, and forensic institutions.

In conclusion, the context of disappearances, missing people and unidentified remains reflects significant technical and institutional challenges in Mexico. Issues such as the limitations in forensic resources, non-standardized databases, and the yet-to-be-unified national genetic registry require a multi-faceted strategic response. Addressing these complexities requires significant investments in forensic capacity, stronger coordination at the national and international levels, and the inclusion of victims' families as key stakeholders in the search for truth and justice.[13] The subsequent sections detail how the Human Identification Program directly addresses these technical needs through strategic international cooperation.

3. *International Cooperation and UNFPA's programme on Human Identification in Mexico*

In November 2021, the UN Committee on Enforced Disappearances (CED), conducted a visit to Mexico upon invitation of the government. This visit resulted in a comprehensive set of recommendations that addressed areas such as the prevention and eradication of enforced disappearances, strengthening search and investigation mechanisms, ensuring justice and accountability and enhancing forensic capacities. These recommendations highlighted the need to address the 'forensic crisis' (CED/C/MEX/VR/1, Sec. I. f). Notably, the CED emphasized the importance of fingerprint identification technologies and standardized data management systems for missing persons and unidentified remains.

In response to these recommendations and at the request of the National Search Commission of Mexico with generous support by the German and Norwegian governments, the United Nations Population Fund (UNFPA), the UNs population and development agency with a mandate in Civil

12 United Nations (2022), CED/C/MEX/VR/1 Sec. III. C para. 29.

13 United Nations (2022), CED/C/MEX/VR/1 Sec. IV. C para. 31: 'The seriousness of disappearances and their diverse and intense impact on victims and Mexican society as a whole require the adoption and urgent implementation of a national policy to prevent and eradicate disappearances.'

Registration, Vital Statistics and Identity Management, initiated a Human Identification Program (IDH) in late 2022.

The program's primary focus is supporting the implementation of a nationwide fingerprint matching system for human identification efforts in Mexico. The program provides technical assistance to the Mexican government, in collaboration with federal and state authorities.

It also works closely with their implementing partners, the University of Hamburg and the University of Frankfurt, with Hamburg focusing on fingerprints and Frankfurt focusing on the processing of nearly 5000 DNA samples that have resulted in several academic publications.

Before the kick-off of the UNFPA supported Program, official and public Mexican data shows that in 2020 only 3 of 32 state forensic services matched on a regular basis fingerprints of deceased with the largest antemortem date base of Mexico: the National Electoral Institute, INE, that contains the registry of 98 million Mexicans. By 2024, the number of state forensic services increased to 24 states (see section: Example of cooperation: Fingerprint Matching with the INE).

Example of the cooperation with Zacatecas: The case of Zacatecas is the most successful to date. In October 2023, a cooperation agreement was signed between UNFPA and the State Prosecutor's Office. Since then, the Prosecutor's Office has systematically compared the fingerprints of unidentified individuals with those in the National Electoral Institute (INE). As of today, the state has no backlog of fingerprints to be compared and carries out this process on a daily basis. 298 previously unknown deceased have been identified and restituted with their families.

Additionally, nearly 200 genetic samples were sent to the Institute of Forensic Medicine at the University of Frankfurt, where they are being analyzed, and hypotheses for identification through fingerprints are being developed. Currently, it is one of the first states that has begun to compare fingerprints with the National Registry of Persons of Honduras in order to identify missing migrants.

4. Obstacles to Identification and the Need for a Multi-Pronged Approach

UNFPAs Human Identification programme approach is based on the Disaster Victim Identification Unit of Interpol, the primary human identifiers used for identifying individuals are fingerprints, DNA profiles and forensic odontology.[14] These are considered reliable and unique to an individual, making them the most important tools for identification. There are also secondary identifiers such as tattoos, scars, or other physical marks, medical records or implants and anthropometric measurements. The primary identifiers are given the highest priority because they are more scientifically robust and less prone to errors or fraud compared to secondary identifiers.

In addition, other important actors, such as the International Committee of the Red Cross (ICRC) or the International Commission on Missing Persons (ICMP) have contributed significantly to the international efforts of human identification. In the context of Latin America, non governmental organizations such as the Guatemalan Forensic Anthropology Foundation (FAFG) and Argentine Forensic Anthropology Team (EEAF) have played an important role in the identification of victims of military dictatorships.

Human identification is not rocket science. It is not an easy task, but not one without a solution. At the end of the day it is about comparing ante mortem with post mortem data. One can have the best forensic experts at their disposal, yet if the data collected cannot be compared in an efficient and accessible database there will be no results. This is why data collection, data storage and data management play a crucial role in an efficient forensic system.

According to Interpol, there are three primary methods of human identification. The first is fingerprint analysis, one of the most widely used techniques, which relies on the unique patterns of ridges and minutiae found on an individual's fingers. Because fingerprints are distinctive and remain unchanged throughout a person's life, they serve as a crucial tool in forensic identification. The second method is DNA analysis, which identifies individuals based on their genetic material. This method is particularly valuable when fingerprints are unavailable or damaged, as DNA can be extracted from various biological samples such as blood, hair, or tissue, and compared against databases to establish identity. The third method involves dental records, which are often used when other forms of identification are not feasible. Since teeth are unique to each individual, dental records

14 Disaster Victim Identification. Interpol 2025, available at: https://www.interpol.int/en/How-we-work/Forensics/Disaster-Victim-Identification-DVI (accessed 10 July 2025).

can be compared to establish identity, particularly in cases involving severe decomposition or burn victims.[15]

With regards to the primary and secondary identifiers, Mexico faces the following obstacles:

- **DNA**: While the General Law on Disappearance of 2017 mandates the State Prosecutor's Office to implement a nationwide, standardized DNA database, the integration of the internationally recognized CODIS system has only recently commenced. This process is expected to take considerable time, as the FBI requires and emphasizes prior standardization protocols. As a matter of current practice, the current landscape is marked by a significant diversity of DNA databases utilized by forensic services across different states. Additionally, during the recent administration, the National Search Commission initiated the implementation of a separate database, known as M-FISys.[16]
  This diversity of DNA data formats represents a key technical challenge for the Mexican forensic system.
  The lack of standardization in DNA data represents one of the most critical challenges for the Mexican forensic system[17], particularly in addressing past cases and the identification of bodies in advanced stages of decomposition. While DNA analysis holds substantial potential for human identification and remains indispensable for numerous cases in Mexico, its current limitations underscore the urgency of adopting a multi-pronged strategic approach. Such an approach should prioritize the utilization of readily available tools, such as fingerprint matching, to meet immediate identification needs while concurrently strengthening and expanding DNA infrastructure.
- **Fingerprints:** The Mexican forensic system utilizes the Automated Fingerprint Identification System (AFIS), a fingerprint recognition technology used to identify and investigate individuals through their fingerprint

15 Disaster Victim Identification. Interpol 2025, available at: https://www.interpol.int/en/How-we-work/Forensics/Disaster-Victim-Identification-DVI (accessed 10 July 2025).

16 Revista Digital de Ciencia Forense 2023, available at: recif.unam.mx (accessed 10 July 2025).

17 United Nations (2022), CED/C/MEX/VR/1 Sec. III. C paras. 29 et seq.: 'The lack of adequate coordination between state and national databases is a significant factor contributing to the ongoing forensic challenges in Mexico, often leading to delays in the identification of human remains.'

impressions. This system is widely employed in forensic and security applications, as well as in various governmental and private sectors. This database records the fingerprints of individuals in prison, public security personnel, or individuals with a criminal record.[18] However, concerns regarding the quality of the data persist, as individuals can potentially register under multiple aliases, thereby limiting the accuracy of matches for identification purposes.

Furthermore, the overall number of individuals registered in AFIS remains relatively low, which constrains its utility as a comprehensive identification tool. To address these limitations, Mexican authorities have recently begun to cross-match fingerprints with the National Electoral Institute (INE), which contains the records of over 98 million citizens. This initiative represents a significant step toward enhancing the scope and accuracy of fingerprint-based identification within the country.

- **Teeth profile:** Regarding dental identification, this process is not widely used in Mexico due to several factors. One of the main reasons is the lack of standardized dental databases, as there is no centralized or mandatory national registry of dental records that allows for systematic comparison of information. Additionally, there is limited access to dental records, as many individuals do not visit the dentist regularly, particularly in rural or low-income communities, making it difficult to obtain detailed dental histories. Dental identification is not prioritized in national or international protocols implemented in Mexico, and to this day, there is a preference for fingerprinting and DNA, with governmental efforts primarily focused on these two methods.
- **Secondary identifiers**: Second identifier methods in human identification are essential when primary methods are unavailable or impractical. As noted by Holz et al., relying solely on primary identifiers in Mexico may be counterproductive, as DNA analysis is both costly and time-consuming, taking several months to complete.[19] In some cases, fingerprints or dental data may not be available. Consequently, secondary identification methods, such as tattoos, photographic comparisons, and medical or surgical records, are crucial. Tattoos, for example, can carry personal symbols or dates linking individuals to their remains.

18 AFIS: A Tool for the Identification of Missing Persons and Individuals with Criminal Records (2023), available at: https://oem.com.mx/elheraldodechihuahua/local/afis-herramienta-para-la-identificacion-de-desaparecidos-y-personas-con-antecedentes-14530407 (accessed 10 July 2025).

19 Holz et al. 2022.

In order to fully utilize the collection and matching of secondary identifier information, such as tattoos or scars, there needs to be an exchange of information between different states or even within a state, facilitated by a centralized database. The ICRC offered its AM/PM database to the Mexican government, which accepted this support. Since then, AM/PM has been implemented nationwide with significant results. However, nearly all forensic services continue to maintain their own data collection systems, often still in Excel files saved on platforms like Dropbox, Google Drive, etc.
One example of the lack of standardization is the absence of a protocol for categorizing tattoos in Mexico. While one forensic expert may categorize a tattoo as a bird, another might classify it as an animal. If another expert then searches for a seagull, the query will yield no results.

The lack of adequate coordination between state and national databases is a significant factor contributing to the ongoing forensic challenges in Mexico, often leading to delays in the identification of human remains. When a body remains unidentified, the remains are typically buried in a forensic or public cemetery. While bodies are now buried individually, for many years, they were buried collectively, further complicating future identification efforts as bodies and body parts may have shifted or become mixed due to soil movement.

5. Example of cooperation: Fingerprint Matching with the INE

Based on the reliability and permanence of fingerprints, the IDH Program focuses on implementing a system for taking and matching fingerprints that support the efforts of the Mexican government to identify unknown bodies.

As a result of this technical support and collaboration, concrete identification figures demonstrate the program's impact: 3,760 identities of previously deceased individuals were recovered in 2023, 6,429 identities in 2024, and 5,467 in the first nine months of 2025. Furthermore, this cooperation has led to the first identification of a Honduranian citizen who passed away violently in Zacatecas, with the deceased being handed over to Honduras thanks to the support of the ICRC and a GIZ project in Honduras.[20]

---

20 García 2025.

Before the donation of the 300 portable scanners used to capture the fingerprints of deceased individuals, a software was developed to facilitate the conversion of fingerprints that were initially taken on paper. When these records are digitized, the software allows the conversion of the digitized fingerprints into the format used by the National Electoral Institute (INE).

The software is an application designed based on a process of flow logic to meet the INE's requirements and ensure that the fingerprint comparison is carried out efficiently. Simplified, the process begins with obtaining the ten-print card, taken by the designated person at each prosecutor's office. This card is digitized by the Prosecutor's Office using an office scanner and the generated file is stored on the computer operating the system. The file in PDF format is then uploaded to the application where the fingerprints are cropped according to the measurements and quality standards previously established by the INE.

The system generates a compressed file in wsq format from the cropped images, along with a text file that organizes and structures the information. This compressed file can then be sent to the INE either individually or in bulk, ensuring that each case is identified with a unique, non repeating number.

Initially, the process was driven in collaboration with the Tamaulipas Prosecutor's Office. Along with the Prosecutor's Office, it was implemented in a computing environment with the support of the civil society organization Data Cívica A.C., carrying out the necessary checks and validations. These included verifying uniqueness and consistency between the manual and automated processes, in collaboration with the INE. This work has been an excellent example of cooperation between federal and state authorities, Mexican forensic professionals, civil society and international cooperation.

Now, since the donation of the portable scanners, expert personnel from the Prosecutor's Office and Forensic Institutes can directly capture the fingerprint from the body of the deceased, even if it is in the process of decomposition, by implementing the appropriate techniques of lofoscopy and skin rehydration.

6. No policies without the participation Role of Civil Society and Families

According to the International Convention for the Protection of All Persons from Enforced Disappearance, each victim has the right to know the truth regarding the circumstances of the enforced disappearance, the progress and results of the investigation and the fate of the disappeared person. This principle underscores the profound importance of truth and transparency in addressing disappearances, as the absence of reliable information exacerbates the suffering of families and leaves them trapped in a state of uncertainty.

The lack of information about the whereabouts and condition of the missing person causes prolonged suffering as the families cannot close the cycle or fully accept the loss. The uncertainty can lead to emotional and physical deterioration, especially amongst mothers and wives, who often take on additional responsibilities, such as leading the search or supporting the family. Therefore, it is essential for authorities to ensure that families are included in decision-making processes regarding the search and access to justice.

The participation of families in the identification process is crucial, as they can provide essential details such as physical descriptions, dental characteristics, tattoos, scars and genetic information. Additionally, they often share narratives about the time and circumstances of the disappearance, helping to guide investigations toward potential search locations. Successful collaborations between civil society and authorities in addressing the forensic challenges have been crucial in improving the identification of missing persons and the resolution of forensic cases.

On the other hand, as part of the activities of the Human Identification Program, there is ongoing engagement with collectives and families in the entities to ensure transparency of the Program's efforts and progress with the State Prosecutor's Offices and Forensic Institutes of each state. Meetings have been held in Colima, Durango, San Luis Potosí, Tamaulipas, Veracruz, and Zacatecas.

Additionally, the Human Identification Program has facilitated the organization of five national meetings of the International Network of Associations of Missing Persons during 2024 and 2025: one in January 2024 in Mexico City, another in June 2024 also in Mexico City, a third in October 2024 in Aguascalientes, one in February 2025 in Michoacán, and another in May 2025 in Mexico City. Each meeting saw the participation of over 200 attendees. These gatherings are designed to foster dialogue and promote the exchange of experiences between families, collectives and authorities, with the aim of enhancing collaboration in addressing issues related to forced disappearances.

7. Conclusion: Towards a National Human Identification Policy

The analysis of the current situation of disappearances and unidentified deceased persons in Mexico reveals a complex forensic and institutional situation. However, the Human Identification Program (IDH) has successfully supported the Mexican government, and its efforts to implement the CED recommendation on matching fingerprints are recognized as a major step forward. This progress has been instrumental in strengthening institutional capacities and promoting technological and international cooperation in human identification. One of the main achievements has been the systematic implementation of fingerprint matching between the forensic institutions and the National Electoral Institute (INE), which has led to an exponential increase in the number of identifications. This demonstrates that, when political will, technical expertise, interinstitutional collaboration and international cooperation converge, tangible results are possible.

Nevertheless, structural challenges of Mexico's forensic system persist. Efforts are underway towards standardizing national DNA databases, solving fragmented data management systems, and strengthening interinstitutional cooperation and harmonizing the forensic databases maintained by different institutions. Overcoming these challenges will require sustained investment, long-term institutional commitment, and a clear roadmap to integrate all existing records into a unified national forensic system.

Finally, families and civil society organizations remain at the core of the search and identification process, reminding us that the human dimension must always remain central to any public policy in this field.'

In conclusion, there is a national consensus and commitment about the need to create a national human identification policy involving all institutions responsible for search, restitution and justice in Mexico.[21] A successful policy would require legislation to focus on implementing policies that streamline the identification process, such as national protocols for all institutions to promote standardized procedures and facilitate information sharing. UNFPA will continue to support these national efforts.

21 Cf. https://cebp.slp.gob.mx/noticias/2024/12/16/reuni%C3%B3n-nacional-sobre-procesos-de-identificaci%C3%B3n-humana/ (accessed 10 July 2025).

Bibliography

BBC. (2017). Mexico's deadly secret: Hundreds of bodies found in mass graves. BBC News. URL: https://www.bbc.com/news/world-latin-america-39272332 (accessed 10 July 2025).

Birngruber, Christoph G. et al. 2020. 'The use of tattoos to identify unknown bodies'. *Rechtsmedizin.* 30.4. 219–24. URL: https://doi.org/10.1007/s00194-020-00396-y (accessed 10 July 2025).

Dittmar, Victoria. 2020. 'Buried truth: A Look at Mass graves in Mexico'. Insight Crime. URL: https://insightcrime.org/news/analysis/buried-truth-mass-graves-mexico/ (accessed 10 July 2025).

Fortuna, Maria et al. 2022. 'Unidentified Bodies in the Mexican Context'. *Forensic Anthropology.* 5.3. 195–205. URL: https://journals.upress.ufl.edu/fa/article/view/1797/2036 (accessed 10 July 2025).

Fortuna, Maria et al. 2020. 'Unidentified bodies in the Mexican context.' *Forensic Anthropology*, 5.3. 195–205. URL: https://journals.upress.ufl.edu/fa/article/view/1797/2092 (accessed 10 July 2025).

García Martínez, J. L. and Rodríguez, A. P. 2023. Estudio forense de las víctimas de violencia en el contexto de la inseguridad en México: Análisis de los casos forenses. Revista Mexicana de Medicina Forense, 10(1), 21–40. https://revmedforense.uv.mx/index.php/RevINMEFO/article/view/3061 (accessed 10 July 2025).

Garciá, Raúl. 2025. 'Indentifican y repatrian cuerpo de joven hondureño en Zacatecas: primer caso histórico'. El Sol de Zacatecas. URL: https://oem.com.mx/elsoldezacatecas/local/identifican-y-repatrian-cuerpo-de-joven-hondureno-en-zacatecas-primer-caso-historico-24661008 (accessed 10 July 2025).

Holz, Franziska et al. 2022. 'A guide to classify tattoo motives in Mexico as a tool to identify unknown bodies'. *International Journal of Legal Medicine.* 136. 1105–111. URL: https://doi.org/10.1007/s00414-022-02814-0 (accessed 10 July 2025).

Huhle, Rainer. 2019. *La desaparición forzada en México: una mirada desde los organismos del Sistema de Naciones Unidas.* 2nd ed. Oficina del Alto Comisionado de las Naciones Unidas para los Derechos Humanos. URL: https://hchr.org.mx/publicaciones/la-desaparicion-forzada-en-mexico-una-mirada-desde-los-organismos-del-sistema-de-naciones-unidas-2da-edicion/ (accessed 10 July 2025).

Mendoza-Castellanos, Metzeri Arumi and Pérez-Flórez, Aurora Marcela. 2023. 'Herramientas de almacenamiento, cotejo y análisis de datos genéticos para la identificación forense en México'. *Revista Digital de Ciencia Forense.* 2.1. 61–81.

Semple, Kirk. 2018. 'In Mexico, morgues are so overwhelmed that a refrigerated truck is storing corpses'. *The New York Times.* URL: https://www.nytimes.com/2018/09/18/world/americas/mexico-morgue-corpses-truck.html (accessed 10 July 2025).

Rufino, Adriana. 2024. 'Desenterrando verdades: reflexiones en torno a la búsqueda forense y los procesos de exhumación en las fosas de Tetelcingo y Jojutla'. A dónde van los desaparecidos. URL: https://adondevanlosdesaparecidos.org/2024/01/18/desenterrando-verdadesreflexiones-en-torno-a-la-busqueda-forense-y-los-procesos-de-exhumacion-en-las-fosas-de-tetelcingo-y-jojutla-en-el-estado-de-morelos/ (accessed 10 July 2025).

Tzuc, Efraín and Sánchez, Mayela. 2024. Quinto Elemento Lab. Sexenio AMLO: 72 mil cuerpos, crisis forense. URL: https://quintoelab.org/project/sexenio--amlo-72-mil-cuerpos-crisis-forense (accessed 10 July 2025).

United Nations. 2018. Guidelines for a legislative framework on civil registration, vital statistics, and identity management. United Nations Department of Economic and Social Affairs. URL: https://desapublications.un.org/publications/guidelines-legislative-framework-civil-registration-vital-statistics-and-identity (accessed 10 July 2025).

Enforced Disappearances – The South African Experience

Gerhard Kemp

Abstract: Enforced disappearance was a key feature of the State's efforts to suppress resistance during apartheid South Africa. It remains part of the unfinished business of dealing with the past in post-apartheid South Africa. The country's ratification in 2024 of both the Apartheid Convention and the Enforced Disappearance Convention point to renewed efforts to align South African law and policy with the international legal frameworks aimed at combating systemic crimes including enforced disappearance. This chapter put these efforts in historical, domestic, and international legal perspective and concludes with a brief discussion of recent developments that may impact on the way in which cases of enforced disappearance are dealt with.

1. Introduction

The Republic of South Africa deposited its instrument of accession to the International Convention for the Protection of All Persons from Enforced Disappearance[1] ('the Enforced Disappearance Convention') on 14 May 2024. On the same day, South Africa also acceded to the International Convention on the Suppression and Punishment of the Crime of Apartheid[2] ('Apartheid Convention'). It should be noted that South Africa is a state party to the Rome Statute of the International Criminal Court[3] and has incorporated this treaty into domestic law via the Implementation of the Rome Statute of the International Criminal Court Act 27 of 2002 ('the

1 Treaty text, available at: https://treaties.un.org/doc/Publication/CTC/Ch_IV_16.pdf (accessed 2 July 2025).

2 Treaty text, available at: https://treaties.un.org/doc/Treaties/1976/07/19760718%2003-04%20AM/Ch_IV_7p.pdf (accessed 2 July 2025).

3 Treaty text, available at: https://treaties.un.org/doc/Treaties/1998/07/19980717%2006-33%20PM/Ch_XVIII_10p.pdf (accessed 2 July 2025).

ICC Implementation Act'). Both apartheid[4] and enforced disappearance of persons[5] are forms of crimes against humanity under the Rome Statute.

Both the Apartheid Convention and the Enforced Disappearance Convention entered into force for South Africa on 13 June 2024. South Africa's decision to accede to both these instruments on the same day was by design. Forced disappearance was a feature of the apartheid state[6] and the unresolved cases remain a deeply problematic issue thirty years after the formal end of apartheid. The relevance and enforceability of the crime of enforced disappearance under the Implementation Act for enforced disappearance cases from the apartheid-era is considered further below.

This paper explores the phenomenon of enforced disappearance in the context of apartheid as an international wrong and crime against humanity, with particular reference to the paradigmatic case study of South Africa. It also analyses the attempts to deal with the consequences of this phenomenon in the post-apartheid era. Finally, the paper offers some thoughts on the broader lessons and perspectives from a South African point of view and in light of country's recent accession to the Enforced Disappearance Convention.

2. The phenomenon of 'enforced disappearances' in the South African context

By its nature, the phenomenon of enforced disappearance makes it difficult to determine exact numbers of victims. Some definitional variation may also add to the uncertainty. In the South African context, a good point of departure is the work of the Truth and Reconciliation Commission ('TRC'). The TRC had a very specific temporal and material mandate, namely to determine the truth about 'gross human rights violations' committed between 1960 and 1994.[7] This temporal mandate did not cover the whole of official apartheid (which was established in 1948 after the election victory of the National Party in the white minority parliamentary elections), but rather the period following the Sharpeville massacre up to the first democratic elections in 1994 – the latter being regarded as the end of official apartheid. The period of 1960 to 1994 is associated with the consolidation of apartheid policies (such as racial segregation, forced

---

4 Art 7 (a) (j) Rome Statute of the ICC.

5 Art 7 (a) (i) Rome Statute of the ICC.

6 Kemp/Kattan 2024.

7 For an overview, see Kemp 2023, 153–76.

removals, racial classification, and racist labour laws), and the concomitant intensification of the resistance to apartheid, which included the armed struggle by the various liberation movements.

The TRC[8] was created by the Promotion of National Unity and Reconciliation Act ('TRC Act').[9] The TRC Act did not use the term 'forced disappearance' as we would have it in international law today, but rather used the term 'abduction'. It should be noted, of course, that the Enforced Disappearance Convention was not yet adopted by the international community, although, the TRC Report referred to the work of the UN Working Group on Enforced or Involuntary Disappearances and in particular the working definition of 'a disappearance' contained in the Draft International Convention on the Protection of all Persons from Forced Disappearance. The TRC also referred to the working definitions developed by human rights groups such as Amnesty International. As noted, the TRC Act used the term 'abduction', which was understood to mean enforced disappearances at the hands of the state, persons who had gone missing in exile or combat, and other missing persons.[10] Guided by the TRC Act and in light of the emerging international concept of enforced disappearance, the TRC settled on a definition of 'abductions'.[11] This definition of abductions/forced disappearances, covered conduct by the state and by non-state actors. This is because the mandate of the TRC was to investigate gross human rights violations by the apartheid state and by the liberation movements.[12] As for missing persons, the TRC differentiated this category from 'abductions/disappeared', as previously mentioned. Although the TRC considered a large number of missing persons cases reported to the Commission, in many of these cases the TRC could not link the apparent disappearance to a political cause and intent on the side of the state or non-state actors could not be established. Such a finding would then lead the TRC to conclude that the state or non-state actor was not responsible for the disappearance. A sub-category of 'missing persons cases', was the 'missing in action' cases. The armed forces of the apartheid state operated beyond the borders of

8 For general background, see Villa-Vicencio/Verwoerd 2000; Krog 1999; Orr 2000; Boraine 2000; Meiring 1999; Van de Vijver 2000.

9 Promotion of National Unity and Reconciliation Act 34 of 1995 (the 'TRC Act').

10 Truth and Reconciliation Commission of South Africa Report, 1998 ('TRC Report') vol. 6 (4) ch. 1, para. 11, available at: https://www.justice.gov.za/trc/report/finalreport/volume%201.pdf (accessed 2 July 2025).

11 TRC Report vol. 6 (4) ch. 1, para. 14.

12 Kemp 2023, 173.

the country, including in countries like Angola, Namibia (then still under South African control) and elsewhere in Southern Africa. Soldiers sometimes went missing and there were instances where it was unclear whether they died in battle or were taken prisoner. While the authorities usually provided some kind of support to the relatives, the TRC noted instances where families were denied relief 'because the state has refused to confirm that their loved ones were on lawful missions for the country'.[13]

The TRC adopted the general approach that a disappearance did not qualify as such, if the 'fate or whereabouts of the disappeared are known, if a body is found, or if it becomes known that the victim is dead.'[14] In terms of potential cases of disappearance, the TRC used two types of classifications: 'Temporary disappearance', that is, an unacknowledged, long-term incommunicado type of imprisonment. And, the second type, where the disappeared person has been killed or has died in unknown circumstances without being traced. The latter was the most common type of disappearance that the TRC had to deal with.[15]

In terms of the modus operandi of the perpetrators of forced disappearance, the TRC noted a few common practices. The most significant of these were the secrecy surrounding the planning and execution of a disappearance. In most cases, the perpetrators remained unknown. This is due to the policy of secrecy, compounded by the fact that disappearance decisions were usually centralised, even though the process of execution was decentralised. The TRC noted that disappearances 'are usually planned by small secret groups within the armed forces, where orders for implementation are delegated through various channels that are often difficult to trace.'[16] In apartheid South Africa, the practice of disappearance involved several units within the police and military. These units were largely autonomous and were independently funded to facilitate the secrecy around the abductions and killings. This element of secrecy also made it possible for the apartheid state to deny knowledge of the existence of disappearance as a state policy. The TRC rejected the apartheid state's efforts to deny knowledge of disappearance practices and concluded that, 'the high rank of the state personnel involved, their easy access to funds and resources, and evidence emerging from amnesty applications by former security force personnel

13 TRC report vol. 6 (4) ch. 1, para. 36.
14 TRC report vol. 6 (4) ch. 1, para. 18.
15 TRC report vol. 6 (4) ch. 1, para. 19.
16 TRC report vol. 6 (4) ch. 1, para. 21.

negate the [claim of ignorance].' Further, the TRC held that '[one] cannot but draw the conclusion that the former state was centrally involved [in the disappearances], not only in sanctioning this tactic, but also in planning and providing funds and resources.'[17]

The nature of the conflict between the apartheid state and the liberation movements provided further cover for the State to deny knowledge of disappearance. The TRC found instances where the apartheid state blamed the liberation movements for disappearances, or tried to convince family members that the disappeared had gone into exile to join the liberation movements. The TRC also found instances where the apartheid state had staged elaborate hoaxes to hide its own complicity. On the rare occasions where the apartheid state did acknowledge a disappearance, common accompanying explanations were to allege that the disappeared had committed suicide, or were shot and killed during an attempt to escape custody.[18]

The nature of the apartheid state and the way in which the various organs of state functioned contributed to the 'conspiracy of silence' on the practice of enforced disappearance. At a more fundamental level, the TRC also noted the lack of vigilance on the side of the judiciary and the willingness of the 'beneficiaries of the former state' (i.e., the minority white population) to accept state propaganda as contributing to the systematic nature of the practice of enforced disappearance. The TRC concluded that 'the judiciary and civil society had a large role to play in allowing disappearances and killings to continue'.[19]

But why did the apartheid state and the non-state actors perpetrate disappearances? The short answer is that the apartheid state shared the same desire as other oppressive regimes to remove people who they considered to be a threat to the status quo. There is a certain cold logic to it. Rather than having to spend resources on criminal trials (even though the trials may very well be unfair), the state simply get rid of its most troublesome opponents by disappearing them. This happened numerous times during apartheid and is still the subject of re-opened judicial inquiries, as will be explained further below. Apart from the immediate result of removing a perceived opponent of the regime, there is the secondary result of intimidation of family, friends, and political comrades; in short, disappearances can have devastating chilling effect. Finally, and as noted in the TRC Re-

17 TRC report vol. 6 (4) ch. 1, para. 23.
18 TRC report vol. 6 (4) ch. 1, paras. 24 et seq.
19 TRC report vol. 6 (4) ch. 1, para. 26.

port, a practice of disappearances can also be an effective way to avoid international pressure. This is because the fate of political prisoners (for example Nelson Mandela, the most famous of the political prisoners held by the apartheid state) proved to be a rallying point for international campaigns and diplomatic pressure, but the issue of the disappeared simply never received the same attention.[20] This in itself provided a strong *raison d'être* for the continued practice of disappearance by the state, even as the international campaign against apartheid gathered momentum in the 1980s.

3. *The factual and legal findings of the TRC*

At the time of the finalisation of the TRC Report, the Commission had received more than 1500 victim statements concerning missing or disappeared persons. The fate of around 477 persons remained uncertain. The majority of the cases were from the period 1985 to 1994. The TRC noted in the final report that it was not possible for the Commission to give an accurate number of cases. This was due to the fact that apparent disappearances were solved through investigations or as a result of amnesty applications before the Amnesty Committee of the TRC. The data then had to be re-coded to reflect the outcome. Thus, for example if, due to these processes, an apparent disappeared person was found to have been killed (by state agents or otherwise), then the coding had to change from disappearance to killing.[21] Nevertheless, the TRC did reach certain conclusions with regard to the various categories of disappeared and missing persons. For present purposes, the main conclusions regarding the category, 'enforced disappearances', will be noted.

First, it is important to briefly note the relevant legal and investigatory powers that were at the disposal of the TRC which enabled the Commission to make certain findings and recommendations. The TRC Act[22] provided the TRC with the powers to hold special investigative hearings on abductions and disappearances. In addition, the amnesty process (which was premised on full and truthful disclosure by applicants of the facts related to alleged gross human rights violations) and the exhumation process related to many of the investigations of gross human rights violations,

20 TRC report vol. 6 (4) ch. 1, para. 31.

21 TRC report vol. 6 (4) ch. 1, para. 37 and relevant footnotes.

22 TRC Act, 1995, section 29.

further assisted the TRC in its findings and recommendations pertaining to disappearances. Indeed, the amnesty process proved to be pivotal in helping the TRC with its investigations into disappearances. The general investigatory powers of the TRC included the power to subpoena those it 'believed had information about an incident or violation to appear before a special panel of the Commissioners and to answer questions.'[23]

From the TRC's findings on enforced disappearances, two things stand out. First, abductions of political activists and members of the armed wings of the liberation movements by the security forces of the apartheid state were quite common. Not all of these abductees were killed; some were recruited to become spies or informers for the apartheid state. A second cohort of disappearance cases related to persons held as detainees awaiting trial. The typical modus operandi was then for the Security Branch of the apartheid state's police to kill detainees whom they did not wish to release, but in the absence of sufficient evidence, could not bring to court for trial. A third group of disappeared were those activists and liberation fighters who were held in detention and who had died as a consequence of torture. The typical practice was then for the Security Branch to forge release papers and other documents to suggest that they were not responsible for the disappearance.[24]

As mentioned, the mandate of the TRC concerned 'gross human rights violations' perpetrated as part of the 'conflict of the past', meaning the period 1960 to 1994. While the TRC was careful not to create moral equivalence between the policies and practices of the apartheid state, on the one hand, and the actions of the liberation movements on the other hand, the final report of the Commission did mention certain findings of gross human rights violations, including disappearances, attributed to non-state actors (the liberation movements, such as the African National Congress (ANC), and other political movements, such as the Zulu nationalist Inkatha Freedom Party (IFP)). For instance, in the early 1990s, and before the end of apartheid, a violent political conflict raged in the KwaZulu-Natal province between the ANC and the IFP. The conflict was fuelled by the apartheid state, but the TRC nevertheless found that several instances of gross human rights violations, including disappearances, were perpetrated by supporters of the rival political movements.[25]

23 TRC report vol. 6 (4) ch. 1, para. 40.
24 TRC report vol. 6 (4) ch. 1, para. 52.
25 TRC report vol. 6 (4) ch. 1, paras. 53–8.

Another instance of non-state perpetration of disappearances occurred outside South Africa's borders. During apartheid, many anti-apartheid activists, and members of the (then banned) liberation movements went into exile. The majority of these South Africans in exile were members of the ANC. The TRC Report noted that fifty-five persons disappeared after having gone into exile. The circumstances of exile necessitated some degree of secrecy, mostly for reasons of security and to escape the oppressive and often lethal reach of the apartheid state. When the liberation movements were unbanned in the early 1990s, and after apartheid officially ended in 1994, most persons in exile returned to South Africa. Some opted to stay on and to continue with their political work overseas. However, some never returned and have not been accounted for by friends or family. This is the cohort of persons that the TRC eventually regarded as disappeared. The TRC noted that in cases of disappearance in exile, the 'specific responsibility' to assist in establishing the fate of the missing, rests on the liberation movement in question (if it was common cause that a missing/disappeared person belonged to a certain organisation). The ANC, the largest and most prominent of the liberation movements, maintained a record of its membership. The ANC even made effort to inform families of the deaths of loved ones in exile or in combat, despite the obvious risk that such communication to people in South Africa would carry. After the unbanning of the ANC in 1990, the organisation created a dedicated office at its headquarters to deal with queries about missing and potentially disappeared persons. Other, smaller liberation movements, such as the Pan Africanist Congress of Azania (PAC), could not match the ANC's ability to deal with missing and disappearance cases. Indeed, the TRC noted that the PAC submitted very little information to the TRC and also failed to conduct internal enquiries into alleged gross human rights violations (including disappearances) committed in exile.[26]

4. Investigating disappearance cases from the apartheid-era (specifically: the TRC mandate-era)

While many of the disappearance cases came to the attention of the TRC through the amnesty process, the TRC was ultimately not in a position

26 TRC report vol. 6 (4) ch. 1, para. 71.

to fully investigate these cases. This is despite the Commission's initial attempt to investigate all the cases, rather than to prioritise cases with the strongest leads. It should also be noted that the TRC was mandated to investigate, through its Investigation Unit, other instances of gross human rights violations (and not only disappearances) perpetrated within the temporal mandate. The financial and institutional limitations of the TRC impacted on its ability to fully investigate apartheid-era disappearances and this had the unfortunate consequence of not only unresolved cases, but also a sense of injustice. Indeed, several amnesty applications concerning disappearances and abductions were granted (on the basis of full admissions by the applicants) but with the families of the victims left in the dark as to whether the disappeared were still alive, simply because the TRC lacked the capacity to investigate the matter beyond the amnesty applicant's admission of the original abduction or disappearance. The TRC did note in its report that such unresolved cases had to be taken further by the post-apartheid state's criminal justice system, notably the prosecuting authority.[27]

The matter of post-TRC investigations and (lack of) prosecutions are dealt with below.

5. The TRC recommendations regarding disappearances

As noted above, the TRC initially tried to investigate all gross human rights violations, including disappearances. This could ultimately not be done for lack of capacity. Nevertheless, the TRC 'tried as best it could to carry out its mandate to compile a list of the disappeared and those abducted and establish their fate and whereabouts'.[28] An incomplete task, then, but not one without significance. Indeed, as the TRC noted in their report, its investigations, hearings, and processes did manage 'to act as catalyst by bringing disappearance cases to the fore'. While it did not solve all cases, a large number were solved, thus enabling families to gain some measure of closure.[29] But several cases remained unresolved, which brings us to the TRC recommendations.

First, the TRC noted that it had a specific mandate, but that the responsibility to take the investigations and, where appropriate, prosecutions of

27 TRC report vol. 6 (4) ch. 1, paras. 82–6; 94.
28 TRC report vol. 6 (4) ch. 1, para. 95.
29 TRC report vol. 6 (4) ch. 1, para. 95.

gross human rights violations from the apartheid-era (including disappearances) further, rests on the post-apartheid, democratic state. Secondly, the TRC noted the relevant international legal framework which informs the matter of disappearances. As mentioned earlier, the TRC is a product of South Africa's transition from apartheid to democracy in the 1990s; its creation preceded the adoption of the Enforced Disappearance Convention. Nevertheless, the TRC was cognisant of developments in international human rights law pertaining to enforced disappearances. In particular, the TRC noted in its report the work of the UN Working Group on Involuntary or Enforced Disappearances, which issued a General Comment to Article 19 of the 1992 Declaration on the Protection of All Persons from Enforced Disappearance.[30] The TRC noted that the Declaration imposes a duty on states to establish the fate and whereabouts of disappeared persons, which is in itself an important remedy for victims. Article 19 of the Declaration provides:

The victims of acts of enforced disappearances and their family shall obtain redress and shall have the right to adequate compensation, including the means for as complete a rehabilitation as possible. In the event of the death of a victim as a result of an act of enforced disappearance, their dependents shall also be entitled to compensation.

In light of its statutory mandate, and mindful of the relevant international human rights and normative context, the TRC have made certain recommendations for taking the matter of disappearances further. In brief, these were:

The establishment of a special task force within the office of the National Director of Public Prosecutions, with the mandate to further investigate individual cases, confirming the disappeared and, where appropriate, making a finding conferring victim status on the disappeared. For purposes of further investigations, the TRC recommended that the special task force should distinguish between enforced disappearances, persons missing in exile, persons missing during periods of unrest, and cases of indeterminate cause.

The task team should include the 'possibility of identifying gravesites and facilitating exhumations in conjunction with civil society groupings working within this arena'.[31]

30 Report of the Working Group on Enforced or Involuntary Disappearances, E/CN. 4/1998 / 43, 12 January 1998 at 16.

31 TRC report vol. 6 (4) ch. 1, para. 110.

6. Post-TRC investigations and further developments

The post-apartheid state acted on the TRC recommendations by creating a Missing Persons Task Team (MPTT). It forms part of the National Prosecuting Authority (NPA) and by the end of 2022 the remains of more than 170 missing persons have been recovered.[32] The TRC officially recognised 477 persons as missing or disappeared, out of a cohort of around 2000 suspected missing persons from the apartheid-era.[33] Experts generally believe the TRC figure of 477 to be an undercount.[34]

While the work of the MPTT is continuing, there is another dimension to the post-TRC period to briefly note in this context. The work of the MPTT is important for reasons of closure for families in search of information about their loved ones. But there is also the imperatives of accountability and justice. In this regard the post-TRC period has been a failure, or, at least, a serious disappointment. The TRC recommended, in its final report, that the NPA pursue criminal prosecutions of a cohort of individuals responsible for gross human rights violations who were either unsuccessful in their amnesty applications, or who failed or refused to apply for amnesty. This recommendation involved around 300 cases. However, twenty years after the publication of the TRC report and recommendations, very little progress has been made in the investigation and prosecution of apartheid-era gross human rights violations.[35] In a remarkable case before the Supreme Court of Appeal, the State acknowledged that a decision was taken at some point between 2003 and 2017 to not continue with any post-TRC prosecutions of gross human rights violations committed during apartheid. The Supreme Court of Appeal described this decision as 'perplexing and inexplicable'.[36] Indeed it was. This case before the Supreme Court of Appeal prompted a change in policy at the NPA. There now seems to be a renewed interest in the investigation of apartheid-era gross human rights violations and this even led to the historic first indictment of two individuals for the crime against humanity of apartheid (albeit on

32 Available at: https://www.news24.com/news24/southafrica/news/perished-under-apartheid-npa-task-team-recovers-remains-of-179-missing-persons-20221126 (accessed 2 July 2025).

33 Khulumani Support Group, available at: https://khulumani.net/ (accessed 2 July 2025). See also, Sarkin 2015, 21–48.

34 Aronson 2011, 262–81.

35 Woolaver 2022, 423–36; Kemp in Vormbaum 2023, 473–87.

36 *Rodrigues v National Director of Public Prosecutions* [2021] 3 All SA 775 (SCA).

the basis of customary international law, rather than statutory law, since the ICC Implementation Act of 2002 does not operate retrospectively or retroactively).[37] Most of these cases concern gross human rights violations like torture and murder and not only disappearance cases. However, the change of policy at the NPA will hopefully lead to accountability for the remaining disappearances identified by the TRC and in the course of the work done by the MPTT.

7. Is there a legal basis to prosecute individuals for apartheid-era enforced disappearance cases?

It was noted that the crime of enforced disappearance (as a crime against humanity) is now a statutory crime under South African criminal law via the ICC Implementation Act of 2002. However, this statute does not have retrospective or retroactive operation and individuals accused of perpetrating the crime of enforced disappearance committed before 2002 may have to be prosecuted for a crime that existed at the time of the commission of the offence, for instance the common law crime of kidnapping.[38] The material elements of the common law crime of kidnapping and the crime of enforced disappearance do not overlap perfectly, so this course of action is not entirely satisfactory.

An alternative option is to view unsolved enforced disappearance cases as 'continuing' crimes against humanity, as incorporated into South African law via the ICC Implementation Act of 2002. A 'continuing crime' in the Rome Statute of the ICC is 'a violation of a primary obligation targeting a potentially ongoing situation that has been committed and then maintained'.[39] Some have (correctly) noted that enforced disappearance is the 'archetypical continuing crime', since it 'involves not only the initial act of abducting, arresting or detaining a victim, rather, its defining feature is the continuing 'refusal to acknowledge that deprivation of freedom or give information on the fate or whereabouts' of the victim'.[40]

A purposive reading of the ICC Implementation Act, in conjunction with a good faith consideration of South Africa's international obligations

37 Kemp/Nortje 2023, 405–30; Kemp 2025.

38 The common law crime is defined as 'unlawfully and intentionally depriving a person of liberty of movement and/or his custodians of control'. Kemp 2022, 340.

39 Nissel 2004, 661.

40 Du Plessis/Gevers/Moodley 2021.

under both the Rome Statute of the ICC and the Enforced Disappearance Convention, can arguably provide the necessary legal basis to prosecute apartheid-era enforced disappearance cases as continuing crimes.

8. The way forward

Article 2 of the Enforced Disappearance Convention provides that an 'enforced disappearance' is

> considered to be the arrest, detention, abduction or any other form of deprivation of liberty by agents of the State or by persons or groups of persons acting with the authorization, support or acquiescence of the State, followed by a refusal to acknowledge the deprivation of liberty or by concealment of the fate or whereabouts of the disappeared person, which place such a person outside the protection of the law.

This definition of 'enforced disappearance' was not employed by the TRC, as we have seen. The TRC rather opted for a broader conceptualisation of 'disappearance' to include conduct by non-state actors. Now that South Africa is a state party to the Enforced Disappearance Convention, it may be a good opportunity for the country to reflect on its own contribution to this crime against humanity and to reflect on ways to make the international legal regime on enforced disappearance more effective. But first, South Africa needs to finish the task of dealing with its own past. It is not only a domestic legal and moral imperative, flowing from the work of the TRC, but also constitutes an international obligation to hold criminally responsible those who perpetrate the crime of enforced disappearance. South Africa has already domesticated this crime against humanity via the Implementation of the Rome Statute of the ICC Act. Nevertheless, during the 2022 parliamentary debate[41] on South Africa's accession to the Enforced Disappearance Convention, it was noted that the relevant parliamentary committee is of the view that the Convention must be incorporated into domestic law. At the time of writing, no draft legislation was yet put forward, and it is presumed that this may follow in the years to come and may provide South Africa with the opportunity to craft a discrete crime of enforced disappearance and a concomitant enforcement regime under

41 Parliament of South Africa, Hansard, available at: https://pmg.org.za/hansard/35662/ (accessed 2 July 2025).

domestic criminal law. As for the disappearances from the apartheid-era, the State should commit to finishing the work allocated to it by the TRC and hold to account those who kidnapped, detained, and disappeared persons. The legal framework for that exists under the available common law and statutory criminal law (including, as noted, the possibility to prosecute enforced disappearance as a continuing crime), but what is needed now, with the window of opportunity fast closing, is a firm institutional, political, and financial commitment by the State.

Bibliography

Aronson, Jay. 2011. 'The strengths and limitations of South Africa's search for apartheid-era missing persons'. *International Journal of Transitional Justice.* 262–281.

Boraine, Alex. 2000. *A country unmasked – Inside South Africa's Truth and Reconciliation Commission.* Oxford: Oxford University Press.

Du Plessis, Max, Gevers, Christopher and Moodley, Celeste. 2021. *Expert Memorandum on the Crime of Enforced Disappearance and its Prosecution under the Rome Statute Act as a Continuing Crime.* Johannesburg. URL. https://unfinishedtrc.co.za/wp-content/uploads/2022/12/2021-03-29-FHR-Opinion-Crime-of-Enforced-Disappearance-as-Continuing-Crime.pdf (accessed 2 July 2025).

James, Wilmot and Van de Vijver, Linda (eds.). 2000. *After the TRC – Reflections on truth and reconciliation in South Africa.* Cape Town: David Philip Publishers.

Kemp, Gerhard. 2022. *Criminal Law in South Africa.* 4th edition. Cape Town: Oxford University Press.

Kemp, Gerhard. 2023. 'From apartheid to democracy in South Africa'. In Czeguhn, Ignacio and Thiessen, Jan (eds.). *Dictatorship, Democracy, and Transitional Justice in Global Legal History.* Berlin: Duncker & Humblot. 153–76.

Kemp, Gerhard. 2023. 'Späte Aufarbeitung in Südafrika'. In Vormbaum, Moritz (ed.). *Spätverfolgung von NS-Unrecht.* Berlin: Springer. 473–87.

Kemp, Gerhard and Nortje, Windell. 2023. 'Prosecuting the crime against humanity of apartheid: The historic first indictment in South Africa and the application of customary international law'. *Journal of International Criminal Justice.* 21.2. 405–30.

Kemp, Gerhard and Kattan, Victor. 2024. *The significance of South Africa's accession to the 1973 Apartheid Convention and suggestions for improving the treaty text.* URL: https://opiniojuris.org/2024/05/31/the-significance-of-south-africas-accession-to-the-1973-apartheid-convention-and-suggestions-for-improving-the-treaty-text/ (accessed 2 July 2025).

Kemp, Gerhard. 2025. *Criminal court in South Africa confirms charges in historic first prosecution of the crime against humanity of apartheid.* URL: https://opiniojuris.org/2025/04/29/criminal-court-in-south-africa-confirms-charges-in-historic-first-prosecution-of-the-crime-against-humanity-of-apartheid/ (accessed 2 July 2025).

Krog, Antjie. 1999. *Country of my Skull.* London: Vintage.

Meiring, Piet. 1999. *Kroniek van die Waarheidskommissie – Op reis deur die verlede en die hede na die toekoms van Suid-Afrika.* Vanderbijlpark: Carpe Diem.

Nissel, Alan. 2004. 'Continuing crimes in the Rome Statute'. *Michigan Journal of International Law.* 25.3. 653–89.

Orr, Wendy. 2000. *From Biko to Basson – Wendy Orr's search for the soul of South Africa as a commissioner of the TRC.* Johannesburg: Contra.

Sarkin, Jeremy. 2015. 'Dealing with enforced disappearances in South Africa (with a focus on the Nokuthula Simelane case) and around the world: The need to ensure progress on the rights to truth, justice and reparations in practice'. *Speculum Juris.* 29.1. 21–48.

Villa-Vicencio, Charles and Verwoerd, Wilhelm (eds.). 2000. *Looking back reaching forward – Reflections on the Truth and Reconciliation Commission of South Africa.* London: Zed Books Ltd.

Woolaver, Hannah. 2022. 'Prosecuting apartheid-era international crimes in South Africa'. In Jessberger, Florian, Vormbaum, Moritz and Burghardt, Boris (eds.). *Strafrecht und Systemunrecht – Festschrift für Gerhard Werle.* Tübingen: Mohr Siebeck. 423–36.

From the European Court of Human Rights to Domestic Trials: The Search for Criminal Accountability for Enforced Disappearances in Türkiye[1]

Burcu Yaşar

Abstract: The European Court of Human Rights was the first judicial forum to uncover enforced disappearances in Türkiye in the 1990s. In the following decade, the harmonisation process with the European Union prompted comprehensive reforms, which in turn led to the (re)initiation and intensification of investigations into past crimes. In this context, Turkish courts began adjudicating cases previously examined by the ECtHR. This paper traces the journey of one such case from Strasbourg to domestic courts to shed light on past and present legal and judicial approaches to enforced disappearances. By focusing on recurring issues and inconsistencies with the international framework, it argues that a lack of accountability for enforced disappearances persists.

1. Introduction

On Saturday, 25 May 2024, the Saturday Mothers (also referred to as Saturday People), a movement of human rights advocates and mostly female relatives of the victims of enforced disappearances, held their 1000th gathering on Galatasaray Square, İstiklal Street, in Istanbul.[2] The movement began its weekly sit-ins on the famous public square on Saturday, 27 May 1995 to demand the investigation of the fate and whereabouts of people who were forcibly disappeared after the military coup in the 1980s and the state of emergency of the 1990s.[3] Confronted with a lack of acknowledgment and accountability for serious human rights violations, criminal defence lawyers on the ground joined forces with a London-based charity with

1 For this work I interviewed with Gülistan Zeren and Özlem Zıngıl and wholeheartedly thank them for their valuable insights.

2 Topcu 2024.

3 Daşlı 2024, 373.

human rights expertise to invoke the individual application mechanism under the European Convention on Human Rights (ECHR).[4] Türkiye[5] had recognised the right to individual petition in 1987 and accepted the compulsory jurisdiction of the European Court of Human Rights (ECtHR) in 1990.

The ECtHR examined many complaints of gross violations, including torture, extra-judicial execution (also referred to as 'unresolved killings'), enforced disappearances and forced displacement, arising in the context of operations conducted by Turkish security forces against the Kurdistan Workers' Party (PKK) in south-eastern Türkiye.[6] When the ECtHR found these complaints admissible because it considered internal domestic remedies to be ineffective, it became the first judicial forum to examine conflict-related complaints and facts of the 1990s.[7] To establish the disputed facts of unprecedented cases, the European Commission, a former ECHR organ,[8] held fact-finding hearings in Türkiye with witnesses and state officials.[9] The outcome was ample case law in both quantitative and qualitative terms. In 51 applications concerning approximately one hundred disappeared persons, the ECtHR found violations of various articles of the ECHR. Eleven applications were deemed inadmissible, and seven applications were resolved through friendly settlements between the government and the applicants.[10]

---

4 Initially and in many instances, individual applications concerning state violence were lodged without any transnational link. See Kurban 2020, 185–229.

5 In this report, the new official name of the Republic of Türkiye, as communicated by the Turkish government to the Council of Europe and international organisations in 2022, has been used. The original title of the European case law dating back this change is preserved for referencing purposes.

6 Çalı 2010, 325–32; Kurban 2020, 133–82.

7 Çalı 2010, 312–20.

8 The monitoring organs under the ECHR were composed of a commission and a court before the establishment of the permanent court by the Protocol 11 to the ECHR, restructuring the control machinery established thereby (ETS No. 155). The Protocol was adopted in 1994 and entered into force in 1998.

9 Çalı 2010, 312 et seq.

10 The Preface written by Emel Ataktürk Sevimli in Sevdiren 2016, 7–11. Truth Justice Memory Center (*Hakikat Adalet Hafıza Merkezi*) (Center for Memory), an Istanbul-based non-governmental organisation focusing on accountability for gross human rights violations and transitional justice, confirmed in 2014 that 311 people forcibly disappeared between 1980-2000. This finding is based on various sources such as the ECtHR judgments, parliamentary reports, civil society databases, case files and witness statements. See in Turkish Alpkaya/Altıntaş/Sevdiren et al. 2014, 131; See in

However, the binding case law of the ECtHR did not directly lead to the investigation and prosecution of the enforced disappearances in the years following the judgments because the official policy of denial continued to prevent truth revelation and accountability.[11] Still, political and bureaucratic engagement with the European Union (EU) and the Council of Europe created momentum for change. After Türkiye was granted the status of candidate for EU membership in 1999, the Turkish government drew up a National Programme for Adoption of the Acquis, clearly outlining its plan to align the national framework with the legislation of the EU member states in light of political criteria of democracy and human rights. The plan included a commitment to ensure the effective implementation of international conventions, notably the ECHR.[12] In the next decade, comprehensive reforms occurred in both the legal and administrative systems.[13] Significant structural changes transformed civil-military relations and diminished the military's influence on civil authority and matters related to internal security and terrorism.[14] Against this backdrop the reforms paved the way for the prosecution of some military officials and other individuals for their alleged involvement in state-sponsored crimes.[15]

In the wake of these reforms, the domestic judicial authorities have dealt with the complaints of enforced disappearances, some of which were previously examined by ECHR organs. This paper takes a closer look at the journey of these complaints, shedding light on past and present legal and judicial approaches to enforced disappearances. The paper follows the route of *Akdeniz* from Strasbourg to domestic courts in Diyarbakır and Ankara, where the case is commonly referred to as the *Kulp case* after the location of the events. This case reflects the wider issues and legal obstacles encountered in cases concerning enforced disappearances. By focusing on these issues and obstacles, the paper demonstrates the persistent lack of accountability for enforced disappearances. It first overviews the enforced disappearance cases examined by the ECtHR (Section 2). Then, it presents the national amendments implemented since the grant of the EU candidacy, highlighting key changes in the criminalisation of international crimes

English Alpkaya/Altıntaş/Sevdiren et al. 2013 (Note that the English version covers the data of 2013).

11 Çalı 2010, 317–25.

12 Türkmen 2013, 258.

13 Çalı 2010, 311–37.

14 Şarlak 2020, 185–9.

15 Sinclair-Webb 2012, 12-5.

and procedural law on custody measures (Section 3). After examining the *Kulp* case, it provides an analysis of the legal and judicial approach to these enforced disappearances, including an analysis of the case law of the Constitutional Court of the Republic of Türkiye (Section 4). It provides a conclusion in Section 5.

2. *Strasbourg case law*

The first ECtHR judgment concerning enforced disappearances in Türkiye resulted from an application lodged with the European Commission of Human Rights (ECommHR) in May 1994 by the mother of a disappeared person, who witnessed her son being surrounded by gendarmes and village guards before his disappearance.[16] When she approached the local authorities about his whereabouts, she was informed that he had not been taken into custody and had instead been kidnapped by the PKK.[17] The Turkish government objected to the facts submitted by the applicant, claiming that they were fabricated. The government submitted that the applicant did not exhaust domestic remedies under criminal and administrative law.[18] This submission was dismissed for being outside the time limit, but the court noted that the investigative authorities did not take the applicant's statement and did not inquire further to substantiate the explanation that her son was kidnapped by the PKK.[19] Based on the fact-finding hearings conducted by the ECommHR in Ankara, the ECtHR established the fact that the applicant's son was held by security forces without official records. Unregistered detention constituted a serious failing of the procedural guarantees against deprivation of liberty under Article 5 of the ECHR given that it concealed the perpetrators' identities and hindered accountability.[20]

In *Çakıcı v. Turkey*, the ECtHR took note of the general unreliability and inaccuracy of custody records in addition to finding that the applicant's brother was taken into custody without any documentation. Registration practices generally excluded the recording of location changes or holding

16 See Cárdenas in this anthology, 221. ECtHR 1998, Kurt v. Turkey, Reports of Judgments and Decisions 1998-III, paras. 14–53; Turhan 2000, 204–58.

17 ECtHR 1998, Kurt v. Turkey, Reports of Judgments and Decisions 1998-III, paras. 16–8.

18 Ibid. paras. 76–81.

19 Ibid. paras. 82–3.

20 Ibid. paras. 118–29.

in transit, making the records insufficient to establish a detained person's whereabouts at a particular time.[21]

Akdeniz and others concerned the unacknowledged detention and disappearance of 11 villagers during a military operation. The Turkish government submitted that a military operation was carried out in October 1993 between the Kulp district of Diyarbakır and two neighbouring provinces; however, the facts about the operation and the security forces' involvement in the detention of missing men were disputed.[22] In fact-finding hearings, the ECommHR delegates heard nine applicants, other family members and villagers, two public prosecutors, two gendarme commanders and the commander of the military forces who conducted the operation.[23] The ECommHR established the facts as follows. The concerned area was situated in mountainous terrain and consisted of dispersed hamlets and houses. Some villagers were rounded up by soldiers as guides to show them the PKK bases and were questioned about their involvement in providing food and shelter to the PKK. Eleven disappeared persons were detained, ten of them being tied up in an open area for about seven days. At least some of them were seen being taken away by a security force helicopter and had been missing since then.[24] Two months after the events, the Kulp public prosecutor initiated an investigation before it referred the case to the Diyarbakır State Security Court on the basis that the PKK had kidnapped the missing men.[25] The Diyarbakır State Security Court took statements from some witnesses between 1994 and 1997 and issued a decision of non-jurisdiction, arguing that there was no evidence of a terror-related crime.[26]

The ECtHR took note of the lapse of time between the disappearance and the court's assessment (seven years), unregistered detention and the lack of substantiated explanations regarding the whereabouts of missing persons. In addition, its own case law indicated a general situation of impunity for the acts of the security forces in this region during the period in question. The court presumed that 11 men died following their detention.[27] It found striking omissions in the investigation of the unregistered deten-

21 ECtHR 1999, Çakıcı v. Turkey [Grand Chamber], no. 23657/94, ECHR 1999-IV, para. 105.
22 ECtHR 2001, Akdeniz and Others v. Turkey, no. 23954/94, para 57.
23 Ibid.
24 Ibid. paras. 10–38
25 Ibid. para. 50.
26 Ibid. para. 52.
27 Ibid. paras. 84–9.

tions and deaths of the detained persons. No investigative action was taken to uncover the extent or nature of the operation despite the fact that some eyewitnesses were heard.[28] Furthermore, the transfer of the case between two courts did not contribute to the effectiveness of the investigation.[29] Consequently, the ECtHR found a violation of the right to life (Article 2), the prohibition of inhuman and degrading treatment (Article 3), the right to liberty and security (Article 5) and the right to an effective remedy (Article 13). In addition, the court found non-compliance with the obligation not to hinder the right to petition (the former Article 25) because the applicants were summoned after they lodged their complaints before the EUCommHR. In many other cases concerning enforced disappearances, the ECtHR repeatedly found violations of the mentioned rights.[30]

3. *Domestic legal developments*

3.1 Domestic legal transformations in the early 2000s

Following the ECtHR's first judgment on enforced disappearance in Türkiye in 1998, Turkish criminal justice and constitutional law underwent considerable changes in light of the national strategy to fulfil the EU criteria. In less than two decades, substantial constitutional amendments took place, including the abolition of the death penalty,[31] the strengthening of the power of international human rights treaties vis-à-vis national laws[32] and the reform of the fundamental rights framework.[33] The 2010 constitutional reform lifted the impunity for the military leaders of the 1980 military coup and established the right to lodge an individual application before the Constitutional Court in cases of violations of fundamental rights that are covered by the ECHR.[34]

In the criminal justice area, both the new Turkish Criminal Code no. 5237 (TCC) and the new Code of Criminal Procedure no. 5271 (CCP)

---

28 Ibid. para. 92.
29 Ibid.
30 For an overview of the ECtHR cases concerning enforced disappearances in Türkiye, see Altıntaş in Alpkaya/Altıntaş/Sevdiren et al. 2013, 109–31. Sethi 2001, 29–31.
31 Death penalty had not been implemented since 1984.
32 Constitution Article 90(5).
33 Türkmen 2013, 259.
34 Constitution Article 148.

were adopted in 2004. The criminal legislation aimed to embrace a modern criminal theory geared towards, among others, protecting the rule of law, the principle of humanism and human rights.[35] The amendments drew extensively from continental jurisdictions. The areas of changes included provisions on the criminalisation of international crimes, prevention of torture, custody procedures, accountability of security forces and remedies for the victims.[36]

As in the political area, legal amendments also concentrated on regulating the boundaries between the military and civil domains. National security courts, special terror courts and martial courts were dissolved in 2004, 2014 and 2017, respectively. This empowered the courts with general jurisdiction to handle crimes against the state and military and terror-related crimes.[37] By 2008, more than 100 high-level military staff were prosecuted for alleged coup attempts. After the 2010 reform, two retired military generals who had led the 1980 coup were also prosecuted for overthrowing parliament and the constitutional order.[38]

Furthermore, a parliamentary Sub-Committee on the violations of the right to life focusing on terrorism and violence was established in 2011 under the permanent Commission on Human Rights Inquiry of the Grand National Assembly of Türkiye (Parliamentary Commission on Human Rights). The Sub-Committee interviewed victims and political and civil society representatives and published its findings and recommendations in 2013.[39] In this period, the judicial authorities increasingly investigated and prosecuted crimes committed in the 1990s. The *Kulp* prosecutions analysed in this paper arose in the same period. The public peace process conducted by the Turkish government and the PKK between 2013 and 2015 facilitated the public debate in the broader societal context.[40] Consequently, the socio-legal landscape of the 2010s generally raised expectations of accountability and justice for enforced disappearances and past crimes among human rights advocates, lawyers and affected families.[41]

---

35 Sözüer 2007, 718; Türk Ceza Kanunu Tasarısı ve Adalet Komisyonu Raporu (The Proposal of the Turkish Criminal Code and the Report of the Justice Commission), 1/593. Period 22. 2nd Legislative Year, 2.

36 Çalı 2010, 327–8.

37 Yenisey/Nuhoğlu 2023, 272.

38 Sinclair-Webb 2012, 12–6.

39 Bakıner 2022, 51–60.

40 Savran 2020, 783.

41 Sinclair-Webb 2012, 8–60.

3.2 Material Law

One of the most significant changes introduced by the new TCC (no. 5237) in the context of the EU harmonisation process was the criminalisation of genocide and crimes against humanity. Türkiye was involved in the negotiations of the Rome Statute and was incentivised by the EU to ratify the statute but has not signed it to date.[42] Türkiye has also not signed the International Convention for the Protection of All Persons from Enforced Disappearance.

Article 77 defines crimes against humanity, formulated based on the Nuremberg Charter and the French Penal Code.[43] The definition differs, nonetheless, from the Rome Statute.[44] Some of the most significant inconsistencies can be outlined as follows. Firstly, a notable difference is that the prohibited acts do not include enforced disappearance, which is also not established as a distinct crime by the TCC. The act of deprivation of liberty is criminalized in an individual form[45] and constitutes one of the prohibited acts of crimes against humanity under Article 77. The acts of enforced disappearances could, therefore, be considered under the acts of deprivation of liberty.[46] Another striking difference is that the Turkish definition requires a specific intent with a discriminatory motive instead of knowledge of an attack against civilians.[47] Moreover, the discriminatory grounds are limited to political, philosophical, racial or religious grounds, thus excluding other grounds such as disability, age or sexual orientation.[48] In addition to these inconsistencies, acts must be systematic in nature to be considered crimes against humanity. This aspect, which is absent from the definition of enforced disappearances under the International Convention for the Protection of All Persons from Enforced Disappearance, creates an additional layer of difficulty for the prosecution of enforced disappearances.

42 Bozbayındır 2013, 19–39.
43 Ibid. 62–3.
44 Ibid. 62–94; Tezcan/Erdem/Önok (2014, 71–81) criticizes non-reliance on Rome Statute.
45 Article 109 of the TCC establishes the crime of deprivation of personal liberty, which punishes unlawful restrictions to the freedom of a person to move or to remain in a particular place.
46 Önok 2010, 33; Sevdiren 2016, 28; Werle/Jessberger 2014, 361 et seq.
47 Ambos/Hall/Hayes et al 2016, 175 et seq.; Bozbayındır 2013, 62–94; Sevdiren 2016, 144 et seq.; Werle/Jessberger 2014, 377–9.
48 Sevdiren 2016, 144 et seq.

In theory, international crimes might find application in relation to acts committed after the entry of force of the new provisions because of a strict interpretation of the principle of legality.[49] To date international crimes have not been used in the investigations of past crime.[50]

3.3 Statute of Limitations

Crimes of genocide and crimes against humanity are not subject to any statute of limitations under the TCC, in accordance with the Rome Statute and customary international law.[51] The TCC generally provides for a longer statute of limitations for non-international crimes such as murder than the former legislation. However, these longer periods do not apply to the investigation of the acts committed in the 1990s, judicial authorities instead applying the former provisions in favour of the suspects and accused.[52] This has tremendous consequences for complaints of enforced disappearances (see Section 4).

3.4 Procedural Law

3.4.1 Police custody

Police custody must be necessary for the investigation and rely on concrete evidence that creates a suspicion of the commission of an offence.[53] The requirement of concrete evidence was introduced by an amendment in 2014 to change the former requirement of 'indications'.[54] As a matter of principle, custody must be ordered by the prosecutor. Article 90(2) of the

---

49 Artuk/Gökçen/Alşahin et al. 2021, 157–61; Demirbaş 2021,125–31. Sevdiren argues that international crimes as established by the general principles of law and customary international law should directly apply in domestic law in accordance with the Article 7(2) of the ECHR and the Article 15(2) of the International Covenant on Civil and Political Rights (ICCPR) because international human rights instruments shall prevail over national laws under the Article 90(5) of the Turkish Constitution. See Sevdiren in Alpkaya/Altıntaş/Sevdiren et al, 2013, 100–3.

50 See Section 4.2.

51 Schabas 2016, 1107–10; TCC Articles 76(4), 77(4) and 78(3).

52 For an opposing view, see Sevdiren in Alpkaya/Altıntaş/Sevdiren et al., 2013, 100–3. See also Contesse in this anthology, 65 et seqq.

53 CCP Article 91(2).

54 Law no. 6526, 21 February 2014, Date of Official Journal: 6 March 2014, Article 6.

CCP allows police custody when the prosecutor cannot be immediately contacted, if there are grounds for detention or arrest and it is necessary to avoid undue delay.

3.4.2 Custody duration

The 1982 Constitution allowed up to 15 days of police custody for collective crimes, extensible under military rule, in war or under a state of emergency. This enabled very extensive periods of deprivation of liberty without judicial review, increasing prisoners' vulnerability to disappearances, torture or ill-treatment. Custody periods have been amended through a set of constitutional and procedural reforms. In 2001, the Constitution reduced the upper limit of custody for collective crimes to 4 days.[55] The proposal of 7 days was rejected in parliamentary discussions based on ECtHR case law and the recommendations of the European Committee for the Prevention of Torture and Inhuman or Degrading Treatment or Punishment.[56] In wartime or a state of emergency, the custody period can be prolonged.[57]

The initial police custody must not exceed 24 hours under CCP Article 91(1). For collective crimes, this period can gradually be extended by the prosecutor three times on justified grounds, not exceeding one day for each order of extension.[58] The suspect does not need to be present before the prosecutor during the decision on extension.[59] Statutory limitations exclude the time necessary for the transportation of the individual to the court. In 2005, the CCP was amended to limit the transportation time to 12 hours.[60]

3.4.3 Custody registry

Persons taken into custody must be recorded in the custodial prison registry.[61] Mandatory information includes the identity of the person and the

55 Constitution Article 19(5).
56 132. Birleşim (The Protocol of the 132. Session) 2001, 21. Period. 70. Volume. 102–7, available at: https://www5.tbmm.gov.tr/tutanaklar/TUTANAK/TBMM/d21/c070/tbmm21070132.pdf (accessed 24 October 2024).
57 Constitution Article 19(5). See Section 3.4.4. below.
58 CCP Article 91(3).
59 Ünver/Hakeri 2024, 894 et seq.; Yenisey 2015, 474.
60 CCP Article 91(1).
61 Regulation on Capture, Custody and Interrogation (Regulation on Capture) Article 11.

officials who ordered the measure, the date and time of entry and release, temporal leaves, the reason for custody, the date and summary of the pre-custody medical examination and the identity of the persons informed of the custody.[62] Further information may be included non-exhaustively. Chief prosecutors are responsible for monitoring activities connected to the registry, custody cells and interrogation rooms.[63]

3.4.4 New police custody power and state of emergency

A new police custody power introduced to the CCP in 2015 created a significant deviation from the ordinary regime of custody. New Article 91(4) of the CCP authorises police commanders to take custody measures up to 48 hours for suspects caught in the act of catalogue crimes. The catalogue encompasses a wide range of crimes, including 'crimes involving force and violence committed during social events,' terror crimes, crimes committed during gatherings and demonstrations and breach of curfews. Turkish legal scholars have heavily criticised this provision for disrupting the criminal justice system centred on the prosecutor, where police do not have investigative powers.[64] For instance, the prosecutor is required to be involved in interrogations and the notification of arrested individuals' relatives. Procedural guarantees remain in limbo in the absence of the immediate involvement of the prosecutor.[65] Therefore, the new measure significantly deviates from the exceptional nature of deprivation of liberty and creates an 'extraordinary' measure within the ordinary regime.[66]

In addition, the custody period was prolonged during the nationwide state of emergency between July 2016 and 2018, when Türkiye derogated from Article 15 of the ECHR. The period was first increased to 30 days, which was incompatible with the ECHR.[67] It was then reduced to 7 days,

62 Ibid. Article 12.

63 CCP Article 92(1); Regulation on Capture Article 26(2).

64 Ünver/Hakeri 2024, 904–5.

65 Yenisey 2015, 470–2. In contrast, the Constitutional Court found Article 91(4) of the CCP to be compatible with the Constitution. Constitutional Court, E. 2015/41, K. 2017/98, 4 May 2017, paras. 131-67, Anayasa Mahkemesi Kararlar Dergisi. 54.1. 277–447.

66 Yenisey/Nuhoğlu 2023, 363.

67 Muižnieks 2016, Measures taken under the state of emergency in Turkey. Strasbourg: Council of Europe Commissioner for Human Rights. URL: https://www.coe.int/e

with an upper limit of 14 days under State of Emergency Law no. 684 (Article 10).[68]

Even after the lifting of the state of emergency, a general tendency towards prolonged custody in the ordinary regime persisted.[69] In 2014, terror-specific custody periods had been reduced and then completely lifted.[70] When the state of emergency was lifted in 2018, they were temporarily re-introduced on the grounds of security deficits potentially caused by the removal of state of emergency laws.[71] This allowed the extension of the custody period by a decision of the judge within the ordinary regime up to 6 days and 12 days for individual and collective crimes, respectively.[72] The extended periods for terror crimes were applicable until July 2022.[73]

3.4.5 Procedural guarantees

The constitution and criminal procedure laws provide for procedural guarantees regarding deprivation of liberty.[74] The suspect or accused has a right to be informed of the accusations, the grounds of deprivation of liberty and his or her rights, including to silence and legal assistance, immediately after any measure has been taken for the safety of the suspect or other individuals.[75] Deprivation of liberty shall be immediately notified to the relatives of the detained person.[76] The detained person has a right to judicial review of

n/web/commissioner/-/measures-taken-under-the-state-of-emergency-in-turkey (accessed 24October 2024).

68 The Constitutional Court rejected the claim that these periods constitute a disproportionate intervention to the fundamental rights. Constitutional Court, E. 2018/92, K. 2019/67, 25 July 2019, para. 71, Anayasa Mahkemesi Kararlar Dergisi. 56.2. 971–95.

69 Ünver/Hakeri 2024, 927 et seq.

70 Yenisey 2015, 474 et seq. fn. 684.

71 Yenisey/Nuhoğlu 2023, 363.

72 The extension of custody was possible without a decision of pre-trial detention based on the workload of judicial authorities. Anti-Terror Law no. 3713, former Temporary Article 19. The Constitutional Court found by 7 against 6 votes that the extended custody periods were compatible with the Constitution. Constitutional Court, E. 2018/137, K. 2022/86, 30 June 2022, Anayasa Mahkemesi Kararlar Dergisi. 60.1. 1–356.

73 Yenisey/Nuhoğlu 2023, 363–4.

74 Constitution, Article 19(4–9).

75 CCP Article 90(4); Law of Police Powers (no. 2559) Article 13(4); Regulation on Capture Article 6(4); Ünver/Hakeri 2024, 891–3.

76 Constitution Article 19(6).

the deprivation of liberty.[77] Any damages caused by non-compliance with procedural standards must be compensated by the state.[78]

The duty of notification to the relatives first received constitutional protection in the 1961 Constitution and has undergone a few changes since then. Article 30 of the 1961 Constitution prescribed that the relatives of an arrested or detained person must be immediately notified when the suspect or accused is brought before the judge. The 1982 Constitution established in Article 19(6) that the notification of the arrest or detention must be immediate unless there are compelling reasons for ensuring the secrecy of the investigation. The constitutional amendment of 2001 established the duty of immediate notification without any conditions.[79]

In addition to the constitutional provision, the CCP and the Law of Police Powers contain multiple conflicting provisions, which have generated debates as to the process of notification. The CCP requires in Article 95(1) an order of the prosecutor for the notification of arrest (*yakalama*), taking of custody and prolongation of the custody period.[80] Thus, it establishes a supplementary procedural requirement of prosecutorial order in contrast to the Constitution.[81] This inconsistency has been criticised by legal scholars.[82] Furthermore, the scope of the person or persons who shall be notified remains unclear.[83] There have been discussions about whether the terminology used for notified persons (*yakınlarına*)[84] could cover persons other than close blood relatives.[85]

If the arrested person is a foreign national, the consulate of his or her nationality must be notified, unless he or she objects in writing (CCP

77 Ibid. Article 19(8).
78 Ibid. Article 19(9).
79 Ibid. Article 19(6).
80 Regulation on Capture Article 8(1).
81 Ünver/Hakeri 2024, 898–9; Yenisey/Nuhoğlu 2023, 356. On the other hand, the Law of Police Powers Article 13(5) does not include the order of prosecutor.
82 Öztürk/Tezcan/Erdem et al. (2023, 457) argue that the requirement of prosecutorial order hinders the notification if the prosecutor is not yet aware of any police custody. Ünver/Hakeri (2024, 898–9) argue that the prosecutorial order could cause delays, making it a practical challenge to make the notification without a delay. They argue therefore for an upper time limit for notification.
83 Kaya Göçmen 2021, 201–4; Özen 2023, 694 et seq.
84 The word "yakın" literary means "close". It is also defined as a "friend, companion or relative with whom one has a close relationship". (*Güncel Türkçe Sözlük* [current Turkish Dictionary], Turkish Language Association, available online at https://sozluk.gov.tr/).
85 Kaya Göçmen 2021, 203; Özen 2023, 742; Ünver/Hakeri 2024, 900.

Article 95(2)).[86] This provision was adopted in 2004 in accordance with public international law. The wording of CCP Article 95(2) does not specify whether the notification of the consulate is a non-exclusive alternative of notification of relatives. This leads to ambiguity as to whether relatives of the foreign national must also be notified in addition to the consulate. This question is especially relevant if the arrestee objects to the notification to the consulate. Notification to the consulate should be understood as supplementary to the notification of relatives.[87] In fact, close relatives are entitled to request a release from the judge.[88] Therefore, the notification of relatives may be necessary to allow foreign nationals to exercise the right to challenge a protective measure and prevent *incommunicado* detention, especially if the detainee objects to the notification of the consulate.[89]

4. Domestic case law

Investigative and prosecutorial authorities are obliged to seek the material truth on an *ex officio* basis.[90] Courts can conduct discovery on the crime scene and appoint experts through their own motions if necessary.[91] The principles of orality and immediacy govern the prosecution stage. Witnesses must be heard in a public trial.[92]

An important impact of constitutional and legal reform has been the (re-)initiation of domestic inquiries into acts committed by security forces in the past two decades. In this section, the domestic inquiries that followed the ECtHR's *Akdeniz* judgment (*Kulp* case) will be summarised before analysing the domestic process and jurisprudence.

86 Ünveri/Hakeri (2024, 899) criticise the requirement of written form because it may not be immediately realisable in practice due to translation and other aspects.
87 Öztürk/Tezcan/Erdem et al. 2023, 457.
88 CCP Article 91(5).
89 On notification to relatives, see Cornelius in this anthology, 81 et seqq.
90 Centel/Zafer 2015, 679–81; Yenisey/Nuhoğlu 2023, 755.
91 CCP Article 63(1) and Article 83.
92 CCP Article 210(1).

4.1 Post-Akdeniz trials: the Kulp case

In the aftermath of the *Akdeniz* judgment, one of the most significant developments was the discovery of a mass grave containing the bones of 11 disappeared persons in 2004 in the area where they were last seen. Upon this discovery, the Parliamentary Commission on Human Rights issued a report, interviewing witnesses and officials and analysing forensic results and official records. The Parliamentary Commission on Human Rights opined that the detention and disappearances of some individuals took place during a counter-terrorism operation and that criminal prosecution was essential to prevent similar crimes.[93]

In 2013, nine years after the discovery of the mass grave, the commander who conducted the operation – at this point a retired brigadier general – was charged with murder, establishing an organisation to commit crimes and inciting the public to armed rebellion.[94] The prosecution was initiated before the 7th Assize Court of Diyarbakır, shortly before it was transferred to the 7th Assize Court of Ankara on security grounds.[95] The hearings were held publicly and monitored by civil society, political party and diplomatic representatives.[96] The accused was defended by a team of defence lawyers. The families of the disappeared persons were participants in the case and were also represented by their lawyers.

The accused denied the charges against him, stating that he fulfilled his duties in accordance with the laws and the orders of the military and the state of emergency administration.[97] In 2016, a legal amendment established that ministerial permission was a prerequisite for the investigation of soldiers' acts that arose from their duties under the state of emergency. The prosecuting court made requests to ministerial and military institutions about the nature of the 1993 operation to establish if it fell under the state of emergency rule. Public institutions stated that they found no information

93 Diyarbakır Public Prosecutor's indictment dated 11 October 2013 (Investigation no: 2013/2531; Indictment no: 2013/687).

94 Former TCC (no. 756) Articles 450(4–5), 149 and 313(2).

95 CCP Article 19.

96 The summary of the trial process in this section is prepared based on the protocols of the hearings monitored by the Center for Memory. The protocols of the hearings, the indictment, newspaper articles as well as a timetable are publicly available on an online database at: https://www.failibelli.org/dava/yavuz-erturk-kulp-davasi/#dava-notlari (accessed 18 October 2024).

97 Ataktürk Sevimli/Kılıç/Zeren et al. 2021, 54.

or documents regarding this operation. The legal amendment additionally generated a discussion in the courtroom on whether military courts shall exercise jurisdiction to adjudicate.[98] The jurisdiction issue was solved when the military courts were lifted by the constitutional referendum in April 2017, which is why the court waited for the entry into force of the referendum results.

The court made further requests to public institutions for evidence collection. Yet, the names of the staff members who served in the 1993 operation were not disclosed to the court. The request to take statements from military staff was subsequently rejected on the basis that it would not contribute to the case. The statements of three witnesses of the participant families were included in the case file on the 18th hearing in February 2018, before the hearing in which the prosecutor presented his opinion on the merits of the case and two hearings before the court gave its judgment. The witnesses were heard a month before by the local court of Diyarbakır upon a request for legal assistance by the prosecuting court. The bench rejected the argument that the witness testimonies constituted new evidence that could create a basis for detention, as any prior requests for detention. The bench also rejected further requests for the extension of the inquiry and the collection of further evidence.

In the final hearing, on 19 September 2018, the 7th Assize Court of Ankara gave its judgment in parallel to the opinion of the prosecutor heard in the previous hearing. It ruled that the accusations of establishing an illegal organisation were time-barred based on the 7.5-year statute of limitation under the former TCC (no. 765). The accused was acquitted of abetting the murder of 11 persons and sedition of the public. In 2020, the Regional Court of Justice of Ankara upheld the judgment. In 2024, the Court of Appeals annulled the acquittal and ruled that the prosecution of the two crimes was also time-barred based on the maximum statutory period of 30 years prescribed by the former TCC.

4.2 Analysis

The domestic process following the *Akdeniz* judgment ceased due to the statute of limitations without providing the complainants the truth about

98 Law no. 6722 amending Law for Provincial Administration no. 5442, 23 June 2016, Date of Official Journal: 14 July 2016, Article 12.

the disappearance of their family members. In *Akdeniz*, the ECtHR had found striking omissions in the investigation of the disappearance and presumed death of the victims. Even after the discovery of the victims' bones, these omissions were not remedied in the post-ECtHR judgment period. Despite the fact that a prosecution against an accused person was initiated, the inquiry was not expanded to find further witnesses, to collect further evidence and uncover the circumstances of the military operation.

Some problems at the prosecution stage may be observed. The transfer of the case from the jurisdiction of the events (Diyarbakır) to another jurisdiction 1,000 km away (Ankara) created an obstacle to evidence collection and examination since the domestic court did not have direct contact with the crime scene and witnesses.[99] The transfer of disappearance cases to geographically distant areas based on general grounds is a common practice.[100] The transfers not only hindered effective and timely fact-finding and the right to a natural judge but also complicated the participation of the complainants and their lawyers in the trials.[101]

Another problem is the disconnection of the examination of the merits of the case from other cases of enforced disappearances. A vast body of studies and sources, including parliamentary reports, court judgments, governmental statements and documents from the last three decades, has demonstrated patterns of serious human rights violations, committed predominantly in the state of emergency region of 1990s.[102] Against this background, The ECtHR has taken into account the broader context in which unacknowledged detention in the region posed a serious threat to life, given its earlier findings that the deficiencies in criminal law protection at the time fostered impunity among security forces.[103] In the domestic proceedings, however, no connection was established between cases involving similar factual circumstances.[104] When intervening parties sought to provide

99 Ataktürk Sevimli/Kılıç/Zeren et al. 2021, 67.

100 Ibid. 64–7.

101 Ibid. Report of the Working Group on Enforced or Involuntary Disappearances on its mission to Turkey 2016, Human Rights Council. United Nations General Assembly, para. 35, available at: https://documents.un.org/doc/undoc/gen/g16/166/87/pdf/g1616687.pdf (accessed 24 October 2024).

102 For an overview of these studies and sources see Kurban 2020, 134–165; Sevdiren 2016, 44–8; Sevdiren in Alpkaya/Altıntaş/Sevdiren 2013, 92–100.

103 Harris/O'Boyle/Bates et al. 2014, 223–4; ECtHR 2000, Timurtaş v. Turkey, no. 23531/94, ECHR 2000-VI para. 85.

104 Ataktürk Sevimli/Kılıç/Zeren et al. 2021, 70–2.

contextual background, their submissions were interrupted and dismissed as irrelevant. In the *Kulp case*, one of the hearings was even suspended to remind the counsel representing the family of the disappeared persons to confine his submissions to the subject matter of the case.[105] Thus, the case was treated as an isolated crime that occurred under ordinary circumstances.

The absence of a crime of enforced disappearance and the consequential application of the statute of limitations constitute significant obstacles to accountability. In most cases involving complaints of enforced disappearances, as in the *Kulp* case, authorities investigate solely murder.[106] This hinders the punishment of enforced disappearances when the standard of proof for murder cannot be met.[107] Moreover, the former TCC (no. 765), which was in force at the time of the events, provides for a statutory limitation of 20 to 30 years in the case of murder. For this reason, it can be assumed that the vast majority of investigations of enforced disappearances in the 1990s are timed-barred as of the date of this publication. As a consequence, the victims of enforced disappearance and their families have not been provided with full reparation.[108]

It should be noted that the domestic process for the *Kulp* case has not been fully finalised given that an individual application claiming fundamental rights violations was lodged before the Constitutional Court.[109] In its previous judgments, the Constitutional Court found a violation of the obligation to conduct an effective investigation under the right to life (Article 17 of the Constitution) on the ground that the investigations concern-

105 Ataktürk Sevimli/Kılıç/Zeren et al. 2021, 72.

106 Ataktürk Sevimli/Kılıç/Zeren et al., 2021, 61.

107 Report of the Working Group on Enforced or Involuntary Disappearances on its mission to Turkey 2016, Human Rights Council. United Nations General Assembly, para. 15, available at: https://documents.un.org/doc/undoc/gen/g16/166/87/pdf/g1616687.pdf (accessed 24 October 2024).

108 Ibid. paras. 42–51. On the contrary, the vigils of the Saturday Mothers/People were repeatedly banned or restricted in violation of the rights of the protestors. See Concluding observations on the second periodic report of Türkiye, 2024, Human Rights Committee, United Nations, paras. 23–4 and 59, available at: https://docs.un.org/en/CMW/C/TUR/CO/2 (accessed 24 October 2024).

109 Interview with Özlem Zıngıl, Lawyer and Program Manager in Center for Memory, Zoom, 23.11.2024.

ing unregistered detention,[110] torture[111] or killing[112] of victims lacked due diligence or reasonable measures. Nevertheless, these judgements reflect a narrow perspective to enforced disappearances. What follows demonstrates the Constitutional Court's approach in relation to the examination of admissibility and merits.

Notably, most complaints of enforced disappearances before the Constitutional Court were found to be inadmissible *ratione temporis*.[113] The *Zeycan Yedigöl* application provides a striking example of this approach. The applicant alleged that her son was taken into police custody on 10 April 1981 and had been missing since then. The criminal process involved three investigations, all of which were time-barred. Two investigations were opened in 1986 and 2012 and became time-barred in 2000 and 2012, respectively. In 2012 a third investigation was formally initiated against the commanders of the 1980 military coup and some police officers, upon the request of the applicant, and was discontinued in the same year. As a matter of principle, the Constitutional Court exercises temporal jurisdiction over decisions and judgments that have finalized after 23 September 2012 (the date marking the beginning of temporal jurisdiction).[114] The Constitutional Court found the application inadmissible with respect to the first and second investigation because they had been closed before that date. The Constitutional Court noted that the state's failure to conduct an effective investigation had certainly occurred prior to that date.[115] While acknowledging the continuous nature of enforced disappearance, it nonetheless held that limitation periods could still be applied.[116] The application was also inadmissible with respect to the third investigation, although it was closed after the date of temporal jurisdiction.[117] This investigation resulted from the prosecution of military commanders, enabled by the constitutional reform that removed their impunity, but it was not considered a new circumstance.[118] The Con-

110 Constitutional Court 2016, Birsen Gülünay, no. 2013/2640, paras. 95–7.

111 Constitutional Court 2016, Hıdır Öztürk and Dilif Öztürk, no. 2013/7832, paras. 9-80 and 196–8.

112 Ibid.; Constitutional Court 2016, Maşallah Güzelsoy, no. 2014/14583, paras. 70–4.

113 Interview with Özlem Zıngıl.

114 Constitutional Court 2015, *Zeycan Yedigöl* [General Assembly], Inadmissibility decision, no. 2013/1566, para. 29.

115 Ibid. para. 35.

116 Ibid. paras. 32–4.

117 Ibid. para. 36.

118 Ibid. paras. 37–43; See Section 3.1 above.

stitutional Court further observed that the third investigation was bound to be as futile as the previous ones.[119] As a result, the court's reasoning confirmed the lack of effective investigations and, moreover, normalized the state's abdication of its right to punish.[120]

Even when a case was admissible, the examination of the merits was restricted. In *Birsen Gülünay*, the Constitutional Court examined the merits only from the perspective of the right to life although it explicitly stated that the case did not concern a 'suspicious death' but a 'suspicious case of disappearance', which has a continuous character.[121] It found a violation of the procedural aspect and not a violation of the material aspect because the standard of proof for death had not been established.[122] Furthermore, the Constitutional Court did not challenge the application of the statute of limitations. Considering the established case-law of the Constitutional Court, one might argue that, in the *Kulp* case, the court might find a violation of the procedural aspect of the right to life because the prosecutions were time-barred before the shortcomings identified by the ECtHR were remedied.[123] However, this is unlikely to lead to new investigations of other potential suspects.

5. Conclusion

Turkish law has undergone profound changes since the beginning of the century, providing a strengthened legal framework for the prevention and punishment of enforced disappearances. In substantial law, the most notable development has been the enactment of international crimes despite some discrepancies with the international framework. In practice, however, the new crimes found no application in cases of enforced disappearances or any other past crime cases. The non-criminalisation of enforced disappearance as a distinct crime remains a significant obstacle to accountability for enforced disappearances. In procedural law, amendments to custody and procedural safeguards provided some guarantees in the area of protection

119 Ibid. para. 42.
120 ibid. paras. 35 and 39.
121 Constitutional Court 2016, Birsen Gülünay, no. 2013/2640, para. 86.
122 Gebeş 2017.
123 In the similar direction, *mutatis mutandis*, Constitutional Court 2016, *İsak Tepe*, no. 2014/4038, para. 80.

of physical integrity.[124] Yet, subsequent amendments such as the new police custody power and anti-terror-related measures significantly restrict the impact of the previous reforms.[125]

The most significant steps towards accountability were taken when the investigations for past crimes intensified in early 2010s. Nonetheless, these domestic processes were hampered by significant obstacles. The criminal inquiries were not expanded to a degree that would uncover the circumstances of disappearances and engage the responsibility of the perpetrators. In the *Kulp* case, the deficiencies in the evidence collection and investigation identified in *Akdeniz* were not sufficiently remedied during the prosecution phase. The transfer of the case and disconnection between past crime cases hampered the effectiveness of the proceedings. Furthermore, domestic courts did not sufficiently distinguish the acts of enforced disappearances from other types of violations, in particular, unresolved killings or unnatural deaths. This has led to a lack of recognition of the act of disappearance as a distinct, continuous crime and the application of statutory limits. Statute of limitation are ultimately the main legal tool that hinders accountability. This perpetrates an uncertain situation for those involved in the cases given that many domestic cases do not lead to any substantial outcome, be it a conviction or an acquittal. As there is no alternative explanation for the circumstances of these disappearances, the need for accountability and truth still persists.

Bibliography

Alpkaya, Gökçen et al. 2013. *Enforced Disappearances and the Conduct of the Judiciary.* Istanbul: Truth Justice Memory Centre. URL: https://hakikatadalethafiza.org/en/publications/enforced-disappearances-and-conduct-judiciary (accessed 24 October 2024).

Alpkaya, Gökçen et al. 2014. *Zorla Kaybetmeler ve Yargının Tutumu.* Istanbul: Truth Justice Memory Centre. URL: https://hakikatadalethafiza.org/yayinlar/zorla-kaybetmeler-ve-yarginin-tutumu (accessed 24 October 2024).

Ambos, Kai et al. 2016. 'Article 7 Crimes against humanity'. In Triffterer, Otto and Ambos, Kai (eds.). *The Rome Statute of the International Criminal Court. A Commentary.* US and Canada: Beck, Hart, Nomos. 144–294.

124 Çalı 2010, 327; Türkmen 2013, 259–60.

125 Muižnieks 2016, Memorandum on the Human Rights Implications of Anti-Terrorism Operations in South-Eastern Turkey. Commissioner for Human Rights of the Council of Europe. URL: https://rm.coe.int/ref/CommDH(2016)39 (accessed 24 November 2024).

Artuk, Mehmet Emin et al. 2021. *Ceza Hukuku Genel Hükümler*. Ankara: Adalet.

Ataktürk Sevimli, Emel et al. 2021. *1990'lı Yıllardaki Ağır İnsan Hakları İhlallerinde Cezasızlık Sorunu. Kovuşturma Süreci*. Istanbul: Hafıza Merkezi. URL: https://hakikatadalethafiza.org/sites/default/files/2022-12/cezasizlik_kovusturmasureci.pdf (accessed 24 October 2024).

Bakıner, Onur. 2022. *Geçiş Dönemi Adaletinin Yokluğunda Resmî Hakikat Arayışı. Türkiye'de Meclis Araştırma Komisyonları*. Istanbul: Hafıza Merkezi. URL:

gecis-donemi-adaletinin-yoklugunda-resmi-hakikat-arayisi-turkiyede-meclis-arastirma-komisyonlari-1.pdf (accessed 24 November 2024).

Bozbayındır, Ali Emrah. 2013. *Turkey and the International Criminal Court. A Substantive Criminal Law Analysis in the Context of the Principle of Complementarity*. Baden-Baden: Nomos. Bern: Stämpfli Verlag.

Centel, Nur and Zafer, Hamide. 2015. *Ceza Muhakemesi Hukuku*. Istanbul: Beta.

Çalı, Başak. 2010. 'The Logics of Supranational Human Rights Litigation, Official Acknowledgment, and Human Rights Reform: The Southeast Turkey Cases before the European Court of Human Rights, 1996–2006'. *Law & Social Inquiry*. 35.2. 311–37.

Daşlı Güneş. 2024. 'Victim Agency, Relational Autonomy and Transitional Justice: Experience of Saturday Mothers'. *The International Journal of Transitional Justice*. 18. 371–86.

Demirbaş, Timur. 2021. *Ceza Hukuku Genel Hükümler*. Ankara: Seçkin.

Gebeş, Melis. 2017. *Zorla Kaybetmeler ve Anayasa Mahkemesi: Hasan Gülünay Kararı Hakkında Bir Değerlendirme*. URL: https://hakikatadalethafiza.org/haberler/zorla-kaybetmeler-ve-anayasa-mahkemesi-hasan-gulunay-karari-hakkinda-bir-degerlendirme#_ftn2 (accessed 24 November 2024).

Harris, David J. et al. 2014. Law of the European Convention on Human Rights. Oxford: Oxford University Press.

Kaya Göçmen, Özen. 2021. *Avrupa İnsan Hakları Sözleşmesi ve Ceza Muhakemesi Kanunu Kapsamında Yakalama ve Gözaltı Koruma Tedbirleri*. Ankara : Seçkin.

Kurban, Dilek. 2020. *Limits of Supranational Justice: The European Court of Human Rights and Turkey's Kurdish Conflict*. New York: Cambridge University Press.

Muižnieks, Nils. 2016. *Measures taken under the state of emergency in Turkey. Strasbourg: Council of Europe Commissioner for Human Rights*. URL: https://www.coe.int/en/web/commissioner/-/measures-taken-under-the-state-of-emergency-in-turkey (accessed 24 October 2024).

Muižnieks, Nils. 2016. *Memorandum on the Human Rights Implications of Anti-Terrorism Operations in South-Eastern Turkey*. Commissioner for Human Rights of the Council of Europe. URL: https://rm.coe.int/ref/CommDH(2016)39 (accessed 24 November 2024).

Önok, R. Murat. 2010. *Uluslararası Ceza Divanı'nı Kuran Roma Statüsü ile Türk Ulusal Mevzuatının Maddi Ceza Hukuku Kuralları Yönünden Uyumuna Dair Rapor*. Ankara: Uluslararası Ceza Mahkemesi Koalisyonu. URL: https://ihop.org.tr/rapor-ucdyi-kuran-roma-statuesue-ile-tuerk-ulusal-mevzuatnn-maddi-ceza-hukuku-kurallar-yoenuenden-uyumu/ (accessed 24 October 2024).

Özen, Mustafa. 2023. *Ceza Muhakemesi Hukuku Dersleri*. Ankara: Adalet.

Öztürk, Bahri et al. 2023. *Nazari ve Uygulamalı Ceza Muhakemesi Hukuku*. Ankara: Seçkin.

Savran, Arin. 2020. 'The Peace Process between Turkey and the Kurdistan Workers' Party, 2009–2015'. *Journal of Balkan and Near Eastern Studies*. 22.6. 777–92.

Schabas, William. 2016. 'Article 29 Non-applicability of statute of limitations'. In Triffterer, Otto and Ambos, Kai (eds.). *The Rome Statute of the International Criminal Court. A Commentary*. US and Canada: Beck, Hart, Nomos. 1107–10.

Sethi, Gobind Singh. 2001. 'The European Court of Human Rights' Jurisprudence on Issues of Forced Disappearances'. *Human Rights Brief*. 8.3. 29–31.

Sevdiren, Öznur. 2016. *Türkiye'nin Cezasızlık Mevzuatı*. Istanbul: Hafıza Merkezi. URL: https://hakikatadalethafiza.org/wp-content/uploads/2016/04/TurkiyeninCezasizlikMevzuati.pdf (accessed 24 October 2024)

Sinclair-Webb, Emma. 2012. *Time for Justice Ending Impunity for Killings and Disappearances in 1990s Turkey*. USA: Human Rights Watch. URL: https://www.hrw.org/report/2012/09/03/time-justice/ending-impunity-killings-and-disappearances-1990s-turkey (accessed 24 October 2024).

Sözüer, Adem. 2007. 'Die Reform des türkischen Strafrechts'. *ZStW* 3, 717–50.

Şarlak, Zeynep. 2020. *A history of the national security state in Turkey*. PhD Dissertation. Universiteit Leiden, Leiden.

Tezcan, Durmuş, Erdem, Mustafa Ruhan and Önok, Murat. 2014. *Teorik ve Pratik Ceza Özel Hukuku*. Ankara: Seçkin.

Topcu, Elmas. 2024. *Turkey: 'Saturday Mothers' protest forced disappearances*. DW. URL: https://www.dw.com/en/turkey-saturday-mothers-protest-forced-disappearance-of-loved-ones/a-69236689 (accessed 24 October 2024)

Turhan, Faruk. 2000. 'Avrupa İnsan Hakları Mahkemesi AİHM Kararları Işığında Kişi Özgürlüğü ve Türkiye. Gözaltında Kayıplar, Hakim Önüne Çıkarma ve Gözaltı Süreleri'. *AHBVÜ-HFD* (Formerly *Gazi Üniversitesi HFD*) 4.2. 204–58.

Türkmen, Füsun. 2007. 'Turkey's Participation in Global and Regional Human Rights Regimes'. In Kabasakal Arat, Zehra F. (ed.). *Human Rights in Turkey*. Philadelphia: University of Pennsylvania Press. 249–61.

Ünver, Yener and Hakeri, Hakan. 2024. *Ceza Muhakemesi Hukuku*. Cilt II. Ankara: Adalet.

Werle, Gerhard and Jessberger, Florian. 2014. *Principles of International Criminal Law*. New York: Oxford University Press.

Yenisey, Feridun. 2015. *Kolluk Hukuku*. Istanbul: Beta.

Yenisey, Feridun and Nuhoğlu, Ayşe. 2023. *Ceza Muhakemesi Hukuku*. Ankara: Seçkin.

Enforced Disappearance as a Crime against Humanity – the Ukrainian Situation

Denys Shylin

Abstract: The chapter deals with the problematic issues related to the definition of enforced disappearance as a crime against humanity. It has been determined that enforced disappearance comprises a gross and complex violation of human rights, which is, in essence, the deprivation of liberty of a person with subsequent refusal to recognize the fact of such deprivation or concealment of the information concerning the fate of that person. In addition to being an offense in itself, enforced disappearance often violates other human rights, including the right to recognition as a person before the law, the right to liberty and security of person and the right not to be subjected to torture or cruel, inhuman or degrading treatment or punishment. Enforced disappearance is considered a violation of human rights that continues until the fate and whereabouts of the disappeared person are clarified. The chapter analyzes the historical genesis of the recognition of enforced disappearance as a crime against humanity. It has been established that the large-scale and systematic practice of enforced disappearances persists in modern conditions.

1. The phenomenon of 'enforced disappearances' in the Ukrainian context

The problem of enforced disappearances has acquired a new meaning for Ukraine due to the ongoing armed conflict on its territory. Since 2014, following the occupation of the Crimean Peninsula and the armed confrontation within certain districts in the Donetsk and Luhansk regions, law enforcement agencies of Ukraine have recorded cases of disappearances and detentions of persons in the territory controlled by the Russian Federation. Similar cases have been also repeatedly documented after the full-scale invasion of the Russian Federation into the territory of Ukraine. Any individual can become a victim of enforced disappearances in the course of an armed conflict. In the occupied territories, however, these are primarily the persons having an active civic or pro-Ukrainian position, experience of military service or participation in the anti-terrorist operation in eastern Ukraine, working in local self-government bodies or law enforcement agencies, or simply speaking Ukrainian; the above said categories are exposed to higher risk.

At the same time, the prosecution of persons who cooperate with the occupation authorities in the territories controlled by the Russian Federation, members of illegal armed formations of the self-proclaimed 'Donetsk People's Republic' and 'Luhansk People's Republic', as well as the introduction of criminal liability for collaborative activities after February 24-2022, created the risk that enforced disappearances can also be committed by the Ukrainian authorities. In particular, after the announcement of anti-terrorist operation on the territory of Ukraine in 2014, a number of normative legal acts were adopted, which regulated additional requirements for the preventive detention of persons suspected of the commission of illegal acts.[1]

2. Legal Situation in Ukraine (I)

Over these ten years, Ukraine has taken a number of important steps towards meeting international standards in the field of enforced disappearances prevention. On June 17-2015, the Verkhovna Rada of Ukraine ratified the 2006 International Convention for the Protection of All Persons from Enforced Disappearance.[2] The Convention is an international UN instrument in the field of human rights protection adopted by the resolution

1 The Law of Ukraine 'On Amendments to the Law of Ukraine 'On Combating Terrorism' on Preventive Detention of Persons Involved in Terrorist Activities in the Area of Anti-Terrorist Operation for a Period of More than 72 Hours' // Verkhovna Rada of Ukraine, No. 1630-VII of 12.08.2014, available at: https://zakon.rada.gov.ua/laws/show/1630-18# (accessed 25 December 2024). Text. Instruction on the Procedure for Preventive Detention in the Area of Anti-Terrorist Operation of Persons Involved in Terrorist Activities and Special Regime of Pre-trial Investigation under the Conditions of Martial Law, State of Emergency or in the Area of Anti-Terrorist Operation // Order of the Ministry of Internal Affairs of Ukraine, the Prosecutor General's Office of Ukraine, the Security Service of Ukraine // Verkhovna Rada of Ukraine, No. 1038/25815 of 27.08.2014, available at: https://zakon.rada.gov.ua/laws/show/z1038-14#Text (accessed 25 December 2024).

2 The Law of Ukraine 'On Ukraine's Accession to the International Convention for the Protection of All Persons from Enforced Disappearance' // Verkhovna Rada of Ukraine, No. 525-VIII of June 17, 2015, available at: https://zakon.rada.gov.ua/laws/show/525-19#n2 (accessed 25 December 2024). List of countries that have acceded to the Convention for the Protection of All Persons from Enforced Disappearance, available

of the UN General Assembly on December 20–2006 No. A/RES/61/177 and entered into force on December 23, 2010.[3] Its signing was preceded by the Declaration on the Protection of All Persons from Enforced Disappearances, adopted by UN General Assembly Resolution No. 47/133 of December 18 1992,[4] which is still effective. The rules of the Declaration became a set of principles for all states regarding the prohibition of enforced disappearances as established in international human rights law and international customary law, and provided for the award of compensation to victims of the above said acts.

Under the 2006 International Convention for the Protection of All Persons from Enforced Disappearance, enforced disappearance occurs when a person is arrested, detained, abducted against his or her will or otherwise deprived of his or her liberty by agents of the State or by a person or group of persons whose acts are in some way aided and abetted by the State. Such deprivation of liberty is accompanied by a refusal to recognize the fact of deprivation of liberty of the person concerned or concealment of information about the fate or whereabouts of the disappeared person. As a result of such behavior, the disappeared person is outside the protection of the law, which deprives them of the possibility to seek legal remedies and guarantees and puts them in a situation of complete defenselessness. This, in turn, makes them vulnerable to other human rights violations, such as torture, sexual violence or even murder.

The 2006 International Convention for the Protection of All Persons from Enforced Disappearance divides acts of enforced disappearance into two categories: isolated cases and acts that constitute a crime against humanity.[5] Article 5 stipulates that 'widespread or systematic practice of enforced disappearances constitutes a crime against humanity as defined in applicable international law and entails the consequences provided for in such applicable international law.'

---

at: https://tbinternet.ohchr.org/_layouts/15/TreatyBodyExternal/Treaty.aspx?CountryID=183&Lang=EN (accessed 25 December 2024).

3 International Convention for the Protection of All Persons from Enforced Disappearance // Verkhovna Rada of Ukraine, Convention, International Instrument of 20.12.2006, available at: https://zakon.rada.gov.ua/laws/show/995_154#Text; (UN website: http://surl.li/rtnxp) (accessed 25 December 2024).

4 Resolution 47/33 of the UN General Assembly of December 18, 1992 'Declaration on the Protection of All Persons from Enforced Disappearance' // Verkhovna Rada of Ukraine, International Instrument, available at: https://zakon.rada.gov.ua/laws/show/995_225#Text (accessed 25 December 2024).

5 Anderson 2006, 270.

3. *Enforced disappearance as a crime against humanity*

Enforced disappearance as a crime against humanity was first recognized during the Paris Colloquium at the Institute of Human Rights of the Paris Bar Association in 1981; the first draft of the International Convention against Enforced Disappearances stated that 'the practice of enforced or involuntary disappearances constitutes a crime against humanity.'[6]

Resolution 828/1984 of the Parliamentary Assembly of the Council of Europe emphasizes that 'the definition of enforced disappearance as a crime against humanity is essential in the context of prosecuting and punishing those responsible for it.'[7] Within the framework of the First Colloquium on Enforced Disappearances held in Bogotá in 1986, it was noted that 'States have an obligation to take effective measures, without exception, to prevent acts of enforced disappearance, which constitute a crime against humanity.'

In its judgment in the case of Godinez Cruz v. Honduras,[8] the Inter-American Court of Human Rights held that enforced disappearances are often qualified as a crime against humanity in doctrine and international practice despite the absence of any international convention that would enshrine this. Later, in 2004, in the decision in the case of Comerciantes v. Colombia,[9] the Inter-American Court of Human Rights found that no specific conditions and prerequisites are required to qualify enforced disappearance as a crime against humanity. Moreover, in 2006, the Inter-American Court of Human Rights, in its judgments in four cases of enforced disappearance that occurred within the framework of Operation Condor, defined acts of enforced disappearance as a systematic state practice of terrorism for which the state concerned must be held responsible.[10]

---

6 Scovazzi 2007, 286.

7 Council of Europe. Resolution 828/1984 of 26 September 1984 / Parliamentary Assembly, available at: https://assembly.coe.int/nw/xml/XRef/Xref-XML2HTML-en.asp?fileid=16239&lang=en (accessed 25 December 2024).

8 IACtHR, Godinez Cruz v. Honduras, judgement of 20 January 1989, available at: www.corteidh.or.cr/docs/casos/articulos/seriec_05_ing.pdf (accessed 25 December 2024).

9 IACtHR, 19 Merchants v. Colombia, judgement of 5 July 2004, available at: http://www.corteidh.or.cr/docs/casos/articulos/seriec_109_ing.pdf (accessed 25 December 2024).

10 IACtHR, Goiburu v. Paraguay, judgement of 22 September 2006, available at: www.corteidh.or.cr/docs/casos/articulos/seriec_153_ing.pdf (accessed 25 December 2024).

These statements, resolutions, and judgments, however, fail to contain any qualification of enforced disappearance as a crime against humanity: neither the systematic nor widespread nature of such acts were mentioned. In the process of drafting and organizing the UN Declaration of 1992, the Inter-American Convention on Enforced Disappearance of Persons of 1994 and especially the International Convention for the Protection of All Persons from Enforced Disappearance of 2006, the above resolutions and decisions were referred to and–representatives of the participating States held long discussions on the mandatory systematic or widespread nature of acts of enforced disappearance in the context of a crime against humanity.[11] As a result, enforced disappearance is presently considered a crime against humanity solely where there is a systematic or widespread practice.

It was for the first time that the Preamble to the 1992 UN Declaration on the Protection of All Persons from Enforced Disappearance stated that 'systematic nature of acts of enforced disappearance constitutes a crime against humanity by its very nature.' Since 1992, the wording 'systematic practice' has become the standard for recognizing an act of enforced disappearance as a crime against humanity. It should be noted that a similar provision is guaranteed in the Inter-American Convention on Forced Disappearance of Persons of 1994. During the development of the text of the 1992 UN Declaration on the Protection of All Persons from Enforced Disappearance, a number of representatives of the UNWGEID (Working Group on Enforced or Involuntary Disappearances) emphasized the difference between a single act of enforced disappearance and its systematic practice. Ultimately, this position was enshrined in this document. During the development of the Inter-American Convention on Enforced Disappearance of Persons of 1994, a similar distinction was made between a single act and a systematic practice of enforced disappearance, which qualified only the latter as a crime against humanity.

The delegations that developed the Rome Statute of the International Criminal Court were rather were reluctant to include enforced disappearance in the list of crimes against humanity (similar to the inclusion of the crime of apartheid) due to insignificant practice of prosecuting the acts in question at that time. By the time of the signing of the Rome Statute in 1998, enforced disappearance was not considered a crime under customary international law being a comparatively new crime found in 'an emerging

11 Wilder 2001, 69.

norm that originated in treaty law.' In contrast, B. Finucane believes that the prosecution of enforced disappearances originates from international humanitarian law rather than human rights law. The researcher argues that the first case law on enforced disappearances can be found in the decisions of the Nuremberg Military Tribunal (for example, in the prosecution of Wilhelm Keitel). Finucane also argues that on the onset, criminal prosecution for enforced disappearance was carried out in a limited context, namely enforced disappearance committed during an armed conflict by a belligerent in the occupied territory.[12] Nevertheless, most state representatives (especially Latin American delegations) supported the inclusion of acts of enforced disappearance in the list of crimes against humanity.

According to the UN International Law Commission, the inclusion of enforced disappearance as a crime against humanity in this document was due to its extremely cruel and serious character. The definition enshrined in the Rome Statute is inherently based on customary international law. According to most scholars, Article 7 of the Rome Statute repeats what was previously recognized in customary international law and states the declarative recognition of effective customary law. According to Anderson K.,[13] whereas, at an earlier stage, a direct link existed between crimes against humanity and armed conflicts, at present, crimes against humanity are recognized to occur both in armed conflict and in peacetime. *Opinio juris* of enforced disappearance before the adoption of the International Convention for the Protection of All Persons from Enforced Disappearance in 2006 was based on the UN Declaration on the Protection of All Persons from Enforced Disappearance of 1992, the Inter-American Convention on Enforced Disappearance of 1994, decisions of the Inter-American Court of Human Rights, resolutions of the Parliamentary Assembly of the Council of Europe, etc. In addition, the prohibition of enforced disappearance is enshrined in Rule 98 of customary international humanitarian law.

The idea of enshrining acts of enforced disappearance as a crime against humanity in the Rome Statute of the International Criminal Court was supported by the following states: Costa Rica, Chile, France, Jordan and Mexico. Representatives of the United Kingdom emphasized that despite the fact that at that time enforced disappearances were not established as crimes against humanity in any international legal act, 'they would readily support such inclusion if the definition of the act were clearer.' For the

12 Finucane 2010, 174.
13 Anderson 2006, 268.

representatives of Syria, the concept of 'enforced disappearance of persons' was unclear since 'it can be used in relation to liberal movements fighting for their independence.' This decision also remained unsupported by the representatives of India.

Ultimately, the Rome Statute of the International Criminal Court included acts of enforced disappearance in crimes against humanity in Article 7.1.i 'when committed as part of a widespread or systematic attack against the civilian population.' Thus, an isolated act of enforced disappearance committed outside the context of such an attack against the civilian population does not constitute a crime against humanity. The term 'widespread' is a quantitative element by its nature; it was interpreted in the case law of the International Criminal Tribunal for Rwanda for the first time as 'the widespread nature of the attack and the significant number of victims.'[14] In turn, 'systematic' is a qualitative indicator. International criminal ad hoc tribunals have interpreted this term in practice, referring to the 'organized nature of violent acts and the impossibility of their accidental occurrence.' Moreover, crimes characterized by a non-random repetition of a similar act on a regular basis reveal the essence of a systematic nature. This interpretation is fully consistent with acts of enforced disappearance as a crime against humanity. This approach has been repeatedly applied in the judgments of the Inter-American Court of Human Rights, including in the case of Velasquez Rodriguez v. Honduras.[15]

The judgment of the International Criminal Tribunal for the Former Yugoslavia in the case of Kunarac and others (June 12 2002, IT-96-23 & 23/1-A, see paras. 71-105) sets out the following contextual elements of a crime against humanity: 1) existence of an attack; 2) the direction of this attack against the civilian population; 3) the attack at issue must be widespread or systematic; 4) the perpetrator was aware that the attack was taking place. This definition limits the list of deprivations of liberty that may lead to enforced disappearance to arrest, detention or abduction. Further, two new elements have been added: 1) the inclusion of political organizations in the list of subjects of acts of enforced disappearance; 2) the purpose of leaving a person without the protection of the law for a considerable period of time has been defined. The interpretation of this

14 Gasser 2008, 251.

15 IACtHR, Velasquez Rodriguez v. Honduras, judgement of 29 July 1988, available at: www.corteidh.or.cr/docs/casos/articulos/seriec_01_ing.pdf (accessed 25 December 2024).

definition is provided in the document 'Elements of the Crime' adopted by the Preparatory Commission of the International Criminal Court,[16] according to which: 1. the perpetrator of the crime: a) arrested, detained or abducted one or more persons; or b) refused to recognize the fact of arrest, detention or abduction, as well as to provide information about the fate or whereabouts of such person or persons; 2. a) following or during this arrest, detention or abduction there was a refusal to recognize the fact of such deprivation of liberty and to provide information about the fate or whereabouts of this person or persons; or b) this was denied after or during the above said deprivation of liberty; 3. the perpetrator knew that: a) such an arrest, detention or abduction would, in the ordinary course of events, be accompanied by a refusal to acknowledge the deprivation of liberty or to provide information about the fate or whereabouts of this person or persons; or b) such a refusal occurred following or during the deprivation of liberty; 4. the above said arrest, detention or abduction was carried out by or with the authorization, support or acquiescence of a State or political organization; 5. the refusal to acknowledge the deprivation of liberty or to provide information about the fate or whereabouts of this person or persons was made by or with the authorization, support or acquiescence of a State or political organization; 6. the perpetrator intended to leave the above said person or persons without protection of the law for a long period of time; 7. the act was committed as part of a widespread or systematic attack against the civilian population; 8. the perpetrator knew that the act constituted part of a widespread or systematic attack against the civilian population or intended it to be part of such an attack.

Actus reus of the crime – this document makes an objective distinction between two alternative types of behavior: deprivation of liberty and concealment of information about the fate and whereabouts of a disappeared person. Deprivation of liberty must be supported by the state or a political organization or occur with their consent. It is necessary that in response to a request from family members for information about the fate of a disappeared person they are denied this information. Deliberate submission of false information is considered a refusal to provide information. In addition, the person who deprived an individual of liberty should not necessarily be the same person who concealed the information. The second type of behavior is the refusal to immediately provide information following a person's abduction. Given the complex nature of this crime, it is

16 McCrory 2007, 552.

recognized that several actors are generally involved in the act of enforced disappearance.

Mens rea of the crime – intent is a mandatory element of this crime. This issue is regulated by Article 30 of the Statute of the International Criminal Court. In the context of the first type of behavior, the intent must include the refusal to provide the necessary information. In the latter case, the perpetrator must be aware that the victim whose fate is being concealed was previously abducted under the first alternative conduct or elsewise deprived of his or her liberty. In addition, the perpetrator must act with the intent to deprive the victim of the protection of the law for a long period of time. Further, the commission of this crime should not be based primarily on personal intentions, but rather on the policy of the state or the activities of a political organization. The inclusion of this crime in the Rome Statute of the International Criminal Court indisputably contributed to the prevention of the practice of enforced disappearance, as a result of which a number of States Parties have introduced this crime into their domestic criminal legislation: Australia, Azerbaijan, Great Britain, Canada, the Netherlands, Germany, New Zealand, etc. For example, in 2002, the Criminal Code of Australia enshrined crimes against humanity in accordance with the provisions of the Rome Statute of the International Criminal Court, and also established a 17-year sentence for committing an act of enforced disappearance. The Crimes Against Humanity and War Crimes Act of Canada stipulates that crimes against humanity, as defined in Article 7 of the Rome Statute of the International Criminal Court, are 'crimes under customary international law.'

Thus, it can be concluded that the practice of enforced disappearance qualifies as a crime against humanity under the condition that: 1) it is carried out as part of a widespread or systematic attack against the civilian population; 2) the actor was aware that such an action was an element of a widespread or systematic attack against the civilian population; 3) the actor was aware that such deprivation of liberty would be accompanied by a refusal to acknowledge this fact, as well as to provide information about the whereabouts and fate of the disappeared persons; 4) the actor intended to leave the person without the protection of the law for a long period of time; 5) the deprivation of liberty was carried out by or with the authorization, support or consent of a state or political organization.

The widespread and systematic practice of enforced disappearances persists in the current context. For example, the 2023 UNWGEID report emphasized that

> UNWGEID expresses its concern about the spread of acts of enforced or involuntary disappearance in Ukraine, which constitutes the most serious violation of human rights... This practice was systematic and used unlawfully by the military forces of the Russian Federation.

Similarly, following its visit to Libya, UNWGEID noted the widespread nature of the practice of enforced disappearances.[17] As of today, Ukraine has registered over 55,000 missing persons, including nearly 48,000 persons who had gone missing under special circumstances. The State has located around 2,500 unidentified bodies. Around 4,000 bodies had been identified through cooperation between State bodies and a procedure for identification had been developed.[18]

Thus, the widespread or systematic practice of enforced disappearance constitutes a crime against humanity under customary international law, international criminal law and international human rights law.

The adoption of the 2006 International Convention for the Protection of All Persons from Enforced Disappearance, the first binding universal international legal instrument to guarantee the human right not to be subjected to enforced disappearance, was prompted by the widespread practice of this crime as well as the existence of a significant number of gaps in international legal protection of human rights. The most significant gap was the absence of international obligations of states to codify enforced disappearance in domestic legislation, along with the establishment of appropriate penalties as well as the principle of universal jurisdiction over this crime.

The 2006 International Convention for the Protection of All Persons from Enforced Disappearance provides an officially recognized definition of enforced disappearance, which reveals the legal nature and constituent elements of this crime. The constituent elements of the crime of enforced disappearance that reveal its essence are: 1) deprivation of liberty against a

---

17 UNGWEID, Report 2023 A/HRC/54/22// UNGWEID. – 2023, available at: http://www.ohchr.org/EN/Issues/Disappearances/Pages/Annual.aspx (accessed 25 December 2024).

18 Experts of the Committee on Enforced Disappearances Commend Ukraine's Law on Missing Persons in Special Circumstances, Ask Questions on Secret Detentions and the Forced Transfer of Children to the Russian Federation, available at: https://www.ohchr.org/en/news/2024/09/experts-committee-enforced-disappearances-commend-ukraines-law-missing-persons-special#:~:text=As%20of%20today%2C%20Ukraine%20had,located%20around%202%2C500%20unidentified%20bodies (accessed 25 December 2024).

person's will; 2) the perpetrators of enforced disappearance are exclusively representatives of the state or persons acting with the authorization or support of the state; 3) refusal to recognize the fact of deprivation of liberty and to inform about the fate and whereabouts of the person in question; 4) leaving a person outside the protection of the law. Despite the fact that the definition does not mention non-state actors, the Convention enshrines the obligation of States Parties to take the necessary measures to investigate acts committed by persons or groups of persons acting without the authorization, support or consent of the State.

The 2006 International Convention for the Protection of All Persons from Enforced Disappearance guarantees the broadest possible protection against enforced disappearance, including all cases of enforced disappearance, not solely those that constitute a crime against humanity.

An enforced disappearance is considered a crime against humanity where it occurs as part of a widespread or systematic attack against the civilian population under Article 7 of the Rome Statute of the International Criminal Court. With regards to the *actus reus* of this crime, it makes an objective distinction between two alternative types of behavior-deprivation of liberty and concealment of information about the fate and whereabouts of the disappeared person. Deprivation of liberty must be supported by the state or a political organization or occur with their consent. Furthermore, it requires that family members be denied this information in response to a request about the fate of the disappeared person. Deliberate submission of false information is viewed as a refusal to provide a response. In addition, the perpetrator who deprived the person of liberty need not be the same actor who conceals the information. Intent is also a mandatory element of this crime. The actor must act with the intent to deprive the person of the protection of the law for a long period of time. Thus, acts of enforced disappearance are committed primarily not on the basis of individual beliefs and intentions, but within the framework of state policy. The inclusion of this crime in the Rome Statute of the International Criminal Court undoubtedly contributed to the prevention of enforced disappearance with account of the fact that a number of States Parties have incorporated this crime into their domestic criminal legislation.

4. Legal Situation in Ukraine (II)

Under the domestic law of Ukraine, namely the Criminal Code of Ukraine, the crime of enforced disappearance is enshrined in Article 146-1, in the section entitled 'Criminal offenses against the will, honor and dignity of a person.'

Thus, Ukraine has assumed international obligations to implement international law into national legislation. The Law of Ukraine 'On the Legal Status of Persons Missing in Special Circumstances' defines the legal status of persons missing in special circumstances and provides legal regulation of social relations with regard to the acquisition of the legal status of persons missing in special circumstances, registration, search and social protection of such persons and their families.[19]

Leonid Tymchenko, Deputy Minister of Internal Affairs of Ukraine, participating in the 27th session of the UN Committee on Enforced Disappearances which took place in Geneva, Switzerland on September 23-24 2024, informed the members of the UN Committee on the fulfillment of Ukraine's obligations under the International Convention for the Protection of All Persons from Enforced Disappearance, in particular, on the search for persons missing in special circumstances.

Therefore, Article 3 of the Convention is reflected in Article 5 of the Law of Ukraine 'On the Legal Status of Persons Missing in Special Circumstances.' It is also this Law that implements Article 4 of the Convention on the introduction of enforced disappearance as an offense in domestic criminal law (Article 146-1 of the Criminal Code of Ukraine). In order to implement the Rome Statute, the Verkhovna Rada of Ukraine adopted in the first reading a draft law that provides for the addition of articles to the Criminal Code on crimes against humanity, which would include enforced disappearance within the meaning of Article 5 of the Convention.

Given the desire to ensure the requirements of the Convention, namely, the proper recording and investigation of each case of enforced disappearance, Ukraine is taking measures to establish its competence to exercise jurisdiction over the crime of enforced disappearance in each case where

19 The Law of Ukraine 'On the Legal Status of Persons Missing in Special Circumstances', available at: https://zakon.rada.gov.ua/laws/show/2505-19#n7 (accessed 25 December 2024).

this crime is committed in the sovereign territory under the jurisdiction of Ukraine, as well as where the disappeared person is a citizen of this state.[20]

5. Conclusion

To summarize, it should be noted that the efficient prevention of enforced disappearances in Ukraine could help to end the Russian Federation's war against Ukraine and would significantly contribute to the strategic goal of our state, which is a comprehensive, just and sustainable peace in Ukraine for the security of the whole world.

Bibliography

Anderson, Kristen. 2006. 'How Effective is the International Convention for the Protection of All Persons from Enforced Disappearance Likely to be in Holding Individuals Responsible for Acts of Enforced Disappearance?'. *Melbourne International Law Journal*. 7. 245–77.

Scovazzi, Tullio and Citroni, Gabriella (eds.). 2007. *The Struggle against Enforced Disappearance and the 2007 United Nations Convention*. Leiden: Martinus Nijihoff Publishers.

Wilder, Tayler. 2001. 'Background to the Elaboration of the Draft International Convention for the Protection of All Persons from Enforced Disappearance'. *The Review of International Commission of Jurists*. 63. 63–72.

Finucane, Brian. 2010. 'Enforced Disappearance as a Crime Under International Law: A Neglected Origin in the Laws of War'. *The Yale journal of international law*. 35. 171–97.

Gasser, Hans-Peter. 2008. 'Protection of the Civilian Population'. In Fleck Dieter (ed.). *The Handbook of International Humanitarian Law*. Oxford: Oxford University Press. 237–323.

McCrory, Susan. 2007. 'The International Convention for the Protection of All Persons from Enforced Disappearance'. *Human Rights Law Review*. 7. 545–66.

20 Deputy Minister of Internal Affairs of Ukraine, participating in the 27th session of the UN Committee on Enforced Disappearances, available at: https://www.kmu.gov.ua/news/delehatsiia-uriadu-ukrainy-na-choli-z-leonidom-tymchenkom-vziala-uchast-u-sesii-komitetu-oon-z-nasylnytskykh-znyknen (accessed 25 December 2024).

Part 2:
Legal and Extra-Legal Response Possibilities

Towards the Criminalisation of Enforced Disappearance under Chilean Law

Juan Pablo Mañalich

Abstract: The chapter presents a description and an assessment of a draft bill currently under discussion in the Chilean Congress that points to the criminalisation of enforced disappearance as an 'ordinary' offence, beyond its current status, under Chilean domestic law, as a crime against humanity. After sketching the historical and legal context to which the legislative proposal answers, which is considerably conditioned by the political and social impact of the *desaparecidos*-cases under Pinochet's dictatorship, the original and the subsequent version of the draft bill are contrasted. The analysis of both texts focuses on the connection between the two central components of the offence's definition, namely the deprivation of the victim's liberty, on the one hand, and either the refusal to provide information or the concealment of her fate or whereabouts, on the other. Highlighting some difficulties emerging from how that connection is shaped under the last version of the Chilean legislative proposal, the chapter closes with a comparison between the main provisions of the draft bill and the recently enacted § 234b of the German Penal Code ('StGB').

1. The historical and legal context

On December 17 2014, a draft bill seeking the explicit criminalisation of enforced disappearance as an ordinary offence under the Chilean Penal Code was submitted to the Chilean Congress by a group of deputies.[1] This took place approximately five years after Chile ratified both the International Convention for the Protection of All Persons from Enforced Disappearance ('the International Convention') and the Inter-American Convention on Forced Disappearance of Persons ('the Inter-American Convention'). After being passed by the Chamber of Deputies on August 23 2017, there has not

1 Bulletin No. 9818-17.

been any significant progress towards passing the draft bill by the Senate since the end of May 2022.[2] A significant concern has been raised regarding the possible implications of the enactment of these new provisions under the requirement of mandatory retroactive application of legislation that is less severe than the law in force when the given offence was perpetrated. This worry points thus to how the proposed provisions stand to the provisions penalising 'traditional' crimes such as kidnapping and unlawful detention by a public official, under which high-ranking agents of the Pinochet dictatorship involved in the *desaparecidos*-cases have been, and are still being, punished.[3]

If they come to be enacted, these new provisions would then coexist, under Chilean domestic law, with the penalisation of enforced disappearance as a crime against humanity. Indeed, under Art. 6 of the 2009 Act No. 20357, which implements the penalisation of most of the international crimes that, *ratione materiae*, fall within the jurisdiction of the International Criminal Court, conduct constitutive of enforced disappearance is made punishable under the (general) condition that it be part of a generalised or systematic attack against a civil population, whereas the attack must respond to a policy either of the state or its officials, on the one hand, or of an organised group fulfilling certain conditions, on the other. Hence, currently at stake is both whether enforced disappearance ought to be independently criminalised as a specific offence without any connection to an attack against a civil population and whether, without such a detached criminalisation, the Chilean state has failed to comply with the requirements that bind it as a party to both the International and the Inter-American Convention.

Regarding the first question, it should be clear that the penalisation of enforced disappearance under the general constraints of the 'context element' and the 'political element' that shape the structure common to all crimes against humanity has a much narrower scope than the one envisioned by those two conventions. Although both treaties define 'enforced disappearance' as requiring that the act of deprivation of liberty or freedom of the (immediate) victim(s) be performed either 'by agents of the [s]tate' or 'by persons or groups of persons acting with the authorization, support[,] or acquiescence of the [s]tate,' this is by no means tantamount to a require-

2 This, as of December 22 2025.
3 Guzmán Dalbora 2009, 55–71.

ment that such an act be part of generalised or systematic attack against a civil population.

However, to acknowledge that the current penalisation of enforced disappearance as a crime against humanity is far from covering the full extension of the form of behaviour defined by both treaties does not suffice to answer the second question in the affirmative. The crucial consideration hereto points instead to the precise reach of the criminalisation duty that both the International and the Inter-American Convention impose on the states that are parties to them. While Art. 4 of the International Convention merely requires that each state party takes 'the necessary measures to ensure that enforced disappearance constitutes an offence under its criminal law,' Art. III of the Inter-American Convention demands from state parties that they undertake 'the legislative measures [...] needed to define the forced [*sic*] disappearance of persons as an offense,' which 'shall be deemed continuous or permanent as long as the fate or whereabouts of the victim has not been determined.' To fulfil the criminalisation duty thus imposed, the given state party must at least adopt an explicit definition of '[en]forced disappearance,' which does not necessarily mean that the adopted definition ought to be semantically equivalent to the definition formulated in the same convention.[4]

In what follows, I will first describe the main aspects of the central provision formulated in both the original and the current version of the Chilean draft bill, upon which I will offer a critical assessment of the legislative proposal. For this purpose, it will be helpful to compare the structural features that the offence will eventually have under the proposed new provision with the definitional strategy displayed in the recent enactment of § 234b StGB, which also criminalises enforced disappearance beyond the scope of its treatment as a crime against humanity.

2. *From the original to the current version of the Chilean draft bill*

The draft bill proposing the explicit criminalisation of enforced disappearance as a specific offence originally consisted of a new Art. 147 bis to be introduced in the Chilean Penal Code, formulated in the following terms:

> Anyone who deprives one or more persons of their liberty and who refuses to report or acknowledge the deprivation of liberty or the where-

4 On this issue, in reference to the criminalisation duty imposed by the Inter-American Convention, see Bascuñán 2007, 59–64, 66–8.

abouts of the victim commits the crime of enforced disappearance of persons and shall be punished with imprisonment [ranging from 3 years and one day to 15 years].

As a matter of grading, a higher penalty was correlated with cases in which the victim is either tortured or subjected to similar mistreatments, as well as an ever higher penalty with cases in which the perpetrator causes the victim's death. The provision also contemplated a non-mandatory mitigation of two degrees of punishment for any principal or accessory contributing to the victim reappearing alive, as well as a non-mandatory mitigation of one degree of punishment for any principal or accessory who supplies information that sheds light on the disappearance. The last paragraph of the proposed Art. 147 bis declared that concerning conduct constitutive of enforced disappearance, the provisions that penalise the behaviour of public officials consisting in the disclosure of secrets or the refusal to obey an order issued by a superior would not be applicable.

Focusing on the core definition of the offence, one can highlight the following five features. (1) In line with the Inter-American Convention, the provision was formulated in a way that enables the individuation of conduct affecting more than one (immediate) victim as a single instance of the offence. (2) Differing from the wording of both the International and the Inter-American Convention, the draft bill defined the offence without any requirement that it be perpetrated either by state agents or with the state's authorisation, support, or acquiescence. (3) Following both conventions, the proposed provision did not require the given deprivation of liberty to be (initially) unlawful. (4) Concerning the connection between the deprivation of liberty and the refusal to provide information on the whereabouts of the victim(s) or to acknowledge the deprivation of liberty, the provision explicitly required that the agent or agents who perform the act of deprivation of liberty and the agent or agents who subsequently refuse to provide information be identical. (5) In contrast to the text of both conventions, the offence was defined with no reference whatsoever to the victim(s) being placed outside the realm of effective legal protection as a consequence of the perpetration of the offence.

As a result of its discussion within the first stage of the legislative process, the proposed provisions dispatched by the Chamber of Deputies to the Senate have been significantly transformed. The first notable innovation relates to the localisation of the five new articles that are currently proposed. Indeed, Arts. 148 A to 148 E are meant to be placed within a section of the Penal Code that deals with offences corresponding to 'grievances inflicted by public officials against rights guaranteed by the Constitution.' This placement decision is consistent with a significant adjustment made to the core definition of the offence, which is now formulated as follows under Art. 148 A:

> Any public official or anyone who, with the authorisation, support, or acquiescence of the state, deprives a person of her liberty, followed by the failure to inform or the refusal to acknowledge such deprivation of liberty, or by the concealment of the fate or whereabouts of the victim, shall be punished with imprisonment [ranging from 10 years and one day to 15 years].

In the following paragraph, we read further that

> [t]he same penalty shall be imposed on any public official who, knowing of the occurrence of these circumstances, does not prevent or does not put an end to them, having the necessary power or authority to do so or being in a position to do so.

Art. 148 A also enables the imposition of a more severe penalty if the deprivation of liberty extends for more than 15 days or if the deed results in serious harm 'to the person or interests of the victim.' An even harsher penalty ranging from 15 years and one day to life imprisonment is contemplated for cases in which, 'on the occasion of the enforced disappearance,' either homicide, rape, 'sodomitic rape,'[5] mutilation, or severe bodily injured is perpetrated on the victim. A similar grading solution, although leading to a maximum of 20 years of imprisonment, is meant to apply to cases in which the enforced disappearance provides the context for conduct constitutive of an 'offence against the person' – whereas this expression should be taken as designative of homicide or bodily injury – imputable in virtue of criminal negligence. The last paragraph of Art. 148 A declares that no statutory limitation applies either to the prosecution of, or to the execution of an already imposed penalty for, enforced disappearance.

In turn, Art. 148 B recognises as an aggravating factor that the victim be a pregnant woman, a minor, a person over 65 years of age, or a person affected by some disability condition. In line with the original version of

5 Notwithstanding its clearly homophobic connotation, it should be noted that this expression is currently devoid of legal meaning, since Chilean law no longer criminalises any form of behaviour to which that label could apply.

the draft bill, Art. 148 C makes it a non-mandatory mitigating factor that a principal or accessory to the offence contributes to the victim reappearing alive or supplies information that sheds light on the disappearance. Art. 148 D upholds the solution of making the provisions that penalise the disclosure of secrets and the refusal to obey an order issued by a superior inapplicable to public officials who may thereby shed light on the whereabouts of the victim or contribute to his reappearance. Yet Art. 148 D goes beyond that solution by making unavailable the (justificatory) defence of fulfilling a duty, (legitimately) exercising a right or faculty, or serving an office. Concerning cases involving members of the military forces or the military police as perpetrators, Art. 148 E, explicitly places prosecution within the scope of ordinary jurisdiction and thus outside the scope of military jurisdiction.

The contrast between the original and the current version of the draft bill is salient. Restricting the comparison to the elements of the core definition, one can highlight the following aspects. (1) Conforming with the International Convention rather than with the Inter-American Convention, the currently proposed provision leads to the individuation of conduct affecting a plurality of (immediate) victims as a corresponding plurality of offences. (2) In line with the wording of both the International and the Inter-American Convention, the offence is now defined in a manner that requires that it be perpetrated either by an agent of the state or by someone acting with the authorisation, support, or acquiescence of the state. (3) Just as the initially drafted provision, the new provision does not require the given deprivation of liberty to be (initially) unlawful. (4) Concerning the connection between the deprivation of liberty, on the one hand, and either the refusal to provide information or to acknowledge the previous deprivation of liberty, or the concealment of the fate or whereabouts of the victim, on the other, Art. 148 A does not explicitly require that the person or persons who deprive the victim of her liberty be identical with the agents whose behaviour is constitutive of the subsequent refusal or concealment. (5) As was also the case under the original draft bill, the offence is defined with no reference whatsoever to the victim being placed outside the realm of effective legal protection as a consequence of the perpetration of the offence.

3. The comparison with the German provision

Among the various adjustments introduced to the Chilean draft bill previously outlined, perhaps the most significant is the requirement that the offence be perpetrated either by a state agent or by someone acting with the authorisation, support, or acquiescence of the state. Indeed, the fact that the offence is partially defined by such a requirement should undermine a concern frequently raised among Spanish and Latin-American legal scholars when considering the merit of such a criminalisation decision.

The concern points to the tension between the criminalisation of enforced disappearance and the *temo tenetur* principle. This tension is sometimes analysed in a way that leads to the claim that enforced disappearance would exhibit the structure of a 'crime of suspicion.'[6] This pejorative characterisation is meant to reflect that, under the criminalisation of enforced disappearance, the concrete punishment risked by the agent involved in the deprivation of the victim's liberty would eventually depend on whether the perpetrator confesses to his previous deed.[7] Yet the concern should be weakened through the consideration that under the requirement that the offence be perpetrated either by a state agent or by someone acting with the authorisation, the support, or the acquiescence of the state, the perpetrator will be placing herself, in virtue of her deed, in a position that makes her at least indirectly answerable to the demand, directly addressed to the state, of shedding light on the situation of the victim.[8] And the fact that the deprivation of the victim's liberty need not be *per se* unlawful implies that such a demand ought not to be construed as grounding a duty of self-incrimination.

In this last regard, the Chilean draft bill appears aligned with the criminalisation decision recently adopted through the enactment of the new § 234b StGB,[9] according to which the offence needs to be perpetrated either by a public official (*Amtsträger*) or by someone whose conduct takes place 'on behalf of or with the approval of a state.' Yet this signalises a first difference that should be noticed. Whereas the Chilean draft bill speaks

6 On this category, see García Pérez 1993, 630–65. See also Modolell 2009, 187.

7 Bascuñán 2007, 66–7.

8 See Ambos/Böhm 2009, 234–5.

9 The provision was introduced through the 'Act for the Further Development of International Criminal Law' (*Gesetz zur Fortentwicklung des Völkerstrafrechts*) of July 30 2024, and is in force since August 3 of the same year. Hereto see the detailed review offered by Geneuss and Jeßberger in the next chapter of this volume.

of '*the* state,' thus purporting to refer to the Chilean state, the German provision speaks of '*a* state,' which seems to refer to any state recognised by the German state (which includes, through an implicit self-reference, the German state itself). The legal implications of this (grammatically) slight but (politically) crucial difference between the two texts should be clear enough.

For present purposes, it seems more important to focus on a further difference concerning the structural connection that connects the two main components of the relevant conduct description. It was already noted that, under the current version of the Chilean draft bill, the deprivation of liberty must be *followed* either by the refusal to provide information or acknowledge its occurrence or by the concealment of the victim's fate or whereabouts. In contrast, the German provision disjunctively combines two forms of behaviour that are thus made alternatively punishable. The first form of behaviour consists in the abduction or deprivation of the victim's 'bodily liberty' (*körperliche Freiheit*), under the condition that it be followed by a refusal to provide information about her fate or whereabouts. The second consists in the concealment of the fate or whereabouts of a person, under the condition that this same person has been previously abducted or deprived of her bodily liberty by a public official or by someone acting on behalf or with the approval of a state. Crucially, the specification of each of these two forms of behaviour does not impose the constraint that the relevant (subsequent or antecedent) condition be fulfilled by the perpetrator herself.

In this way, § 234b StGB explicitly solves a question that the Chilean provision leaves unanswered. Under Art. 248 A, the offence thus defined can only be perpetrated by performing an act of deprivation of the victim's freedom. Thus, the proposed provision does not settle whether the refusal or concealment corresponds to further conduct that the agent of the deprivation of liberty would need to display, on the one hand, or instead only to a circumstance on which the specific criminal significance of the previous deprivation of liberty as an instance of enforced disappearance would objectively depend, on the other. (Under the latter construction, that circumstance would, of course, need to be foreseen by the perpetrator when depriving the victim of her liberty as a matter of *mens rea*.) Both readings raise difficulties, indicating that the strategy of simply reproducing the wording of the International and the Inter-American Convention on this regard is technically inadequate.

A final difference between the Chilean draft bill and the solution adopted through § 234b StGB should be highlighted. The difference in question arises from the fact that only the latter integrates the requirement that the conduct displayed by the perpetrator(s) result in the victim being 'removed from the protection of the law.' Notwithstanding the controversy that still surrounds the phrasing of the corresponding clauses of the definitions laid down in the International and the Inter-American Convention, primarily due to the clause's ambiguity,[10] the complexly articulated criminal significance of the offence seems difficult to depict without any reference to the distinctive effect that its perpetration has for the (immediate) victim. However, the fact that incorporating that reference into the legal definition of the offence may certainly restrict the scope of the given criminalisation decision should not be seen as *per se* problematic or unwelcome. For we should also be concerned with the extent to which a less demanding definition of the offence, as the one contained in the Chilean draft bill, may contribute, perhaps unexpectedly, to its trivialisation.

Bibliography

Ambos, Kai and Böhm, María Laura. 2009. 'La desaparición forzada de personas como tipo penal autónomo'. In Ambos, Kai (ed.). *Desaparición forzada de personas. Análisis comparado e internacional.* Bogotá: Temis. 195–255.

Bascuñán, Antonio. 2007. 'Derechos fundamentales y derecho penal'. *Revista de Estudios de la Justicia.* 9. 47–74.

García Pérez, Octavio. 1993. 'Delitos de sospecha: principio de culpabilidad y derecho a la presunción de inocencia. Los artículos 483 y 485 CP'. *Anuario de Derecho Penal y Ciencias Penales.* 46.2. 629–78.

Guzmán Dalbora, José Luis. 2009. 'Chile'. In Ambos, Kai (ed.). *Desaparición forzada de personas. Análisis comparado e internacional.* Bogotá: Temis. 53–73.

Modolell, Juan Luis. 2009. 'La desaparición forzada de personas en el sistema interamericano de derechos humanos'. In Ambos, Kai (ed.), *Desaparición forzada de personas. Análisis comparado e internacional.* Bogotá: Temis. 180–93.

Pervou, Ionna. 2023. *The Right not to Be Subjected to Enforced Disappearance.* Cham: Springer.

10 In reference to the International Convention, see Pervou 2023, 50–2.

The New Crime of Enforced Disappearance in German Criminal Law

Julia Geneuss and Florian Jeßberger[1]

Abstract: On 6 June 2024 a new offense of 'enforced disappearance of persons' was added to the German Criminal Code (*Strafgesetzbuch*, StGB) as § 234b. After much discussion, with this offence the German legislator implements the *International Convention for the Protection of All Persons from Enforced Disappearance.* This article examines the newly created offense within its international legal context. It explains the structure of § 234b StGB, will offer a deeper understanding of its doctrinal characterization and provide a critical lens through which potential issues in the interpretation and application of the offense can be identified.

1. Introduction

On 6 June 2024 a new offense of 'enforced disappearance of persons' was added to the German Criminal Code (*Strafgesetzbuch*, StGB) as § 234b. This article examines the newly created offense within its international legal context. It explains the structure of § 234b StGB, will offer a deeper understanding of its doctrinal characterization and provide a critical lens through which potential issues in the interpretation and application of the offense can be identified.

The article first outlines the different forms in which enforced disappearances occur and provides a brief overview of the history of their

1 This article is based on the report 'Ein Tatbestand des gewaltsamen Verschwindenlassens im deutschen Strafrecht' the authors wrote in November 2023 for the Deutsches Institut für Menschenrechte (German Institute for Human Rights) as well as on the articles (also in German) Jeßberger/Geneuss, Ein Tatbestand des Verschwindenlassens im deutschen Strafrecht – Völkerrechtliche, straftatsystematische und kriminalpolitische Prolegomena zur Einführung des § 234b StGB-E, Kriminalpolitische Zeitschrift 2024, 95–105, and Geneuss/Jeßberger, Der neue Tatbestand des Verschwindenlassens von Personen (§ 234b StGB), Neue Strafrechtswissenschaft 2024, 372–92.
The authors would like to thank Sophie Konrad for her invaluable assistance in preparing this article.

criminalization (2). It then closely examines two key international legal instruments that address the offense, noting their differences in structure and types of commission (3). Next, the article traces the specific history of its implementation in Germany (4). Subsequently, § 234b StGB is presented and analyzed with respect to its protected legal interests, offense structure, and doctrinal characterization (5). The requirements of the offense are then discussed in detail, with reference to complex interpretive issues (6). Finally, the article addresses questions of sentencing, as well as issues relating to the statute of limitations and the extraterritorial application of criminal law (7).

2. *Enforced Disappearances: Phenomenon and Legal Development*

2.1 The Phenomenon of Enforced Disappearance

The term *forced* or *enforced disappearance of persons* refers to situations in which individuals are detained by others, and both their detention and whereabouts are concealed from third parties, even when inquiries are made.[2] As a result, the individuals 'disappear' and are effectively deprived of protection from third parties, including from the legal system itself. While not always the case, state actors are often involved in these disappearances. Additionally, although not necessarily, the disappeared persons may suffer mistreatment, torture, or even death while in a state of helpless abandonment. The victim of enforced disappearance is, first and foremost, the individual who disappears. However, their family and relatives as well as the social environment often endure years, or even decades, of uncertainty and distress following the disappearance. Moreover, trust in state institutions can erode, either because the authorities themselves are involved in the disappearance or because they are unable to ascertain the whereabouts or fate of the disappeared person.

Disappearances can occur in two forms, systematic and sporadic.[3] The systematic form refers to cases where enforced disappearances happen on a mass scale, typically targeted at a specific social group as part of state-coordinated repression. This practice is most commonly associated with the military dictatorships in Latin America during the 1970s and 1980s, under

2 Instructive on this and the following Grammer 2005 and Cornelius 2006.

3 On this and the following Grammer 2005, 13 et seqq.

the term *desaparecidos*,[4] but it has also occurred in other contexts, such as during the Nazi dictatorship in Germany under the so-called 'Nacht und Nebel Erlass'.[5] Systematic enforced disappearances are generally classified as crimes against humanity under international criminal law. In the Statute of the International Criminal Court (ICC Statute), the crime of enforced disappearance is covered in Article 7(1)(i), (2)(i), and in the German Code of Crimes Against International Law (*Völkerstrafgesetzbuch*, VStGB) under § 7(1) no. 7.

In contrast, sporadic enforced disappearances refer to singular instances not carried out within a systematic context. In these cases, as there is no widespread or systematic attack against a civilian population, the offense of crimes against humanity does not apply. Such disappearances must be addressed under ordinary domestic criminal law rather than international criminal law.

2.2 Legal Development

Efforts to legally address the phenomenon of enforced disappearances began in the 1980s under the auspices of international organizations.[6] In 1992, the UN General Assembly adopted the *Declaration on the Protection of All Persons from Enforced Disappearance*.[7] The *Inter-American Convention on the Forced Disappearance of Persons*, adopted two years later, proved to be more effective.[8] These international instruments do not differentiate between systematic and sporadic disappearances. From the mid-1990s, enforced disappearance was discussed for the first time as an issue of *international criminal law*, particularly during the preparatory work for the creation of an international criminal court. It was finally codified as a specific crime against humanity in the ICC's Rome Statute, adopted in 1998. On 20 December 2006, the UN General Assembly adopted the *International Convention for the Protection of All Persons from Enforced*

4 Grammer 2005, 9 et seqq. with further references.

5 Cornelius 2006.

6 In February 1980, a Working Group on Enforced or Involuntary Disappearances was set up by the then UN Commission on Human Rights. It has been under the authority of the UN Human Rights Council since 2006.

7 GA Res. 47/133 of 18 December 1992.

8 OAS A-60 of 9 June 1994.

Disappearance (CED),[9] which entered into force on 23 December 2010. As of today, 72 states have ratified the Convention, and 26 others have signed it. The Convention explicitly addresses both systematic and sporadic disappearances, likely influenced by the developments in international criminal law.

Through the implementation of international legal instruments, in particular the ICC Statute, enforced disappearances have also been incorporated into domestic criminal law systems.[10] Many states have created an offense of enforced disappearance (only) as a crime against humanity, including Germany under its *Völkerstrafgesetzbuch*. With the introduction of § 234b StGB Germany now joins a group of states that have established an independent offense of enforced disappearance within their ordinary domestic criminal law.

3. *The Crime of Enforced Disappearance: Structure and Types of Commission*

In international law instruments, two types of enforced disappearance can be distinguished, each with its own structure. The first is the so-called 'unitary offense' under human rights law, which is particularly regulated in Article 2 of the Convention and similarly in Article II of the Inter-American Convention. This concept treats enforced disappearance as a multi-act but unified event, classifying the elements of the offense accordingly (see I.). The second is a 'dualistic offense' under international criminal law, which forms the basis of the ICC Statute as a single offense within the category of crimes against humanity. This dualistic offense distinguishes between two related but independent variants (see II.). As national criminal law systems have implemented the provisions of both the Convention and the ICC Statute, some overlap between the two types of offenses has occurred.

9 GA Res. 61/177 of 20 December 2006.

10 For details, see the overview in the above-mentioned article. However, at least in Europe, the significance of state criminal provisions appears to be largely symbolic so far. Only recently did the first proceedings take place in Switzerland in which the criminal offense of enforced disappearance (Article 185*bis* of the Swiss Criminal Code) was charged and tried: Criminal proceedings against the Belarusian Yuri Garawski took place before the Cantonal Court of St. Gallen in September 2023. He was accused of being involved in kidnappings on behalf of Alexander Lukashenko's regime. The defendant was acquitted due to lack of evidence. On the trial, see Gerny 2023.

3.1 CED: A Unitary Human Rights Concept

Article 2 CED defines enforced disappearance as:

> the arrest, detention, abduction or any other form of deprivation of liberty by agents of the State or by persons or groups of persons acting with the authorization, support or acquiescence of the State, followed by a refusal to acknowledge the deprivation of liberty or by concealment of the fate or whereabouts of the disappeared person, which place such a person outside the protection of the law.

Accordingly, enforced disappearance is characterized by three main elements:[11] first, the deprivation of liberty; second, the refusal to acknowledge the deprivation of liberty *or* the concealment of the fate or whereabouts of the disappeared person; and third, the direct or indirect involvement of the state[12] (this is specifically referenced in the first element, concerning deprivation of liberty).

These elements are layered over time: the refusal or concealment must follow the deprivation of liberty. In addition to these three elements, there is a fourth requirement: the individual must be deprived of legal protection. The wording suggests that this consequence must be causally linked to the deprivation of liberty and the refusal or concealment ('as a result of'). It is unclear whether this is an independent element of the offense, which must be proven separately and also be reflected in the perpetrator's intent, or merely a typical consequence of the conduct without an independent effect. The Treaty Committee has left this question open.[13]

---

11 This corresponds to the consistent practice of the Contract Committee, see for example OHCHR, Fact Sheet No. 6 Rev. 4 on Enforced Disappearances, 2023.

12 Non-state actors are not included in Art. 2 of the Convention. However, Art. 3 obliges states parties to take appropriate measures against non-state actors.

13 See also OHCHR, Fact Sheet No. 6 Rev. 4 on Enforced Disappearances, 2023: 'According to article 2 of the Convention, enforced disappearance places the disappeared person outside the protection of the law. This provision confirms that, in every enforced disappearance, the disappeared person is totally defenceless and, as an inherent consequence, is deprived of any form of protection from the law.' This statement can be understood as meaning that the fourth characteristic only has a 'confirming' and not a 'constitutive' effect. Cf. also Citroni 2021, 675 et seqq.

3.2 ICC Statute: Dualistic Offense under International Criminal Law

Although § 234b StGB was created to implement the CED, its structure can only be understood in light of the crime against humanity of enforced disappearance under ICC Statute and *Völkerstrafgesetzbuch.* The Statute defines enforced disappearance of persons as a crime against humanity (Article 7(1)(i)).[14] According to Article 7(2)(i) of the ICC Statute, the crime is defined as:

> the arrest, detention or abduction of persons by, or with the authorization, support or acquiescence of, a State or a political organization, followed by a refusal to acknowledge that deprivation of freedom or to give information on the fate or whereabouts of those persons, with the intention of removing them from the protection of the law for a prolonged period of time.

The Elements of Crimes, adopted by the Assembly of States Parties in 2002, further specify the elements of the offense.[15] They state:[16]

> Article 7(1)(i): Crime against humanity of enforced disappearance of persons [...]
> Elements
> No. 1: The perpetrator
> (a) arrested, detained[25, 26] or abducted one or more persons; or
> (b) Refused to acknowledge the arrest, detention or abduction, or to give information on the fate or whereabouts of such person or persons.
> Footnote 25: The word 'detained' would include a perpetrator who maintained an existing detention.
> Footnote 26: It is understood that under certain circumstances an arrest or detention may have been lawful.

---

14 'For the purposes of this Statute, 'crime against humanity' means any of the following acts committed in the course of a widespread or systematic attack directed against a civilian population and with knowledge of the attack: [...] (i) enforced disappearance of persons [...].'

15 The Elements of Crimes are available at www.icc-cpi.int/sites/default/files/ElementsOfCrimesEng.pdf (accessed 20 July 2025). On the significance of the Elements, see Werle/Jeßberger 2020, mn. 235 et seqq.

16 On the history of the development of enforced disappearance as a crime against humanity in the ICC Statute and on the drafting of the elements of the crime, see Schabas 2017, 449–66; Witschel/Rückert 2001, 98–103.

According to element no. 1, it is generally sufficient if the perpetrator *either* deprives the person of liberty (a) *or* refuses to recognize the deprivation of liberty or to provide information on the person's fate or whereabouts (b). In both types of offense, however, merely committing one of the acts is not sufficient to establish criminal liability. Element no. 2 clarifies that in the first variant of the crime, the act of deprivation of liberty ('arrest, detention or abduction') must be followed by the refusal to acknowledge this deprivation of liberty or to provide information as an objective element of the crime.[17] In the second variant, the act of deprivation of liberty must either precede or accompany the refusal to acknowledge or provide information.[18] Thus, the elements of the crime not only clarify that enforced disappearance has a two-dimensional structure, they also stipulate that both acts are offenses in themselves. Thus, a perpetrator can commit one of these acts without participating in the other, but the complementary act must still be objectively present and reflected in the perpetrator's intent.

This structure remains a key characteristic of the offense of enforced disappearance as a crime against humanity under international criminal law.[19] As the ICC Statute was implemented into national criminal law systems, including Germany's, this structure was retained. § 7(1) no. 7 VStGB reads:[20]

> Whoever, as part of a widespread or systematic attack directed against any civilian population, [...] causes a person's enforced disappearance, with the intention of removing them from the protection of the law for more than just a brief period of time,

17 'No. 2a): Such arrest, detention or abduction was followed or accompanied by a refusal to acknowledge that deprivation of freedom or to give information on the fate or whereabouts of such person or persons; or [...].'

18 'No. 2b): Such refusal was preceded or accompanied by that deprivation of freedom.'

19 To date, the International Criminal Court has had little case law on the crime against humanity of enforced disappearance. In the Public Redacted Version of 'Decision Pursuant to Article 15 of the Rome Statute on the Authorization of an Investigation into the Situation in the Republic of Burundi' (ICC-01/17-X-9-US-Exp) of 25 October 2017, Pre-Trial Chamber III comments in more detail on the interpretation of the offense. However, the comments are not relevant for the present purposes.

20 The English translation of the German Code of Crimes against International Law is available at www.gesetze-im-internet.de/englisch_vstgb/englisch_vstgb.html. Translation by Brian Duffett, revised by Jan Christoph Nemitz and Steffen Wirth, updated by the Language Service of the German Federal Ministry of Justice.

(a) by abducting that person on behalf of or with the approval of a State or a political organisation, or by otherwise severely depriving them of their physical liberty, without immediately providing truthful information on that person's fate and whereabouts, or
(b) by refusing, on behalf of a State or a political organisation or in contravention of a legal duty, to provide information immediately on the fate and whereabouts of the person deprived of their physical liberty under the circumstances referred to under letter (a) above, or by providing false information [...]

In addition to the differing structure of the offense and the requirement of a widespread or systematic attack against the civilian population, the offense under the ICC Statute differs from the CED's definition in that the ICC Statute requires the subjective intention to remove the person from the protection of the law for a prolonged period of time, while the Convention treats this as an objective element. Furthermore, the ICC Statute does not require a direct or indirect connection to the state; the perpetrators' connection to a political organization is sufficient.

4. Implementation of the Convention in Germany

Germany signed the Convention on 26 September 2007 and ratified it on 24 September 2009.[21] From the outset, including in its interactions with the *Committee on Enforced Disappearances*, the monitoring body for reviewing states' implementation of the Convention,[22] the German government maintained that the creation of a separate criminal offense for enforced disappearance in its ordinary domestic criminal code was unnecessary for fulfilling the Convention's requirements.[23] It argued that the Convention does not explicitly require state parties to do so and that the conduct it

21 Federal Law Gazette 2009 II, at 932.

22 Supervision is mainly carried out as part of a reporting procedure. The German report was presented to the Treaty Committee in 2014. The German government has commented on the Committee's recommendations on several occasions. Germany's most recent dialog with the Treaty Committee took place in March 2023 as part of the follow-up procedure. The respective statements are available at www.ohchr.org/en/treaty-bodies/ced (country: Germany).

23 The Memorandum on the CED Implementation Act (Denkschrift zum CED-Zustimmungsgesetz), BT-Drs. 16/12592, 8 April 2009, at 33, states: 'There is therefore no legal necessity to create a new criminal offense.' See also Report Germany,

addresses is already adequately covered by existing provisions of German criminal law.

The Committee repeatedly criticized this stance, as well as the lack of implementation in Germany. It concluded that the existing criminal offenses, along with their associated penalties and statutes of limitations, were insufficient to meet the obligations set out by the Convention.[24] The Committee emphasized that enforced disappearance should not be seen as a series of separate crimes, but rather as a singular, complex crime.[25]

In response to the Committee's criticism and the public pressure from civil society, the German government gradually softened its position over the past decade.[26] It informed the Committee that it was still considering whether to create a separate criminal offense for enforced disappearance. However, it did acknowledge that establishing such an offense could have 'symbolic value', even though it would be 'very complex'.[27] In March 2023, the German government declared that it would continue to 'consider the matter' of introducing a distinct offense for enforced disappearance and would keep evaluating the possibility of reform.[28] This shift ultimately led to the drafting of § 234b StGB. According to the explanatory memorandum, the introduction of a separate offense for enforced disappearance is intended to 'address possible doubts about the full implementation of the

CED/C/DEU/1, 23 May 2013, paras. 22 et seqq., 25. Additional Information Submitted by Germany, CED/C/DEU/AI/1, 19 October 2020, paras. 4, 6.

24 Cf. e.g. CED, Concluding Observations, CED/C/DEU/OAI/1, 14 April 2023, para. 9 et seq.

25 CED, Concluding Observations, CED/C/DEU/OAI/1, 14 April 2023, para. 5; see also CED, Concluding Observations, CED/C/DEU/CO/1, 10 April 2014, para. 7; see also Summary Record of the 426th Meeting, CED/C/SR.426, 5 April 2023, Statement Ms. Janina (Country Rapporteur), para. 6; Statement Mr. de Frouville (Country Rapporteur), para. 7.

26 The German government also recognized that, according to another view, the specific injustice of enforced disappearance could only be covered by the creation of a separate criminal offense; Report Germany, CED/C/DEU/1, 23 May 2013, para. 26.

27 Additional Information Submitted by Germany, CED/C/DEU/AI/1, 19 October 2020, para. 6 ('symbolic impact'); Summary Record of the 426th Meeting, CED/C/SR.426, 5 April 2023, para. 20 ('extremely complex offense'). The government also suggested that the interpretation of the Convention's provisions regarding the necessity of such an offense should be left to legal scholars; CED, Twenty-fourth session – Summary record of the 426th meeting, CED/C/SR.426, April 5, 2023, at 4.

28 CED, 24 Session (20 March 2023 – 31 March 2023), Germany, Opening Statement.

International Convention for the Protection of All Persons from Enforced Disappearance [...] in line with the Committee's recommendation [...].'[29]

On 6 June 2024, the German Parliament introduced the offense of enforced disappearance into the Criminal Code as § 234b,[30] alongside a range of other amendments to international criminal law.[31] The Act entered into force on 3 August 2024.[32]

The implementation of a specific offense of enforced disappearance in the *Strafgesetzbuch* is to be welcomed. On the one hand, the special responsibility arising from Germany's past argues in favour of taking a visible stand by independently depicting the specific injustice of enforced disappearances. The memorandum on the CED Implementation Act rightly states: 'The so-called 'Night and Fog Decree' at the time of National Socialist rule is regarded as one of the first recorded incidents of enforced disappearance worldwide.'[33] Criminal disappearances were then also the subject of criminal proceedings after the Second World War.[34] In particular, in the trial of the main war criminals before the International Military Tribunal and in the so-called Jurists' Trial before the US Military Tribunal, acts of enforced disappearance were tried (in each case from the point of view of war crimes).[35] The practice of enforced disappearances was also widespread in the post-war period, particularly in the Soviet occupation

29 Draft Law introduced by the Federal Government, BT-Drs. 20/9471, 27 November 2023, at 35, translation by the authors.

30 Act on the Further Development of International Criminal Law BT-Drs. 20/9471, 20/10015, 20/10131 No. 1.21,
as amended by the Legal Affairs Committee, BT-Drs. 20/11661. The *Bundestag* had previously rejected an amendment by the CDU/CSU parliamentary group (BT-Drs. 20/11668).

31 See Epik/Jeßberger 2024, 801 et seqq. and Raube 2024, 278 et seqq.

32 Federal Law Gazette 2024 I No. 255 of 2.8.2024. Additionally, the introduction of § 234b StGB will lead to further amendments in the Criminal Code (§§ 126 para. 1 no. 5 and 138 para. 1 no. 6 StGB), the Code of Criminal Procedure (§ 100a para. 2 no. 1 lit. i StPO), and the Courts Constitution Act (§ 74a para. 1 no. 6 GVG).

33 Memorandum on the CED Implementation Act (Denkschrift zum CED-Zustimmungsgesetz), BT-Drs. 16/12592, 8 April 2009, at 31, translation by the authors.

34 See also Finucane 2010, 171 et seqq.

35 IMT, judgment of October 1, 1946, in The Trial of German Major War Criminals. Proceedings of the International Military Tribunal sitting at Nuremberg, Germany, Part 22 (August 22nd, 1946 to October 1st, 1946), 453 et seqq., 492 et seqq.; US Military Tribunal, Nuremberg, judgment of December 4, 1947 (Altstötter et al.), in Trials of War Criminals Before the Nuremberg Military Tribunals Under Control Council Law No. 10, Vol. III, 1058.

zone, right up to the time after the founding of the GDR.[36] On the other hand, one would like to think that it would be in keeping with Germany's officially articulated claim to be a 'pioneer' in the protection of human rights and international criminal law to take a clear and decisive position here.[37] This is also stated in the memorandum to the CED Implementation Act:

> By ratifying the Convention, the Federal Republic of Germany intends to live up to the pioneering role it has claimed together with the other European states in the protection of human rights. In order for the Federal Republic of Germany to be able to credibly demand protection from enforced disappearances from other states, it must itself fulfill the international requirements.[38]

5. *§ 234b StGB: Protected Legal Interests, Structure and Doctrinal Characterization*

The newly introduced offense reads:[39]

> § 234b Enforced Disappearance of Persons
>
> (1) Whoever as a public official or on behalf of or with the approval of a state shall be punished with imprisonment for not less than one year
>
> 1. abducts a person or otherwise deprives them of their physical liberty, followed by a refusal to provide information about their fate or whereabouts, or
> 2. conceals the fate or whereabouts of a person who has been abducted or otherwise deprived of their physical liberty by a public official or on behalf of or with the authorization of a state, or refuses to provide information about this,
>
> and thereby deprives them of the protection of the law.
>
> (2) In less serious cases, the punishment shall be imprisonment from three months to five years.

---

36 Cornelius 2010.

37 On the proclaimed pioneering role of Germany and the German judiciary in international criminal law, see Draft Law introduced by the Federal Government, BT-Drs. 20/9471, 27 November 2023, at 10.

38 Memorandum on the CED Implementation Act (Denkschrift zum CED-Zustimmungsgesetz), BT-Drs. 16/12592, 8 April 2009, at 31, translation by the authors.

39 Translation by the authors.

The legal framework for this offense is clearly based on three key provisions: Regarding the *conditions* for criminal liability, the offense follows the definition of enforced disappearance as outlined in Article 2 CED. In terms of its *structure*, § 234b StGB primarily aligns with 7(1) no. 7 VStGB and the relevant provisions of the ICC Statute, including the Elements of Crime. Regarding *legal consequences*, classification within the German criminal law system, and the degree of injustice, § 234b draws from § 234a StGB, the offense of abduction (*Verschleppung*).

5.1 Protected Legal Interests

The offense protects multiple legal interests, addressing the rights of different individuals. First, it protects the individual legal interests of the disappeared person, including their personal freedom, the legal protections granted to them from the state, their human dignity and their mental and possibly physical integrity. In reference to § 234a StGB, it can be assumed that the offense does not solely protect one of these interests but rather their combined interaction.[40]

Additionally, § 234b StGB safeguards the legal interests – specifically, the mental well-being – of third parties who are unaware of the fate of the missing person.[41] This interpretation aligns with international law and is based on the 'parent norm' of the Convention: According to Article 24(1), the term 'victim' is extended to include anyone harmed directly as a consequence of an enforced disappearance. The case law of international human rights courts also recognizes that third parties whose rights are violated can be considered victims, even though the legal issue here is different.[42]

Before this backdrop, the group of individuals whose interests are protected needs to be defined more clearly. While case law from human rights courts has been inconsistent and focused on individual cases in recent years, a focus on close *family relationships*, particularly parents of the disappeared person, is suggested. However, the wording of the Convention

40 On § 234a StGB Sonnen 2023, § 234a para. 3; Eisele 2019, § 234a para. 1.

41 This also applies to the Swiss offense of enforced disappearance (Art. *185bis* Swiss Criminal Code), Swiss Confederation, Report of Switzerland on the national implementation of the 2006 International Convention for the Protection of All Persons from Enforced Disappearance, 19 December 2018, para. 140.

42 On the victim status of relatives in the case law of international human rights courts, see Schniederjahn 2017, 146 et seqq.

is broader and is not limited to family members.[43] In German criminal law, § 373b of the Code of Criminal Procedure (*Strafprozessordnung*, StPO), which defines the term 'injured party' in procedural law, may serve as a point of reference for defining the group of protected persons. According to paragraph 2, when an act results in the death of the directly injured person, the following individuals are considered 'injured parties': spouses or life partners, cohabiting partners in the same household, direct relatives, siblings, and dependants. Including individuals with close personal ties beyond family members also aligns with the rationale of the offense. In the case of enforced disappearance, these individuals must be regarded as *directly* injured parties.

5.2 Structure

Regarding the structure of the offense, § 234b StGB follows the dualistic model already realized in § 7(1) no. 7 VStGB, rather than the uniform human rights offense as outlined in the Convention.[44] § 234b StGB distinguishes between two types of offense.

Offense no. 1 involves deprivation of liberty, followed by a refusal to provide information (*offense of deprivation of liberty*). The refusal to provide information does not necessarily need to be carried out by the perpetrator who deprived the individual of their liberty, but it is a genuine objective element of the offense and must be covered by the perpetrator's intent, i.e. at least *dolus eventualis*. Offense no. 2, a mirror image of the first offense, punishes the concealment of the fate or whereabouts of a person who has (probably: previously) been deprived of their liberty or the refusal to provide corresponding information (*offense of concealment and refusal to provide information*). Here, not only must the concealment or refusal to provide information be intentional, the offender's intent, again at least *dolus eventualis*, must also include the fact that the person has been deprived of their liberty. And again, the perpetrator of the concealment or refusal to provide information need not be the same person as the one responsible for the deprivation of liberty. In both offense variants, it is essential that the disappeared person is deprived of the protection of the law as a result of either deprivation of liberty followed by refusal to provide information or

43 As also understood by von Braun/Diehl 2011, 214, 220.

44 Cf. Jeßberger/Geneuss 2024b, 95, 97 et seqq.

the concealment or refusal to provide information with prior deprivation of liberty.

The dualistic structure illustrates the phenomenon of enforced disappearance as a multi-act event. The individual acts typically occur over time and may involve different persons. It is characterized by its collective nature, which can vary in time and space. The 'specific wrong' of enforced disappearance is adequately grasped only when both acts – in both variants – combine to form a legal unit of assessment, resulting in the overarching outcome of removal from the protection of the law.

5.3 Doctrinal Characterization

The offense has a multi-act permanent character (*Dauerdelikt*). Two distinct states can be identified, each with its own permanent component. Deprivation of liberty describes a permanent state that begins with the suspension of an individual's freedom of movement and ends only when this restriction no longer exists, such as when the victim is released or dies. It can also be assumed that a permanent temporal component lies in the concealment of the fate or whereabouts of the person concerned or the corresponding refusal to provide information. This creates or maintains a state of ignorance, similar to the offense of bankruptcy under § 283 StGB, as confirmed by the Federal Court of Justice (*Bundesgerichtshof*) for concealment.[45] Notification obligations and an ongoing endangerment situation persist until truthful information is provided or 'unveiled', revealing the individual's fate or whereabouts.[46] In practical application, however, difficult questions of demarcation arise here, especially if the information cannot (or can no longer) be verified. However, unlike the deprivation of liberty variant, the death of the victim is not relevant for the termination of the concealment and refusal offense.

Furthermore, the offense can only be committed by certain perpetrators (*Sonderdelikt*), first and foremost public officials. However, in both variants, 'private individuals' acting on behalf of or with the approval of the state can also be perpetrators, alongside public officials (§ 11(1) no. 2 StGB). In variant no. 1, the deprivation of liberty must be committed by such

45 On bankruptcy, see BGH, decision of 14.3.2016 - 1 StR 337/15, para. 23 = BGHSt 61, 180 et seq.

46 Grammer 2005, 220 et seqq. also instructive on the time of termination.

a qualified perpetrator, though according to the wording the subsequent refusal to provide information is not necessarily required to be carried out by such qualified perpetrator. In practice, however, this will typically also involve a public official or a suitably qualified private individual. In variant no. 2, both the perpetrator of the concealment or refusal to provide information and the one responsible for the (previous) deprivation of liberty must either be a public official or act on behalf of or with the approval of the state.[47]

Lastly, the offense follows another offense (*Anschlussdelikt*) when concealment or refusal to provide information (no. 2) follows an *unlawful* deprivation of liberty. In this case, the violation of legal interests already established by the deprivation of liberty is intensified by the concealment or refusal, extending the impact to additional legal interests. However, the unlawfulness of the deprivation of liberty is not a mandatory requirement. If the deprivation of liberty *is lawful*, § 234b(1) no. 2 StGB does not constitute such a subsequent offense, as the infringement on legal interests and therefore the 'specific wrong' differs from cases of unlawful deprivation of liberty.

6. Elements of the Offense

The following section provides an explanation of the requirements for the two types of offense. It then discusses the overarching elements and requirements of the offense, including considerations of unlawfulness.

6.1 Deprivation of Liberty (para. 1 no. 1)

The first offense related to enforced disappearance involves the abduction of a person or any other act that deprives a person of their physical liberty. The term 'abduction' refers to the offense outlined in § 239a StGB, specifically the crime of kidnapping for extortion. It involves removing a person to a location where their ability to defend themselves is so restricted that

47 This duplication does not follow straightforwardly from the Convention. At least according to the wording, an enforced disappearance would also be assumed if the deprivation of liberty carried out by a public official is subsequently concealed by a non-public official or a private person with no connection to the state.

they are exposed to the perpetrator's unrestrained influence. A change of location is therefore required.[48]

The phrase 'deprives a person of their liberty' is based on § 239 StGB. According to the explanatory memorandum, this is intended to cover any action or omission that completely deprives another person of the ability to move.[49] The term 'other deprivation of liberty' is interpreted broadly and includes situations such as a custodial sentence, arrest by police officers, blocking exits from a building, or forcibly detaining someone or preventing a vehicle occupant from leaving a car.[50] While such acts do not necessarily constitute enforced disappearance, the broad, somewhat 'over-inclusive' definition of the offense is positive, as it ensures no evasive behavior is excluded.[51] In these situations, the second act – refusing to provide information about the fate or whereabouts of the person deprived of their liberty – along with the requirement for the deprivation of liberty to result in the protection of the law, serves as a corrective measure.

The offense of deprivation of liberty can only be committed by a public official, as defined in § 11(1) no. 2 StGB, or by someone acting on behalf of or with the approval of the state. Therefore, there must be at least an indirect connection to the state. However, it is unclear how 'acting on behalf of' or 'with the approval' of the state should be understood. This raises the practical question of whether repeated kidnappings by non-state actors, such as drug cartels, could be considered as being carried out with the state's approval if state authorities fail to investigate or clarify the situation – essentially an implied 'approval by omission'. There are valid reasons to adopt a broad interpretation here. If one assumes that the legislator aimed to implement the Convention comprehensively, the text of the Convention should guide the interpretation in line with international law. Article 2 CED, for example, refers to the 'authorization, support or acquiescence' of the state. In these cases, the state breaches its duty to protect, and the perpetrator need not fear interference from state authorities.[52] The concept of 'approval' in § 234b StGB appears broad enough to encompass acquiescent

48 Eidam 2020, § 239a StGB, para. 7.

49 Eidam 2020, § 239 StGB, para. 10. Draft Law introduced by the Federal Government, BT-Drs. 20/9471, 27 November 2023, at 35.

50 Wieck-Noodt 2021, § 239 StGB, para. 27.

51 On circumvention behavior Grammer 2005, 188.

52 Grammer 2005, 203 et seqq.

behavior by the state.[53] While the reference to the state is explicitly included for the act of deprivation of liberty, it is not mentioned in relation to the refusal to provide information. According to the wording, information could be withheld by any private individual.

6.2 Concealment and Refusal to Provide Information (para. 1 no. 2)

The second type of offense involves concealing a person's fate or whereabouts and refusing to provide information on the matter.

6.2.1 Concealment

There was some debate during the legislative process over which acts should be included in the second variant of the offense. In the original draft bill, only concealment was initially specified. The explanatory memorandum states: '[...] concealment requires the perpetrator to provide false or misleading information with the aim of hiding the whereabouts or fate of the victim.'[54] Concealment in this context involves deception. Mere active denial (e.g., 'I don't know where the person is, I have no information') or simply not responding to inquiries (i.e., omission) does not qualify as concealment.

During expert hearings, the Legal Affairs Committee criticized the draft's focus on concealment as too narrow, as it falls short of the Convention's scope and the definition of enforced disappearance in international law.[55]

6.2.2 Refusal to Provide Information

The Legal Affairs Committee agreed with this critique. To fully implement the Convention, which also addresses the refusal to recognize the depriva-

---

53 Thus, for the Swiss offense of enforced disappearance (Art. 185*bis* Swiss Criminal Code), Swiss Confederation, Report of Switzerland on the national implementation of the 2006 International Convention for the Protection of All Persons from Enforced Disappearance, 19 December 2018, para. 27.

54 Draft Law introduced by the Federal Government, BT-Drs. 20/9471, 27 November 2023, at 36, translation by the authors.

55 Cf. Geneuss 2024 (expert opinion given before the Legal Affairs Committee of the German Bundestag).

tion of liberty as an offense, the offense of refusing to provide information about the fate or whereabouts of the person deprived of liberty must be extended.[56]

It is unclear how the refusal to provide information should be understood, particularly whether a prior request for information is required. The word 'refusal' might initially suggest that an active external request is needed. This was the case when the crime of enforced disappearance was originally formulated in § 7(1) no. 7 VStGB. In that version, refusal to provide information had to be explicitly 'on request'.[57] However, with the 2024 reform of the *Völkerstrafgesetzbuch*, this requirement has been removed. The reasons given for this were gaps in criminal liability – the 'parent norms' of the ICC Statute and the Convention do not provide for such a requirement – as well as the potential risks for inquiring relatives. The reform's explanatory memorandum explicitly states that the use of the word 'denied' does not imply a prior request is necessary.[58] This means that failing to provide information, even without a request, is sufficient to constitute refusal under § 7(1) no. 7 VStGB. A similar interpretation must apply to enforced disappearance under § 234b StGB.

In any case, providing incorrect or incomplete information also qualifies as a refusal to provide information. Likewise, refusal can be assumed if the offender claims they cannot provide any information or only shares their current knowledge, even though they could reasonably be expected to make further inquiries or are obligated to do so.

6.2.3 Omission

The question remains whether the mere failure to notify also qualifies as refusal to provide information. This can only be the case when there is an obligation to inform, creating a legal interest in the information and when the perpetrator is under an obligation to notify, thus assuming a guarantor role. Such obligations are found in Article 104(4) of the Basic Law, as well

56 BT-Drs. 20/11661.

57 When the German Code of Crimes Against International Law was created in 2002, the legislator added the requirement to make an inquiry in order to substantiate the German offense. The explanatory memorandum to the law states that a refusal is inconceivable without prior inquiry, BT-Drs. 14/8524, at 22.

58 Draft Law introduced by the Federal Government, BT-Drs. 20/9471, 27 November 2023, at 29.

as in various provisions of the Code of Criminal Procedure, the Family Court Act, and state police laws.[59] Article 104(4) of the Basic Law ensures notification obligations to prevent individuals from disappearing without a trace.[60]

However, it should be noted that a proposal from members of the CDU/CSU parliamentary group to supplement No. 2 with the phrase 'or does not recognize the deprivation of liberty, fails to recognize it or fails to inform under Article 104(4) of the Basic Law'[61] did not receive the necessary majority in the Legal Affairs Committee.

6.3 Overarching Prerequisite

6.3.1 Success: Withdrawal from the Protection of the Law

§ 234b StGB requires that, for both types of offense, the offender 'thereby deprives the person who has been deprived of their liberty and whose fate or whereabouts have been concealed or information about this has been refused from the protection of the law.' This element of the offense must be committed with intent,[62] and is in addition to the already stipulated outcomes in the two variants (deprivation of liberty or ignorance of the whereabouts and fate of the disappeared person).

According to the explanatory memorandum, this characteristic is expected to be fulfilled 'regularly',[63] with exceptions occurring only in the case of very short-term deprivation of liberty, refusal to provide information, or when the victim is granted access to legal remedies or counsel.[64] In this

59 The failure to notify, i.e. the violation of an obligation to notify, does not necessarily lead to the unlawfulness of the deprivation of liberty itself; see Gusy 2018, Art. 104 GG, para. 72.

60 Cf. only Mehde 2023, Art. 104 GG, paras. 165, 167, 174; Degenhart 2021, Art. 104, para. 25.

61 Cf. BT-Drs. 20/11668.

62 In Art. 7(1) no. 7 of the ICC Statute, the deprivation of the protection of the law is not formulated as an objective element of the offense, but as a requirement of intent ('with the intention of depriving him of the protection of the law for more than a short time'). This corresponds to the parent norm under international criminal law of Art. 7(1)(i), (2)(i) ICC Statute.

63 Draft Law introduced by the Federal Government, BT-Drs. 20/9471, 27 November 2023, at 35.

64 Draft Law introduced by the Federal Government, BT-Drs. 20/9471, 27 November 2023, at 35.

interpretation, the characteristic of deprivation from the protection of the law becomes a relatively minor corrective element. However, considering the broad range of conduct covered by the offense and the low subjective requirements – *dolus eventualis* suffices in all cases – it is reasonable to elevate this constituent success to a genuine gravity threshold.

6.3.2 Unlawfulness of the Deprivation of Liberty

The question arises regarding situations where the deprivation of liberty is justified, such as by official powers. A distinction must be made between the two offense variants.

For offense variant No. 1, while the deprivation of liberty may be justified, it could still be followed by concealment or refusal to provide information, which could be covered by the intent – *dolus eventualis* – of the perpetrator of the (justified) deprivation of liberty. Although the wrongful act and wrongful outcome of the deprivation of liberty are eliminated here by means of a permission, a 'residual wrong' of enforced disappearance remains due to the intent related to the refusal to provide information. However, it is uncertain whether this residual injustice is sufficient to make the perpetrator liable under variant no. 1 (even as a less serious case pursuant to § 234b(2) StGB).

For offense variant No. 2, the situation differs. Here, the deprivation of liberty may also be justified under a permission clause. The fundamental purpose of the provision, which aims at the comprehensive protection of affected individuals, suggests that even lawful deprivations of liberty under domestic law can lead to criminal liability if concealment or refusal to provide information follows. This is consistent with the rationale behind Article 104(4) of the Basic Law and its statutory manifestations. Parliamentary proceedings have also clarified that the offense of enforced disappearance may arise even from lawful deprivation of liberty.[65]

65 Legal Affairs Committee BT-Drs. 20/11661, at 17 ('The object of the concealment or refusal to provide information can also be a deprivation of liberty that is not in itself unlawful.', translation by the authors).

7. Sentencing, Statute of Limitations, Scope of Application

7.1 Sentencing

The range of penalties specified in § 234b StGB – one to fifteen years of imprisonment, with a minimum of three months to five years in less serious cases – is broad, but appears appropriate both in view of the requirements of the Convention and within the system of German penalties.

The Convention does not prescribe a specific penalty range but obliges the state parties to impose appropriate penalties that reflect the exceptional gravity of enforced disappearance. A penalty is considered 'appropriate' within the framework of a suppression convention[66] if it fits seamlessly into the state's legal system, considering the severity of the offense. Thus, the appropriateness of the penalty is not an objective quantum but is determined by the domestic legal context.

Two relevant points, which are also mentioned in the explanatory memorandum, help categorize this offense within the German legal system. First, the crime of concealment under § 234a StGB, which carries a penalty of one to fifteen years, is similar in nature. The explanatory memorandum equates both offenses in terms of their gravity, which seems justifiable, even though § 234a is an endangerment offense, while § 234b is an injury offense. Second, the crime against humanity of enforced disappearance under § 7(1) no. 7 VStGB, with a penalty range of five to fifteen years, is also relevant. The lower penalty range in § 234b reflects that the disappearance is not part of a broader attack on a civilian population, as is required for crimes against humanity.

7.2 Statute of Limitations

Under § 78(3) no. 2 StGB, the statute of limitations for prosecution of enforced disappearance is twenty years. According to § 78a sentence 1 StGB, the period begins 'as soon as the act has been completed'. For the offense of deprivation of liberty, this means the limitation period begins once the abducted person is freed (or dead). In cases of concealment or refusal to provide information, the limitation period begins when the unlawful

66 On the concept of suppression conventions in transnational criminal law, see only Boister 2018.

situation ends and the whereabouts or fate of the disappeared person is known.

7.3 Scope of Application

German criminal law applies to enforced disappearance if the offense is committed within Germany (§ 3 StGB); for this, it is sufficient for one partial act to occur within Germany (§ 9 StGB).

If the offense is committed abroad, German law applies if the offense is also punishable in the foreign jurisdiction or if that jurisdiction lacks criminal authority and other requirements are met (§ 7 StGB). Specifically, the offender must either be a German citizen, a foreigner in Germany who cannot be extradited, or the offense must be committed against a German national. The extended definition of 'victim' also means that the German nationality of a relative or other personally related individual under § 395(1) No. 4 of the Code of Criminal Procedure establishes the scope of application of German criminal law.

In contrast to § 234a StGB The legislator chose not to include enforced disappearance under § 5 StGB.[67] Nevertheless, § 6 No. 9 StGB ensures that all provisions of the Convention are implemented.[68]

8. Conclusion

The creation of an independent offense of enforced disappearance is a positive step from both transnational and domestic criminal policy perspectives. While its practical application may remain limited, it sends an important legal policy signal.

The complexities involved in legislating at the intersection of transnational criminal law, international criminal law, ordinary German criminal

67 § 5 no. 6a) StGB stipulates that German criminal law applies to § 234a in the case of a foreign place of offense and a foreign perpetrator, regardless of the law of the place of offense, 'if the offense is directed against a person who is a German national and that person's domicile or habitual residence is in Germany at the time of the offense'. The English translation of the German Code of Crimes is available at www.gesetze-im-internet.de/englisch_stgb/englisch_stgb.html. Translation provided by Prof. Dr Michael Bohlander. Translation completely revised and regularly updated by Ute Reusch.

68 Draft Law introduced by the Federal Government, BT-Drs. 20/9471, 27 November 2023, at 36.

law, and constitutional law become apparent when analyzing the difficulties in the legislative process. Ultimately, the success of implementing international treaty obligations is determined by the accuracy of the provision's coverage in relation to the treaty's parent norm, while also aligning with national constitutional law and principles of national criminal law. Given the complex nature of enforced disappearance – often involving multiple individuals and spanning temporal and geographic contexts – the difficulties in adequately addressing it within criminal law are evident.

Overall, § 234b StGB can be considered largely successful. The dualistic offense model, as found in international criminal law under § 7(1) No. 7 VStGB, is particularly effective. However, § 234b raises several interpretational and practical questions that stem from the complexity of the enforced disappearance phenomenon.

Bibliography

Boister, Neil. 2018. *An Introduction to Transnational Criminal Law.* 2nd edition. Oxford: Oxford University Press.

Citroni, Gabriella. 2021. 'Consequences of the Lack of Criminalization of Enforced Disappearance at the Domestic Level: The Italian Experience'. *Journal of International Criminal Justice.* 19.3. 675–95.

Cornelius, Kai. 2010. *Vom spurlosen Verschwindenlassen zur Benachrichtigungspflicht bei Festnahmen.* Berlin: Berliner Wissenschafts-Verlag.

Degenhart, Christoph. 2021. 'Art. 104 GG'. In Sachs, Michael (ed.). *Kommentar zum Grundgesetz.* 9th edition. München: C.H. Beck.

Eidam, Lutz. 2020. '§ 239a StGB'. In Matt, Holger and Renzikowski, Joachim. *StGB: Strafgesetzbuch – Kommentar.* 2nd edition. München: Verlag Franz Vahlen.

Eisele, Jörg. 2019. '§ 234a StGB'. *Schönke/Schröder: Kommentar zum Strafgesetzbuch.* 30th edition. München: C.H. Beck.

Epik, Aziz and Jeßberger, Florian. 2024. 'Das Gesetz zur Fortentwicklung des Völkerstrafrechts'. *Juristenzeitung.* 801–8.

Finucane, Brian. 2010. 'Enforced Disappearance as a Crime under International Law. A Neglected Origin in the Laws of War'. *Yale Journal of International Law.* 35. 171–97.

Geneuss, Julia. 2024. 'Schriftliche Zusammenfassung meiner Stellungnahme vor dem Rechtsausschuss des Deutschen Bundestages am 31. Januar 2024 zu dem Gesetzentwurf der Bundesregierung 'Entwurf eines Gesetzes zur Fortentwicklung des Völkerstrafrechts' BT-Drs. 20/9471'. URL: www.bundestag.de/dokumente/textarchiv/2024/kw23-de-fortentwicklung-voelkerstrafrecht-1005822 (accessed 20 July 2025).

Geneuss, Julia and Jeßberger, Florian. 2024. 'Der neue Tatbestand des Verschwindenlassens von Personen (§ 234b StGB)'. *Neue Strafrechtswissenschaft.* 4. 372–92.

Gerny, Daniel. 2023. 'Historischer Prozess in der Schweiz: Ein Mann aus Lukaschenkos Todesschwadron steht in St. Gallen vor Gericht'. *Neue Zürcher Zeitung*. URL: 2ww.nzz.ch/schweiz/lukaschenkos-scherge-will-in-der-schweiz-aussagen-ld.1745635 (accessed 20 July 2025).

Grammer, Christoph. 2005. *Der Tatbestand des Verschwindenlassens einer Person. Transposition einer völkerrechtlichen Figur ins Strafrecht.* Berlin: Duncker&Humblot.

Gusy, Christoph. 2018. 'Art. 104 GG'. In von Mangoldt, Herrmann, Klein, Friedrich and Starck, Christian (eds.). *Grundgesetz. Kommentar.* 7th edition. München: C.H. Beck.

Jeßberger, Florian and Geneuss, Julia. 2024. *Ein Tatbestand des gewaltsamen Verschwindenlassens im deutschen Strafrecht*, Deutsches Institut für Menschenrechte. URL: www.institut-fuer-menschenrechte.de/fileadmin/Redaktion/Publikationen/Analyse_Studie/Analyse_Tatbestand_Verschwindenlassen_im_deutschen_Strafrecht.pdf (accessed 20 July 2025).

Jeßberger, Florian and Geneuss, Julia. 2024. 'Ein Tatbestand des Verschwindenlassens im deutschen Strafrecht – Völkerrechtliche, straftatsystematische und kriminalpolitische Prolegomena zur Einführung des § 234b StGB-E'. *Kriminalpolitische Zeitschrift.* 95–105.

Mehde, Veith. 2023. 'Art. 104 GG'. In Dürig, Günter, Herzog, Roman and Scholz, Rupert (eds.). *Grundgesetz. Kommentar.* München: C.H. Beck.

Raube, Svenja. 2024. 'Das Gesetz zur Fortentwicklung des Völkerstrafrechts – Zu den jüngsten Arbeiten am Bau für deutsche Weltrechtspflege'. *Kriminalpolitische Zeitschrift.* 278–97.

Schabas, William A. 2017. 'Defining Enforced Disappearance as a Crime Against Humanity'. In Bidault, Mylène et al. (eds.). *Réciprocité et Universalité: Sources et Régimes du Droit International et des Droits de l'Homme: Mélanges en l'Honneur du Professeur Emmanuel Decaux.* Paris: Éditions Pedone. 449–66.

Schniederjahn, Nina. 2017. *Das Verschwindenlassen von Personen in der Rechtsprechung internationaler Menschenrechtsgerichtshöfe.* Berlin: Duncker&Humblot.

Sonnen, Bernd-Rüdeger. 2023. '§ 234a StGB'. Kindhäuser, Urs et al. (eds.). *Strafgesetzbuch Kommentar.* 6th edition. Baden-Baden: Nomos.

von Braun, Leonie and Diehl, David. 2011. 'Die Umsetzung der Konvention gegen das Verschwindenlassen in Deutschland. Zur Erforderlichkeit eines eigenen Straftatbestandes'. *Zeitschrift für Internationale Strafrechtsdogmatik.* 214–29.

Werle, Gerhard and Jeßberger, Florian. 2020. *Principles of International Criminal Law.* 5th edition. Oxford: Oxford University Press.

Wieck-Noodt, Brunhild. 2022. '§ 239 StGB'. In Erb, Volker and Schäfer, Jürgen (eds.). *Münchener Kommentar zum StGB.* 4th edition. München: C.H. Beck.

Witschel, Georg and Rückert, Wiebke. 2001. 'Article 7(1)(i) – Crime Against Humanity of Enforced Disappearance of Persons'. In Lee, Roy S. (ed.). *The International Criminal Court, Elements of Crimes and Rules of Procedure and Evidence.* New York: Transnational. 98–103.

Human Rights Law Relevant to the Criminal Prosecution of Enforced Disappearances and the Practice of Two Regional Human Rights Tribunals

Claudia Marcela Cárdenas Aravena

Abstract: Since the last decade of the last century, several international instruments have referred to the enforced disappearance of persons, first mentioning it, then defining it, including some rules for international cooperation on the matter and finally providing more specific provisions (e.g. regarding children) and creating a Committee to promote the enforcement of state duties on the matter. Besides the legal instruments, the practice can show us whether its understanding or scope is understood differently by two robust regional tribunals: the Inter-American Court of Human Rights and the European Court of Human Rights. Its practice on the matter is reviewed, for the purpose of identifying commonalities and differences among the approaches of both jurisdictions. Both main contexts of application, the approaches on proof, violated rights, state duties, exercise of the jurisdiction *ratione temporis* and reparations are presented, so that the reader may have a quick look at the main features.

1. Introduction

The expression 'enforced disappearance of persons' was born outside of the law, as the description of a practice that was recognizable in different scenarios, generally associated with the persecution of one or more groups of persons, during the 20th century. The law has reacted to this phenomenon only after the massification of policies on enforced disappearance of persons, as was the case in many Latin-American countries in the 1970s, which followed similar patterns, and the persistent insistence of the relatives of those disappeared.[1] The first field of law which adopted the wording 'enforced disappearances' was human rights law. Relevant documents on the matter show an evolution, from the mere prohibition and description of

1 Dulitzky 2019, 423–51.

enforced disappearances to its formal definition and the obligation of the states to prevent and punish the conduct as a crime (2).

International courts of human rights have issued decisions relevant to different questions related to enforced disappearances. In this chapter, some of the main topics developed in the practice of both the Inter-American and European Human-Rights Courts will be presented. Interestingly, they show partially different approaches (3.).

2. International legal instruments dealing with the phenomenon of enforced disappearances

In 1980, the UN Commission on Human Rights established a Working Group on Enforced Disappearances to examine questions relevant to enforced or involuntary disappearances of persons.[2] In addition to these reports, international law has produced different instruments dealing with enforced disappearances since the beginning of the 1990s.

Since enforced disappearance encompasses both a crime and a violation of human rights, due to the involvement of the state power, international legal instruments on the matter often address both human rights and criminal issues.

A review of the different instruments will show the evolution that has taken place in its provisions. The ICC Statute is left aside, as there is another chapter in this volume that is dedicated to international criminal law.[3]

2.1 Declaration on the Protection of all Persons from Enforced Disappearance (1992)

Article 17 of the Declaration is interesting for the criminal legal approach:

> 1. Acts constituting enforced disappearance shall be considered a continuing offence as long as the perpetrators continue to conceal the fate and the whereabouts of persons who have disappeared, and these facts remain unclarified.

2 Resolution 20 (XXXVI) from 29th February 1980.
3 See the contribution by Aziz Epik in this volume.

> 2. When the remedies provided for in article 2 of the International Covenant on Civil and Political Rights are no longer effective, the statute of limitations relating to acts of enforced disappearance shall be suspended until these remedies are re-established.
> 3. Statutes of limitations, where they exist, relating to acts of enforced disappearance shall be substantial and commensurate with the extreme seriousness of the offence.

Along with declaring that the enforced disappearance is a continuing offence (which is something that will be repeated afterwards in other instruments), it addresses the topic of the statute of limitations stating two rules: when it exists, the extreme seriousness of the offence should be considered, and it shall be suspended if for a period effective remedies are not available. However, that raises the question on the determination of the period of (un)availability of the effective remedies. It seems that it establishes not only an ungrateful and heavy, but questionable burden for the victims to try once and then again to obtain justice and to check whether the remedies provided are (still) available (or available again) or not.

2.2 Inter-American Convention on Forced Disappearance of Persons (1994)

It is not surprising that this regional instrument was adopted prior to the universal instrument on the matter, because the phenomenon of the *desaparecidos* contributed to the name of the crime and this regional phenomenon pushed and shaped the legal instruments to come.

The preamble of the Inter-American Convention on Forced Disappearance of Persons states that enforced disappearance encompasses violations of multiple human rights (para. IV) and reaffirms that when committed systematically, it constitutes a crime against humanity (para. VI). A number of other provisions in this legal instrument is relevant for criminal law and practice.

Article I lists different state obligations regarding enforced disappearance. Section a) is dedicated to the obligations 'Not to practice, permit, or tolerate the forced disappearance of persons.' These are called *material* obligations by the European Court of Human Rights (ECtHR). Its letters b) and c) obligate the states to punish within their jurisdictions those responsible for enforced disappearance and to cooperate with other jurisdictions doing so. This second group of obligations are called *procedural* obligations by the ECtHR. Even if the obligation to punish is not really seen to be a procedural one, it seems to be included in this group since in order to punish, criminal proceedings should first take place. However, in order enable punishment, enforced disappearance should be described as a criminal offence in the applicable criminal law as well. This is provided for in Article III:

> The States Parties undertake to [...] define the forced disappearance of persons as an offense and to impose an appropriate punishment commensurate with its extreme gravity. This offense shall be deemed continuous or permanent as long as the fate or whereabouts of the victim has not been determined.
> The States Parties may establish mitigating circumstances for persons who have participated in acts constituting forced disappearance when they help to cause the victim to reappear alive or provide information that sheds light on the forced disappearance of a person.

The conduct that should be described in the applicable criminal law as enforced disappearance is referred to in Article II:

> For the purposes of this Convention, forced disappearance is considered to be the act of depriving a person or persons of his or their freedom, in whatever way, perpetrated by agents of the state or by persons or groups of persons acting with the authorization, support, or acquiescence of the state, followed by an absence of information or a refusal to acknowledge that deprivation of freedom or to give information on the whereabouts of that person, thereby impeding his or her recourse to the applicable legal remedies and procedural guarantees.

In the text, the – now classical – four parts of the definition are present: (1) deprivation of freedom, (2) involvement of state actors, (3) absence of reliable information on the person that has been deprived from liberty and (4) the deprivation of state protection. The fourth element is phrased as a consequence of the other three. There are different ways to phrase this last element in different legal instruments.

Article IV obliges making the conduct punishable in each state party and contains some provisions on jurisdiction. It establishes a duty to exercise jurisdiction based on the territoriality principle and on the personality principle. It also contains an *aut dedere aut judicare* provision, on the following terms:

> Every State Party shall, moreover, take the necessary measures to establish its jurisdiction over the crime described in this Convention when the alleged criminal is within its territory, and it does not proceed to extradite him.

Regarding the exercise of jurisdiction based on the passive personality principle or the *aut dedere aut judicare* provision, the last paragraph of the article could become relevant:

> This Convention does not authorize any State Party to undertake, in the territory of another State Party, the exercise of jurisdiction or the performance of functions that are placed within the exclusive purview of the authorities of that other Party by its domestic law.

2.3 Convention for the Protection of All Persons from Enforced Disappearances (2006)

The main universal instrument of the enforced disappearance of persons was adopted twelve years after the Inter-American Convention. Many provisions of the United Nations (UN) Convention, as its definition of enforced disappearance in Article 2, were taken from the Inter-American Convention. Additionally, twelve years of application of the Inter-American Convention by the Inter-American Human Rights System (1994-2006) and a number of documents from the Working Group on Enforced Disappearances were available to that point.

The preamble of the UN Convention contains new ideas (compared with the Inter-American Convention), as the recognition that enforced disappearances could be crimes against humanity not only when they are committed in a systematic way, but (broader), when circumstances described in international law are met (when they are committed as part of a systematic or widespread attack on a civilian population) (V); fighting against impunity as a main goal (VI), the right of victims to justice and to reparation (VII) and the right to truth (VIII), phrased as:

> *Affirming* the right of any victim to know the truth about the circumstances of an enforced disappearance and the fate of the disappeared person, and the right to freedom to seek, receive and impart information to this end.

Article 7 is dedicated to penalties. It is similar to the one in the Inter-American Convention, but it contains more detail in providing for the possibility to establish mitigating circumstances and includes the possibility to establish aggravating circumstances:

> Article 7.2 Each State Party may establish:
> (a) Mitigating circumstances, in particular for persons who, having been implicated in the commission of an enforced disappearance, effectively contribute to bringing the disappeared person forward alive or make it possible to clarify cases of enforced disappearance or to identify the perpetrators of an enforced disappearance;
> (b) Without prejudice to other criminal procedures, aggravating circumstances, in particular in the event of the death of the disappeared person or the commission of an enforced disappearance in respect of pregnant women, minors, persons with disabilities or other particularly vulnerable persons.

When one considers that enforced disappearance puts every victim in a situation of extreme vulnerability, this reference is likely to be made to the possible pre-existing vulnerability of the victim.

Article 9 deals with jurisdiction and *aut derere aut judicare* in the same manner as in the Inter-American Convention. Article 11 complements the *aut dedere aut judicare* provision with considerations on the right to a fair trial for the accused.

> 2. [...] the standards of evidence required for prosecution and conviction shall in no way be less stringent [....].
> 3. Any person against whom proceedings are brought in connection with an offence of enforced disappearance shall be guaranteed fair treatment at all stages of the proceedings. [...]

Another novelty in the UN Convention is that it includes some provisions on children, as follows:

> Article 25
>
> 1. Each State Party shall [...] prevent and punish [...]:
> (a) The wrongful removal of children who are subjected to enforced disappearance, children whose father, mother or legal guardian is subjected to enforced disappearance or children born during the captivity of a mother subjected to enforced disappearance;
> (b) The falsification, concealment or destruction of documents attesting to the true identity of the children referred to in subparagraph (a) above.
> [...]

> 4. Given the need to protect the best interests of the children referred to in paragraph 1 (a) of this article and their right to preserve, or to have re-established, their identity, including their nationality, name and family relations as recognized by law, States Parties which recognize a system of adoption or other form of placement of children shall have legal procedures in place to review the adoption or placement procedure, and, where appropriate, to annul any adoption or placement of children that originated in an enforced disappearance.

One may notice that the description of the punishable conduct differs from the one described for adults, considering that children have differences in the way they can exercise their liberty, so that it refers to the 'wrongful removal of children,' and their right to identity is protected.

The last remarkable point of the UN-Convention is the creation of the Committee on Enforced Disappearances (Article 26 et seq) as a way of monitoring the implementation of the convention. The Committee's members consist of ten experts serving in their personal capacity (Article 26). Each State Party shall submit a report to the Committee on the measures taken to give effect to its obligations under this Convention and the Committee is able to issue comments or requests (Article 29). Any requests that a disappeared person should be sought and found may also be submitted to the Committee by any person having a legitimate interest (Article 30.1).

2.4 General Observations of the UN Working Group on Enforced or Involuntary Disappearances

As previously stated, the Working Group on Enforced or Involuntary Disappearances is a UN mechanism that was established with a universal mandate in 1980, by the resolution 20 (XXXVI) of the Commission on Human Rights. It was intended to serve as a channel of communication between victims of disappearance and governments, as well as to assist families in determining the fate or whereabouts of those disappeared. From 1996 to 2013 it has produced a number of general observations on different topics related to enforced disappearances that have been considered in practice. Some of the comments were dedicated to a specific article or provision of the declaration and others related to topics such as rights to truth, children and women affected by enforced disappearance.[4]

3. *Criteria and decisions of human rights tribunals on enforced disappearances*

The practice of two regional Human Rights courts will be examined, namely the Inter-American Court of Human Rights (IACtHR) and the ECtHR. The focus will be on both the main issues they have ruled on and on the different criteria they have developed.

3.1 The Inter-American Court of Human Rights

A large number of cases before the IACtHR involve enforced disappearances. Although the phenomenology is not the same in all cases, a clear majority of the cases deal with the enforced disappearances that occurred in Latin America in the 1970s and 1980s. A good example hereof is the Velásquez Rodríguez v. Honduras case, which was the first case before the IACtHR.

The judgment is from 29 July 1988 and it states how between 100 and 150 persons disappeared in Honduras following the same pattern (para. 147). Ángel Manfredo Velásquez was a student at the Universidad Nacional Autónoma de Honduras. He disappeared on 12 September 1981 in the Tegucigalpa city center. He was kidnapped by a group of men with guns in cars providing no official identification. Even though the kidnappers were not wearing uniforms, it has been established that the kidnapping was committed either by military officials or by people commanded by them. Three *habeas corpus* actions were filed, as well as two criminal complaints. However, no investigations followed up in order to establish the whereabouts of Manfredo Velásquez or to punish those responsible for his disappearance. The case was submitted to the Court in 1986. According to the judgment, the following provisions of the American Convention of Human Rights were violated: Article 1 (obligation to respect the rights), Article 4 (right to life), Article 5 (right to personal integrity) and Article 7 (right to personal liberty).

4 The full text of each general comment is available at: https://www.ohchr.org/en/special-procedures/wg-disappearances/general-comments (accessed 11 May 2025).

Over time, the judgements made by the IACtHR on the matter have discussed different issues, such as the elements of the enforced disappearance, the complexity and multiplicity of the human rights violations involved, the continuous and permanent character of the human rights violations, the particular gravity of the enforced disappearances, and its proof. The main findings of the IACtHR on enforced disappearances are collected in number 6 of its *Cuadernillos de Jurisprudencia de la Corte Interamericana.*[5] The following sections mostly follow the order found here.

3.1.1 The proof of enforced disappearances as a clandestine crime

Regarding the proof of enforced disappearances, the importance of circumstantial or indirect evidence has been highlighted from the very beginning, as it has been shown that the perpetrators usually seek to destroy any direct evidence of the crime.[6] The clandestine nature of the crime and its incidence in the burden of proof has been highlighted as follows:

> This Court points out that forced disappearance is characterized by its clandestine nature, [...] it is the State which has control over the mechanisms to investigate incidents that took place within its territory. Consequently, any attempt to shift the burden of proof to the victims or their next of kin is contrary to the obligation imposed upon the State by Article 2 of the American Convention and Articles I(b) and II of the Inter-American Convention on Forced Disappearance.[7]

This feature is important because of its effects on the access to justice for the victims and because it has been repeated in numerous cases.[8]

3.1.2 Violated rights in cases of enforced disappearances

The discussion on which rights are violated in cases of enforced disappearances might be useful in criminal law, for example, to determine what is subject to protection by the criminalization of the conduct (*bien jurídico protegido, Rechtsgut*).

---

5 Actualized until 2022, available at: https://biblioteca.corteidh.or.cr/adjunto/38897 (accessed 11 May 2025).

6 IACtHR 1988, Velásquez Rodríguez v. Honduras, para. 131; IACtHR 1989, Godínez Cruz v. Honduras, para. 155 and other cases.

7 IACtHR 2005, Gómez Palomino v. Peru 2005, para. 106.

8 The last one (to date) in IACtHR 2024, Muniz da Silva v. Brazil, paras. 78–83.

The IACtHR distinguishes between the violation of the rights of the disappeared person and the violation of the rights of his or her relatives. This is important, because while the violation of the rights of the disappeared are the most obvious, the violations of the rights of the relatives may last for decades and can even be the source of transgenerational damage.[9]

The rights of the disappeared person that are violated by their enforced disappearance are his/her liberty, his/her life, his/her personal integrity and his/her personality.[10]

In their turn, members of his/her family might see their access to justice, their right to truth and right to personal integrity violated.[11] The IACtHR has pointed out the following situations;

> (i) they suffered personal, physical and emotional after-effects resulting from the disappearance of a loved one; (ii) they suffered an irreversible change in their immediate family unit and family life, affecting, *inter alia*, significant sibling relationships; (iii) they were involved in several actions, including the search for justice or information on the victims' whereabouts; (iv) the uncertainty surrounding the whereabouts of the victims has prevented grieving, prolonging the psychological effects of the disappearance on the next of kin, and (v) the State's failure to investigate and collaborate in efforts to determine the whereabouts of the victims and those responsible for the disappearances has exacerbated the different impacts suffered by the next of kin. These circumstances have had effects that persist over time and continue to this day[12].

Moreover, the IACtHR has echoed some general comments by the Working Group on Enforced Disappearances in order to determine violated rights, stating that, 'not knowing the whereabouts of a family member can amount to torture.'[13]

---

9 Bourguignon et al. 2024, 215–20.

10 References on judgements may be found in *Cuadernillos de Jurisprudencia de la Corte Interamericana* 6 2022, 43–63.

11 References on judgements may be found in *Cuadernillos de Jurisprudencia de la Corte Interamericana* 6 2022, 44–80.

12 IACtHR 2014, Rochac Hernández v. El Salvador, para. 12.

13 IACtHR 2022, Movilla Galarcio v. Colombia, para. 173.

The IACtHR has also highlighted the specific impact of enforced disappearances on women:

> According to the General comment on women affected by enforced disappearances, approved by the Working Group on Enforced or Involuntary Disappearances at its ninety-eighth session in 2013, in cases of enforced disappearances, women are affected economically, socially and psychologically: the emotional impact is aggravated by the economic impact, in particular when the woman searches for her loved one and, when the woman also becomes the head of the family, family obligations increase, and there is less time available to deal with everything else.[14]

3.1.3 Understanding of the jurisdiction *ratione temporis*

Both the continuous and pluri-offensive character of the offense of enforced disappearance has consequences for the jurisdiction *ratione temporis* per the understanding of the IACtHR. If the rights of the relatives continue to be violated after the state submitted itself to the jurisdiction of the IACtHR (the so-called *critical date*), it is understood that it can exercise its jurisdiction over these violations, even if the facts that give rise to the original violations of rights have happened before that. Furthermore, if the disappearance continues after the critical date (even if it has commenced before it), the IACtHR has understood it has jurisdiction to rule on the enforced disappearance.[15]

3.1.4 Duties of the state in cases of enforced disappearances

The IACtHR has ruled on the state duty to prevent the commission of the crime, the duty to investigate, the duty to proportionally sanction the gravity of the crime and to adequate the legal order of the State to implement these duties.

Regarding the duty to investigate, the IACtHR has pointed out that the investigation must be a *serious* one that is not done by simply asking the

14 IACtHR 2022, Movilla Galarcio v. Colombia, para. 180.

15 IACtHR 2008, Heliodoro Portugal v. Panama, para. 36; IACtHR 2024, Muniz da Silva v. Brasil, para. 30.

victims to give information.[16] It understands that a lack of investigation can amounts to support for those responsible.

It has also been stated that these serious investigations should happen *ex officio* and without delay, applying due diligence standards[17] and providing the technological and scientific means to obtain and process evidence.[18]

Concerning the duty to sanction proportionally to the gravity of the crime, The Court has ruled that a state is responsible for the application of a rule of domestic law resulting in the imposition of lenient penalties for enforced disappearances as crimes against humanity.[19]

3.1.5 Reparations in cases of enforced disappearances

The IACtHR usually provides a set of reparations that the states have to follow. These are not limited to payments to the victims but cover a variety of other issues. In cases of enforced disappearances these measures encompass the investigation, the identification of the mortal remains of victims, the burial of the victims, health treatment for the victims (both physical and psychological), the construction of memorials and other matters in order to preserve memory, the creation of databases of gene material for the identification of the mortal remains of the victims, human rights education for public servants and public access to the state archives.[20] This variety of measures follows the UN criteria for reparations as stated in the Basic Principles and Guidelines on the Right to a Remedy and Reparation for Victims of Gross Violations of International Human Rights Law and Serious Violations of International Humanitarian Law from 2005.

16 IACtHR 1988, Velásquez Rodríguez v. Honduras, para. 174.
17 IACtHR 2009, Ansualdo Castro v. Peru, para. 154.
18 IACtHR 2009, Radilla Pacheco v. Mexico, para. 222.
19 IACtHR 2024, Vega González et al. v. Chile, para. 335.
20 IACtHR 2024, Muniz da Silva v. Brasil, para. 203 (8–18). Further references on judgements may be found in *Cuadernillos de Jurisprudencia de la Corte Interamericana* 6 2022, 120–47.

3.2 The European Court of Human Rights

The ECtHR initiated its experience in judging cases of enforced disappearances ten years after the IACtHR, with the case Kurt v. Turkey.[21]

The first thing to be observed is that the contexts in which the enforced disappearance has occurred is different from the classical American context: the majority of cases on enforced disappearances before the ECtHR are related to armed conflicts: the conflict between Türkiye and the Kurds; the conflict between Türkiye and Cyprus, conflict in former Yugoslavia, the conflict between Russia and Chechenia are examples of this.[22] More recently, one should add the conflict between Russia and Ukraine.[23] Another interesting group of cases are those related to the *extraordinary renditions*, i.e., the secret surrender to the Central Intelligence Agency of the United States of America of persons suspected of being involved in terrorist activities. In this practice, persons were taken to detention centers in different countries in a way that was considered as enforced disappearances, due to the clandestine nature of the detention and because the action by the authorities in general implied no guarantees for those detainees.[24]

One can find both commonalities and differences in how issues of both regional human rights jurisdictions are treated. The treatment of the selected features will be presented in the same order as *supra* for the IACtHR.

3.2.1 The proof of enforced disappearances as a clandestine crime

A common problem lies in the clandestine nature of the crime of enforced disappearances, leading to a so-called 'wall of silence'.[25]

Until 2000 it was understood that the alleged crime should be proven beyond any reasonable doubt, even if it is not likely that the victims would

21 For further information on Turkish cases, both before the ECCHR and before domestic jurisdictions, see the contribution by Burcu Yaşar in this volume.

22 López 2020, 431–3.

23 ECtHR 2024, Ukraine v. Russia (re Crimea), para. 950-74, 1368 and resolutive part B.2. On enforced disappearances in Ucraine, see the contribution of Denys Shylin in this volume.

24 That was the case in ECtHR 2012, Al Masri v. Macedonia. More references in López 2020, 447–51.

25 Keller/Heri 2014, passim.

have access to the pieces of evidence to do so, and even if the ECtHR does not exercise any criminal jurisdiction.[26]

The criterion on proof changed from 2000 on, with Timurtaş v. Turkey as a leading case, understanding finally that circumstantial evidence suffices in these cases. According to the criteria set there, the state has to explain the injuries of persons that have been detained without being injured or ill; and the state is responsible for the whereabouts of the people that it has detained. The overall context is also considered. In this case, six years had elapsed without any news of the whereabouts of Abdulbahap Timurtaş, who was accused of cooperating with the Kurds. The State could not say what had happened to him, so that it was considered that the allegations of enforced disappearance led to state responsibility. Moreover, it was established that the State should have investigated the case in order to establish responsibilities.[27]

3.2.2 Violated rights

The ECtHR recognizes that disappearance causes a state of continuous violation of human rights for both those disappeared and their relatives.[28]

The Court usually analyses cases of enforced disappearance in connection with Articles 2 (right to life), 3 (prohibition of torture), 5 (right to liberty and security) and 13 (right to an effective remedy) of the European Convention on Human Rights. The latter is read in conjunction with Articles 2 and 3. In some cases, the Court has also declared a violation of Article 8 (right to respect private and family life).

The Court applies a presumption of violation of the right to life when the victim has last been seen alive in life-threatening circumstances and the respondent state fails to provide convincing explanations as to his or her fate and whereabouts. When disappearances occur under these circumstances, the state's obligation to conduct an effective investigation and to identify and prosecute perpetrators does not come to an end upon discovery of the body or presumption of death.[29]

26 ECtHR 1998, Kurt v. Turkey, para. 107.

27 ECtHR 2000, Timurtaş v. Turkey, para. 81–90.

28 ECtHR 2009, Varnava and others v. Turkey, para. 148.

29 ECtHR 2006, Bazorkina v. Russia, paras. 110–2; ECtHR 2009, Varnava and others v. Turkey, paras. 144–5; ECtHR 2008, Osmanoğlu v. Turkey, para. 72.

It has been stated that relatives of disappeared persons may also themselves be victims of a violation of the prohibition of torture, mainly due to the authorities' reactions and attitudes when the situation has been brought to their attention. To assess the occurrence of such a violation, the ECtHR considers the proximity of the family ties, the circumstances of the relationship, the extent to which the relative witnessed the events in question and the involvement of the family member in attempts to obtain information on the disappearance. However, the ECtHR has been reluctant to recognize transgenerational damage in cases of relatives born after the enforced disappearance.[30]

It is interesting to point out that the ECtHR has declared that there is a public interest in knowing the proceedings that are employed, even if it has not necessarily declared that there is a 'right to truth' in a public dimension.[31]

The ECtHR recognizes enforced disappearances as a continuous offence and the various rights that are affected, both for those disappeared and for their relatives:

> A disappearance is a distinct phenomenon, characterised by an ongoing situation of uncertainty and unaccountability [...]. This situation is very often drawn out over time, prolonging the torment of the victim's relatives. It cannot therefore be said that a disappearance is, simply, an 'instantaneous' act or event; the additional distinctive element of subsequent failure to account for the whereabouts and fate of the missing person gives rise to a continuing situation. Thus, the procedural obligation will, potentially, persist as long as the fate of the person is unaccounted for; the ongoing failure to provide the requisite investigation will be regarded as a continuing violation [...].[32]

3.2.3 Understanding the jurisdiction *ratione temporis*

Arguing on effectiveness and on the genuine connection standard, the ECtHR observes restrictive parameters concerning the time that may elapse between the triggering event and the action before the European Human Rights System. Even when considering especially complex situations, it has stated that:

30 ECtHR 2013, Janowiec and others v. Russia, para. 163.
31 ECtHR 2012, Al Masri v. Macedonia, para. 192.
32 ECtHR 2009, Varnava and others v. Turkey, para. 148.

'[T]he lapse of time between the triggering event and the critical date must remain reasonably short [...]. Although there are no apparent legal criteria by which the absolute limit on the duration of that period may be defined, it should not exceed ten years.'[33]

It has decided the above without closing the door to extend these limits under exceptional circumstances.

Interestingly, in cases of disappearances the ECtHR urges not only the states to act diligently, but also urges the relatives to do so:

> In cases of disappearances, just as it is imperative that the relevant domestic authorities launch an investigation and take measures as soon as a person has disappeared in life-threatening circumstances, it is indispensable that the applicants, who are the relatives of missing persons, do not delay unduly in bringing a complaint about the ineffectiveness or lack of such investigation before the Court. [...] [A]pplicants cannot wait indefinitely before coming to Strasbourg. They must make proof of a certain amount of diligence and initiative and introduce their complaints without undue delay.[34]

3.2.3 Duties of the state in cases of enforced disappearances

Even if the ECtHR does not dedicate much text to emphasize the state duties arising in cases of disappearances, it does indicate the duty for the state to investigate in an effective manner.[35]

3.2.4 Reparations

Regarding the reparations, the ECtHR only decides on economic reparations, without demanding the states to take other kinds of measures (as foreseen e. g. in the UN principles on reparations).[36]

---

33 ECtHR 2013, Janowiec and others v. Russia, para. 146.
34 ECtHR 2009, Varnava and others v. Turkey, para. 161.
35 Ibid.
36 As an example ECtHR 2013, Janowiec and others v. Russia, paras. 219–24.

Conclusions

There has been an increasing density of regulation in the international legal instruments regarding enforced disappearances. This started with stating the right not to be subjected to enforced disappearance and subsequently established a whole set of different regulations to date. Many of them are relevant for criminal law, both at an international and national levels. This is a matter of both international criminal law and of transnational criminal law.[37]

Comparing Inter-American and European approaches, in practice one may identify both commonalities and issues that differ.

The commonalities include the same understanding of enforced disappearances, both in the elements of their definition and regarding the crime's nature as a continuous offence that violates the rights of both the disappeared person and of their relatives (including the right not to be subjected to torture for the latter).

Moreover, despite initial different approaches, today both courts rely on circumstantial evidence as sufficient, considering what has been called the clandestine nature of the crime.

Regarding the differences, the first is the different phenomenology of the cases, while cases related to dictatorships are common in the Inter-American System, cases related to armed conflicts and the so-called 'war on terrorism' are prevalent in the European System.

Another difference between both systems is in regard to the understanding of the due-diligence duty. While the IACtHR understands this as a state duty and details its components in every judgment, the ECtHR understands that it exists for the state mainly in the form of a duty to investigate but argues that the victims also have a duty of diligence consistant in bringing their case before the European Human Rights System without undue delay.

Finally, on the matter of reparations, the ECtHR only orders reparations consisting of a sum of money, while the IACtHR orders a variety of different actions as reparations, that may include not only money, but memorials and the obligation to educate state servants in human rights and other measures in line with the UN-law on the matter.

---

37 Using the category as Boister explained it in the European Journal of International Law in 2003.

Bibliography

Boister, Neil. 2003. 'Transnational Criminal Law?' *European Journal of International Law.* 14.5. 953–76.

Bourguignon, Manon, Katz, Muriel and Dermitzel, Alice. 2024. 'Traumatic traces of enforced disappearance through generations.' In Bianchi, Maria Giovanna and Luci, Monica (eds.). *Psychoanalytic, Psychosocial, and Human Rights Perspectives on Enforced Disappearance.* London and New York: Routledge. 215–31.

Dulitzky, Ariel E. 2019. 'The Latin-American Flavor of Enforced Disappearances'. *Chicago Journal of International Law.* 19.2. 423–89.

Keller, Helen and Heri, Corina. 2014. 'Enforced Disappearance and the European Court of Human Rights: A 'Wall of Silence', Fact-Finding Difficulties and States as 'Subversive Objectors''. *Journal of International Criminal Justice.* 12.4. 735–50.

López Guerra, Luis. 'Desapariciones forzadas en la jurisprudencia del Tribunal Europeo de Derechos Humanos'. In Ibáñez Rivas, Juan María, Flores Pantoja, Rogelio and Padilla Cordero, Jorge (eds.) *Desaparición forzada en el sistema interamericano de derechos humanos.* Mexico: Instituto de Estudios Constitucionales del Estado de Querétaro. 431–52.

Enforced Disappearance and International Criminal Law[1]

Aziz Epik

Abstract: This article takes a look at the crime of enforced disappearance as a crime against humanity under Article 7 (1) (i) ICC Statute. Enforced disappearances are not a recent phenomenon but still prevalent in weak governance zones and dictatorial regimes. The crime will therefore likely concern the International Criminal Court in the future. Against this backdrop it is important to reflect on unresolved doctrinal issues that could prove difficult in the application of the offence. After a short introduction to the elements of the crime, four issues are discussed in more detail. First, the question of who qualifies as a perepetrator is addressed. Second, it will be discussed whether the deprivation of freedom needs to be unlawful to qualify as relevant under Article 7 (1) (i) ICC Statute. The third issue concerns the need for an inquiry into the fate and whereabouts of a victim while the fourth point focuses on the intent requirement. The article closes with a summary of its key findings.

1. Introduction

Enforced disappearances are not a recent phenomenon – in fact, *Hitler's* Night and Fog Decree ('Nacht-und-Nebel-Erlass'[2]) was the basis for such a practice in National Socialist Germany.[3] There have also been multiple

1 This chapter is a slightly revised and footnoted version of a presentation given by the author at the University of Hamburg in June 2024. The author would like to thank Ms Anna-Julia Egger for valuable support in the preparation of this manuscript.

2 On the Night and Fog Decree see Cornelius in this anthology, 83–8; Cornelius 2006, 85–98; Finucane 2010, 175–81.

3 Keitel was convicted by the IMT, see IMT, judgment of 1 October 1946. The Night and Fot Decree was characterized as a war crime, but it remained unclear for what underlying act in particular Keitel was conviced. See on this Finucane 2010, 177–8; Gaggioli 2013, 327.

instances where enforced disappearances have been systematically used by states – in particular in the Latin-American context.[4]

However, for a long time, international criminal law has been remarkably reserved on the matter. During the 20th century there was no separate offence of 'enforced disappearance', neither in the Statute of the International Military Tribunal (IMT) nor in the Control Council Law No. 10 – and also not in the Statutes of the International Criminal Tribunal for the former Yugoslavia (ICTY) and the International Criminal Tribunal for Rwanda (ICTR). Acts of enforced disappearance could only be captured as deprivation of liberty, other inhumane acts or persecution[5] – all of which do not cover the specific wrong of the crime.[6]

After important preparatory work during the 1980s, the momentum for drafting and codifying enforced disappearance as a separate offence finally developed in the 1990s.[7] The *Declaration on the Protection of All Persons from Enforced Disappearances*[8] which was adopted by Resolution 47/133 of the UN General Assembly on 18 December 1992 provided a first definition of enforced disappearances in its Preamble:

> *Deeply concerned that in many countries, often in a persistent manner, enforced disappearances occur in the sense that persons are arrested, detained or abducted against their will or otherwise deprived of their liberty by officials of different branches or levels of Government, or by organized groups or private individuals acting on behalf of, or with the support, direct or indirect, consent or acquiescence of the Government, followed by a refusal to disclose the fate or whereabouts of the persons concerned or a refusal to acknowledge the deprivation of their liberty, which places such persons outside the protection of law.*

A similar definition can be found in Article II of the Inter-American Convention on Forced Disappearance of Persons of 9th June 1994[9] and in

4 See the country reports in this anthology by Martins, 49–63, and Contesse, 65–80.

5 ICTY, judgment of 14 January 2000 (Kureškić et al., TC), para. 566; ICTY, judgment of 15 April 2011 (Gotovina et al., TC), vol. 2, paras. 1831–9; ECCC, judgment of 7 August 2014 (Nuon and Khieu, TC), para. 448.

6 See von Braun/Diehl 2011, 218.

7 See for an overview van den Herik/Braga da Silva 2022, para. 180; Brody/González 1997, 365–405.

8 See on this Cardenas in this anthology, 210–1.

9 Article II: 'For the purposes of this Convention, forced disappearance is considered to be the act of depriving a person or persons of hir or their freedom, in whatever

Article 2 of the International Convention for the Protection of All Persons from Enforced Disappearance of 20 December 2006 (UN Disappearances Convention).[10]

The International Law Commission included this definition in its 1996 Draft Code and, finally, after strong initial opposition,[11] the States agreed in Rome to include a separate crime of enforced disappearance as a crime against humanity into Article 7 (1) (i) of the ICC Statute. Some states have included similar definitions in their domestic codes of crimes under international law, such as Germany[12] with section 7 (1) no. 7 of the German Code of Crimes Against International Law (VStGB).

In the following, I want to take a closer look at the crime of enforced disappearance under the ICC Statute. At the outset, a brief remark is warranted: the crime of enforced disappearance is an underlying offence of crimes against humanity as defined in Article 7 (1) and (2) (a) ICC Statute. In order to constitute a crime under international law, a single act of enforced disappearance therefore needs to be committed as part of a widespread or systematic attack directed against any civilian population, with the knowledge of the attack. In addition, the definition of 'attack' in Article 7 (2) (a) ICC Statute requires that the attack must have been committed 'pursuant' to or in furtherance of a State or organizational policy to commit such attack". Both the widespread or systematic character and the policy element make it clear that isolated incidents are not sufficient –

way, perpetrated by agents of the state or by persons or groups of persons acting with the authorization, support, or acquiescence of the state, followed by an absence of information or a refusal to acknowledge that deprivation of freedom or to give information on the whereabouts of that person, thereby impeding his or her recourse to the applicable lagal remedies and procedural guarantees.'

10 Article 2: 'For the purposes of this Convention, 'enforced disappearance' is considered to be the arrest, detention, abduction or any other form of deprivation of liberty by agents of the State or by persons or groups of persons acting with the authorization, support or acquiescence of the State, followed by a refusal to acknowledge the deprivation of liberty or by concealment of the fate or whereabout of the disappeared person, which place such a person outside the protection of the law.'

11 See Giorgou 2013, 1003; Jeßberger/Geneuss 2024, 25 et seq.; van den Herik/Braga da Silva 2022, para. 180 fn. 679 with further references; von Hebel/Robinson 1999, 102. On the characterization as a crime against humanity in human rights instruments see Brody/González 1997, 378–82.

12 Geneuss/Jeßberger in this anthology, 191-2.

enforced disappearances need to be part of a broader attack on a civilian population.[13]

2. The elements of the crime of enforced disappearance

Building on this preliminary observation, I now turn to an analysis of the elements of the crime. According to the legal definition in Article 7 (2) (i) of the ICC Statute

> *'Enforced disappearance of persons' means the arrest, detention or abduction of persons by, or with the authorization, support or acquiescence of, a State or a political organization, followed by a refusal to acknowledge that deprivation of freedom or to give information on the fate or whereabouts of those persons, with the intention of removing them from the protection of the law for a prolonged period of time.*

The material elements of the offence require, first, that a person was arrested, detained or abducted by or with the authorization, support or acquiescence of a State or a political organization.[14] It is notable that the ICC Statute limits the forms of deprivation of freedom to arrest, detention and abduction while other definitions, such as the one in the Disappearances Convention, include an opening clause by additionally referring to 'any other form of deprivation of liberty". However, the ICC Pre-Trial Chamber has held that it 'understands the terms 'arrest, detention or abduction' to cover comprehensively any form of deprivation of liberty of a person against his or her will'.[15]

Second, this deprivation of freedom needs to be followed by a refusal to acknowledge it or to give information on the fate or whereabouts of the person.[16] With regard to the mental element, the standard intent requirement of Article 30 needs to be accompanied by the *intention* of removing the person from the protection of the law for a prolonged period of time.[17]

---

13 On the contextual element of Article 7 ICC Statute see, among others, Werle/Jeßberger 2020, paras. 982–1002.

14 See van den Herik/Braga da Silva 2022, para. 272.

15 ICC, decision of 9 November 2017 (Situation in the Republic of Burundi, PTC), para. 118; see also van den Herik/Braga da Silva 2022, para. 273.

16 See van den Herik/Braga da Silva 2022, para. 272.

17 See Werle/Jeßberger 2020, para. 1105.

The combination of the two parts of the offence – deprivation of freedom and refusal to acknowledge it or to give information about the fate and whereabouts – characterizes the specific wrong of the crime and distinguishes it from a 'mere' deprivation of freedom.[18] It is the connection between the deprivation of freedom and the intended removal from the protection of the law by refusing to communicate that qualifies the conduct as a separate crime.

3. *Enforced disappearance as a complex crime: four key issues*

A plain reading of the definition already makes quite clear that the crime of enforced disappearance is a rather complex one. This analysis will focus on four main issues that warrant closer attention:

First, the question arises as to who may qualify as a perpetrator under this provision: does it include only those who participate both in the deprivation of freedom *and* in the refusal to acknowledge it or provide information, or does it extend to anyone who participates in either part of the offence? Second, does the deprivation of freedom need to be *unlawful*, or can enforced disappearance occur even when the (initial) arrest or detention is in line with international law? Third, does the second part of the definition require that someone has inquired about the fate or whereabouts of the 'disappeared' person? Fourth, does the crime require a special intent – the intention to remove the person from the protection of the law – or is mere knowledge of this consequence sufficient?

3.1 Who is a perpetrator?

The crime of enforced disappearance is seldomly committed by one perpetrator alone. Rather, one or more persons are involved in the deprivation of freedom while others are responsible for the refusal to acknowledge or give information. This is evident in cases where enforced disappearances are committed through a state's apparatus of power.[19]

Consider, for example, the following scenario: Two officers of the *state* police arrest a dissident who is then transported to a black site. Upon

18 See also Citroni 2021, 676; van den Herik/Braga da Silva 2022, paras. 177, 272; Vermeulen 2012, 172.

19 See Citroni 2021, 676.

inquiry of the relatives, an officer of the *municipal* police refuses, in line with his standard orders, to acknowledge any deprivation of freedom or to give information on the fate or whereabouts of the arrested person.

Here, different actors are involved and only by taking their actions together are the material elements of the offence fulfilled. While the state police deprives the victim of his or her freedom, it is the municipal police which refuses to disclose any information.

These actors operate within the same system of a state-sponsored policy of enforced disappearances. However, under the common framework of attribution, it would be difficult to qualify them as co-perpetrators. Although their acts are linked by a state policy, they are distinct actions by separate individuals, lacking direct communication or interaction between them.[20] This is too loose a connection to claim that they followed a common plan as demanded by Article 25 (3) (a) ICC Statute for co-perpetration.[21]

However, the structure of the crime, its historical development and its phenomenology strongly suggest that the offence presupposes a different model of attribution – specific to this offence.[22] Instead of co-perpetration stricto sensu, a person must be qualified as a perpetrator of the crime of enforced disappearance if he or she knowingly acts within a system of enforced disappearances and participates in a manner that would qualify him or her as perpetrator in either part of the offence – deprivation of freedom or refusal to communicate. Thus, a substantial contribution with control over a 'part' of the crime is sufficient to constitute perpetration so long as the other material elements of the crime are objectively present and covered by the intent of each perpetrator.[23]

The position taken here is in line with the Elements of Crimes. An introductory footnote to the elements states:

> *Given the complex nature of this crime, it is recognized that its commission will normally involve more than one perpetrator as a part of a common criminal purpose.*

---

20 See Grammer 2005, 152–4.

21 Werle/Jeßberger 2020, paras. 608 et seq. Similarly in a German context von Braun/Diehl 2011, 226 et seq.

22 See von Braun/Diehl 2011, 220. More generally on the specificities of enforced disappearance requiring a '*sui generis* regime' see Sarkin 2012, 582.

23 See similarly Grammer 2005, 152; Jeßberger/Geneuss 2024, 25.

This suggests that the drafters of the elements also acknowledged that the crime of enforced disappearance deviates from the general rules laid down in article 25 (3) ICC Statute.[24] Furthermore, the first element states that

> *'the perpetrator (a) arrested, detained or abducted one or more persons; or (b) refused to acknowledge the arrest, detention or abduction, or to give information on the fate or whereabouts of such person or persons.'*

By listing the two variants of perpetration in the *alternative*, the elements demonstrate that participation in either is sufficient.[25] The second and third element make clear, however, that the respective other part of the offence must have occurred as well and that the perpetrator has to be aware of this.[26]

This position is also commonly adopted in academic literature[27] and is, to take one example, reflected in the approach taken by the German legislator who included both parts as separate variants of the offence into the definition of enforced disappearance in the German Code of Crimes Against International Law (section 7 (1) no. 7 VStGB).[28]

It is, of course, a significant deviation from the general rule that demands a common plan in order to attribute responsibility as co-perpetrators if a perpetrator does not fulfill all the material elements him- or herself. At the same time, deviations from general rules in the special part are nothing

24 See Grammer 2005, 160.

25 Critizizing the elements of the crime see van den Herik/Braga da Silva 2022, para. 278, who suggest addressing the elements for perpetrators involved in the deprivation of liberty separately from those relevant to perpetrators in volved in the refusal of information. On the structural differences between this definition in the Elements of Crimes, the definition in the ICC Statute and the definition in the UN Disappearances Convention see Jeßberger/Geneuss 2024, 25.

26 2. (a) Such arrest, detention or abduction was followed or accompanied by a refusal to acknowledge that deprivation of freedom or to give information on the fate or whereabouts of such person or persons; or (b) Such refusal was preceded or accompanied by that deprivation of freedom.
3. The perpetrator was aware that: (a) Such arrest, detention or abduction would be followed in the ordinary course of events by a refusal to acknowledge that deprivation of freedom or to give information on the fate or whereabouts of such person or persons; or (b) Such refusal was preceded or accompanied by that deprivation of freedom. See on this Grammer 2005, 161; Jeßberger/Geneuss 2024, 25.

27 See Grammer 2005, 152; Jeßberger/Geneuss 2024, 25; Werle/Jeßberger 2020, para. 1102.

28 On the remaining ambiguities of the definition in section 7 (1) no. 7 VStGB Grammer 2005, 162–3.

novel – consider, for instance, special intents or, in the domestic context, so-called organizational offences.

3.2 Lawful deprivation of freedom?

The second question I want to address is whether a lawful deprivation of freedom is sufficient to establish the first material element of the crime. In the literature, this is generally assumed with a view to an all-encompassing protection of the victim.[29] The elements of crimes acknowledge that 'under certain circumstances an arrest or detention may have been lawful'. The ICC Pre-Trial Chamber also held that the 'crime also includes the scenario in which a victim, initially arrested and detained lawfully, may be 'disappeared' in custody.'[30]

The position taken earlier – that the commission of one part of the offence is sufficient to assume perpetration – could, however, suggest otherwise. One could assume that, if committing either part of the offence can lead to a conviction for a crime against humanity, legal deprivations of freedom should indeed be excluded. Otherwise, the participation in a legal arrest or detention would turn a police officer into an international criminal.

If lawful deprivations of freedom were excluded, however, the second part of the offence would become irrelevant whenever the deprivation of freedom was lawful. That is to say: The refusal to acknowledge or give information would not constitute a crime under international law so long as the deprivation of freedom was not unlawful to begin with. What distinguishes the crime of enforced disappearance from the crime of illegal deprivation of liberty is, however, the removal of a person from the protection of the law regardless of whether the initial deprivation of freedom was in line

29 See Jeßberger/Geneuss 2024, 18; van den Herik/Braga da Silva 2022, para. 273; Vermeulen 2012, 54; Werle/Jeßberger 2020, para. 1102. Differently Ott 2011, 177, who seems to reject an enforced disappearance as long as the initial reason for a lawful detention remains valid.

30 ICC, decision of 9 November 2017 (Situation in the Republic of Burundi, PTC), para. 118.

with (international) law or not.[31] This purpose would be ill-served if lawful deprivations of freedom were excluded.

The supposed friction that arises from the position that participation in either part of the offence is sufficient is easily unmasked as an illusionary problem anyway: even a lawful deprivation of freedom is not a neutral act if committed in the knowledge that it is part of a systematic policy of enforced disappearances and with the intent that an acknowledgement of the deprivation of freedom or information on the fate or whereabouts will be refused by other perpetrators in due course.[32] At the same time, persons involved in the initial lawful arrest in good faith will not posses the necessary *mental element* (knowledge that acknowledgement will be refused) and, therefore, not be liable. There is, thus, no risk of over-criminalization of *bona fide* police officers.

3.3 Inquiry required?

The third and practically important question that needs to be addressed is whether the crime of enforced disappearance demands an inquiry by relatives or other interested parties in the fate and whereabouts of the disappeared person in order to trigger a duty to acknowledge or give information. Some authors have argued that the wording and structure of the offence suggest that such an unwritten element needs to be read into the definition.[33]

I respectfully disagree with this position. While the offence *can* be interpreted in this way – after all, the wording of the provision 'followed by a refusal to acknowledge that deprivation of freedom or to give information' seems to imply an inquiry as there would be no ground for someone to 'refuse to acknowledge' something that he or she has not been inquired upon – this interpretation is certainly not compelling.[34] In particular, the

31 See Grammer 2005, 101–3. See also Gaggioli 2013, 328, according to whom it is irrelevant for the determination of an enforced disappearance whether the deprivation of liberty was arbitrary or not.

32 See, in a similar vein, Vermeulen 2012, 178, who compares enforced disappearances with 'unacknowledged detention' instead of 'unlawful detention'. See also Modolell González 2010, 484.

33 See van den Herik/Braga da Silva 2022, para. 275; Werle/Jeßberger 2020, paras. 1102–3.

34 In the same vein Grammer 2005, 213; Ott 2011, 178 et seq.

second variant – the refusal to give information – can be construed differently if read in light of the development of international human rights law (including through the influence of the efforts to prevent and repress enforced disappearances) towards the recognition of a duty to inform relatives of an arrested person even in the absence of any inquiry.[35]

The ICC Pre-Trial Chamber in its *Burundi* decision also seems to move towards this position. The Chamber held:

> *Whether or not the victim's family lodges a formal complaint, the State authorities are duty-bound to commence an impartial and thorough investigation ex officio without delay into the disappearance of the victim.*[36]

The purpose of protecting persons who have been deprived of their freedom from being removed from the protection of the law also argues in favor of dispensing with the requirement of an inquiry:[37] In dictatorial regimes, inquiring about the fate and whereabouts of a person can especially bring about serious risks for the inquiring person. It would therefore be up to a courageous person who nevertheless inquires in this way to trigger the criminal liability of those involved in the enforced disappearance. This seems contradictory to the intended purpose of the offence.

3.4 Intent requirement

The final issue I want to address concerns the intent requirement.[38] A plain reading could suggest that the crime of enforced disappearance demands a special intent: the intention of removing the arrested or detained person from the protection of the law for a prolonged period of time.[39]

35 This position is supported by the definition of the UN Disappearances Convention. Article 2 reads in this regard 'followed by a refusal to acknowledge the deprivation of liberty or by concealment of the fate or whereabouts of the disappeared person'. The term concealment is more precise in this regard and makes clear beyond doubt that an inquiry is not required.

36 ICC, decision of 9 November 2017 (Situation in the Republic of Burundi, PTC), para. 118.

37 See Grammer 2005, 213; Ott 2011, 178 et seq.

38 Another problem in this context is the interpretation of the 'for a prolonged period of time' element of the intent requirement, see van den Herik/Braga da Silva 2022, para. 277.

39 With this understanding Jeßberger/Geneuss 2024, 26; similarly Modolell González 2010, 477, 485; Ott 2011, 183–6.

This would substantially narrow the applicability of the offence as most persons involved in depriving someone of their freedom or refusing to acknowledge or give information will not act with the special intent – in the sense of a dolus directus of the first degree – of removing them from the protection of the law. However, such an interpretation is neither necessary nor preferable.[40]

First, the wording 'intention' leaves open whether the offence refers to a standard of qualified intent or to the intent requirement as found in Article 30 ICC Statute.

Second, preceding (and following) definitions of enforced disappearance, after which Article 7 was modelled, suggest that the removal of the person from the protection of the law has been seen as a consequence of the refusal to acknowledge or give information and does not need to be purposefully intended by the perpetrator.[41] Take the 1992 definition for example: '*which places such persons outside the protection of law.*' Or the definition of the UN Disappearances Convention with identical wording. These definitions should guide the interpretation of the ICC Statute.[42]

I would therefore suggest that, in accordance with Article 30 (2) (b) ICC Statute[43], the perpetrator must have been aware that his or her acts will remove the person from the protection of the law in the ordinary course of events rather than having purposefully intended to do so.[44]

For now, the ICC seems to suggest an 'evidentiary approach' to the problem. The Pre-Trial Chamber held that 'oftentimes the manner in which the person is deprived of his or her liberty allows the Chamber to infer the intention to remove the victim from the protection of the law'.[45] The decision is ambiguous though as the paragraph on the question of 'intention' starts with the sentence 'As a result of the enforced disappearance, the victim is removed from the protection of the law [...].'[46] It is therefore possible that the ICC will adopt the position outlined above in the future.

40 In a similar vein van den Herik/Braga da Silva 2022, para. 276.

41 See Grammer 2005, 191–3; Vermeulen 2012, 170.

42 See Ott 2011, 177.

43 In relation to a consequence, that person means to cause that consequence or is aware that it will occur in the ordinary course of events.

44 See also van den Herik/Braga da Silva 2022, para. 276; Werle/Jeßberger 2020, paras. 1105 et seq.

45 ICC, decision of 9 November 2017 (Situation in the Republic of Burundi, PTC), para. 120.

46 ICC, decision of 9 November 2017 (Situation in the Republic of Burundi, PTC), para. 120.

It might be advisable to clarify the issue *de lege ferenda*, at least in the elements of crimes.

4. Concluding Remarks

There is plenty more to discuss. For example, the extent to which the crime can be 'privatized' to include the conduct of non-state actors.[47] While I agree that the roots of the crime presuppose the performance of state functions so that the interpretation of the reference to political organizations cannot be streamlined with the interpretation of the policy element in the chapeau of Article 7,[48] I would like to stress that non-state actors nowadays exercise great power in weak governance zones without resembling states.[49]

Let me summarize: I have first argued that the crime of enforced disappearance modifies the rules of attribution so that every person who participates as a perpetrator in either part of the offence is a perpetrator of the crime. Second, this position does not lead to an exclusion of lawful deprivations of freedom from the conduct falling under the definition. Third, the offence does not require an inquiry in the fate or whereabouts of the disappeared person. And, fourth, it does also not require that the perpetrator acts with a special intent in the sense of a dolus directus of the first degree. Most of these issues have not been addressed in case law so far. However, enforced disappearances continue in weak governance zones and dictatorial regimes. It is thus rather a question of when, not if, the ICC will have to deal in more detail with this crime.

Bibliography

Brody, Reed and González, Felipe. 1997. 'Nunca Más: An Analysis of International Instruments on 'Disappearances''. *Human Rights Quarterly*. 19.2. 365–405.

Citroni, Gabriella. 2021. 'Consequences of the Lack of Criminalization of Enforced Disappearance at the Domestic Level'. *Journal of International Criminal Justice*. 19. 675–96.

Cornelius, Kai. 2006. *Vom spurlosen Verschwindenlassen zur Benachrichtigungspflicht bei Festnahmen*. Berlin: Berliner Wissenschafts-Verlag.

47 See on this van den Herik/Braga da Silva 2022, para. 274.
48 See Werle/Jeßberger 2020, para. 1105.
49 In detail on this dichotomy see Giorgou 2013, 1001.

Finucane, Brian. 2010. 'Enforced Disappearance as a Crime Under International Law. A Neglected Origin in the Laws of War'. *Yale Journal of International Law.* 35.1. 171–97.

Gaggioli, Gloria. 2013. 'The prohibition of enforced disappearances: a meaningful example of a partial merger between human rights law and international humanitarian law'. In Kolb, Robert and Gaggioli, Gloria (eds.). *Research Handbook on Human Rights and Humanitarian Law.* Cheltenham and Northampton: Edward Elgar. 320–42.

Giorgou, Irena. 2013. 'State Involvement in the Perpetration of Enforced Disappearance and the Rome Statute'. *Journal of International Criminal Justice.* 11. 1001–21.

Grammer, Christoph. 2005. *Der Tatbestand des Verschwindenlassens einer Person. Transposition einer völkerrechtlichen Figur ins Strafrecht.* Berlin: Duncker & Humblot.

Jeßberger, Florian and Geneuss, Julia. 2024. *Ein Tatbestand des gewaltsamen Verschwindenlassens im deutschen Strafrecht.* Berlin: Deutsches Institut für Menschenrechte. URL: https://www.institut-fuer-menschenrechte.de/fileadmin/Redaktion/Publikationen/Analyse_Studie/Analyse_Tatbestand_Verschwindenlassen_im_deutschen_Strafrecht.pdf (accessed 30 October 2024).

Modolell González, Juan Luis. 2010. 'The Crime of Forced Disappearance of Persons According to the Decisions of the Inter-American Court of Human Rights'. *International Criminal Law Review.* 10. 475–89.

Ott, Lisa. 2011. *Enforced Disappearance in International Law.* Cambridge, Antwerp and Portland: Intersentia.

Sarkin, Jeremy. 2012. 'Why the Prohibition of Enforced Disappearance Has Attained Jus Cogens Status in International Law'. *Nordic Journal of International Law.* 81.4. 537–84.

van den Herik, Larissa and Braga da Silva, Rafael. 2022. 'Article 7'. In Ambos, Kai (ed.). *Rome Statute of the International Criminal Court. Article-by-Article Commentary.* 4th edition. Munich: C.H.Beck.

Vermeulen, Marthe Lot. 2012. *Enforced Disappearance. Determining State Responsibility under the International Convention for the Protection of All Persons from Enforced Disappearance.* Cambridge, Antwerp and Portland: Intersentia.

von Braun, Leonie and Diehl, David. 2011. 'Die Umsetzung der Konvention Gegen das Verschwindenlassen in Deutschland. Zur Erforderlichkeit eines eigenen Straftatbestandes'. *Zeitschrift für Internationale Strafrechtsdogmatik.* 4. 214–29.

von Hebel, Herman and Robinson, Darryl. 1999. 'Crimes within the Jurisdiction of the Court'. In Lee, Roy S. (ed.). *The International Criminal Court. The Making of the Rome Statute. Issues, Negotiations, Results.* The Hague, London and Boston: Kluwer Law International. 79–126.

Werle, Gerhard and Jeßberger, Florian. 2020. *Völkerstrafrecht.* 5th edition. Tübingen: Mohr Siebeck.

The Harms and Political Significance of Enforced Disappearances

Rocío Lorca

'And whatever men do or know or experience
can make sense only to the extent that it can be spoken about.
Men in the plural, that is,
men in so far as they live and move and act in this world,
can experience meaningfulness only because they can talk with
and make sense to each other and to themselves'[1]

Abstract: This chapter explores the harms that constitute the crime of enforced disappearance, as well as its political significance, by looking at the phenomenology of this crime in Latin American dictatorships between the 1960s and 1980s as crimes against humanity. I argue that the harms of enforced disappearance can only be adequately understood by focusing both on what the practice destroys, i.e. identities, and on what the practice seeks to create, i.e. a new kind of political agency. The destructive dimension of these crimes provides grounds for recognising the relatives of the disappeared as direct victims and the denial of information as a way of perpetuating the crime. The constitutive dimension of the crime helps to understand why the public search for the disappeared is such a crucial condition for a genuine recovery of our democracies.

Enforced disappearances are both exceptional and 'normal.' They are exceptional because, as a practice of state terror, they overturn the most basic and cherished features of our social and political life, opening up an indefinite context of exception to legal and moral normativity. But they are also disturbingly 'normal' in the sense of being a systematic, widespread, patterned and predictable way in which authoritarian power is constituted, exercised and maintained over time. Throughout the twentieth century, the practice of enforced disappearance took place in almost every totalitarian regime,

1 Arendt 1958 (2019), 4.

and we continue to see it in many countries around the world today.[2] In this chapter, I explore the different harms that constitute this crime, as well as its political significance. I argue that the harms of enforced disappearances can only be appropriately grasped if we focus both on what the practice destroys as well as on what it creates.

In order to consider the damage caused by enforced disappearances, I would like to clarify what I mean when I talk about this crime. Gabriel Gatti distinguishes between two types of disappearance, according to the nature of the victims and the meaning of the violence unleashed on them. An original and paradigmatic idea of the disappeared, which he calls *el desaparecido modélico* or 'the modelic disappeared,' emerged with the practices of mass enforce disappearances that took place in Latin American dictatorships in the 1960s, 70s, and 80s.[3] From this paradigmatic case, a second conception emerges, namely, 'the transnational disappeared.'[4] This second idea speaks of immutable, general and transnational features elaborated through normative abstractions in national and international legal documents. The transnational disappeared as a concept can encompass many different experiences of enforced disappearances across the globe. Thus, while the 'modelic disappeared' is constituted by discrete historical fact and contextual meaning, the 'transnational disappeared' is constituted by normative abstraction.[5]

The normative analysis offered in this chapter will be referred to the 'modelic disappeared,' i.e., a specific kind of political violence that took

2 See Annual Report of the United Nations Committee on Enforced Disappearances, available at: https://tbinternet.ohchr.org/_layouts/15/treatybodyexternal/TBSearch.aspx?Lang=en&TreatyID=2&DocTypeID=27 (accessed 2 July 2025). See also Duhaime 2023, 19–35.

3 For a brief account of the emergence of the concept and its Latin American origins, see Dulitzky 2019, 426 et seq.

4 In Dulitzky 2019, 444–50 shows how Latin American organizations from civil society pushed and drove the development of international law on this area, both in the books and in practice. Indeed, the first legal document in this area was the Inter-American convention of Forced Disappearance of Persons (1994), and Latin American human rights organizations, activists and scholars were very important in pushing for the inclusion of this crime in the Rome Statute.

5 This process of abstraction, unlike others, was not a top-down process imposed from the North to the South, but, importantly, the result of Latin American human rights organizations' reliance on international legal institutions in their search for truth, justice, and non-repetition. Generally on this, see Lorca 2024, Sikkink 2001 and Dulitzky 2019 arguing that Chile and Argentina have been at the forefront in terms of prosecutions and convictions of people for these kinds of crime, 453.

place in Latin American dictatorships between the 1960s and 80s. I will focus on this particular case of enforced disappearance because of its influence on the international legal framework dealing with this crime[6] and also because, as a well-documented experience, it provides valuable access to understanding the particular harms that enforced disappearance can have on both individual victims and their political communities.

1. *The Latin American* detenido desaparecido

The fact that the concept of the 'disappeared' originated in Latin America does not mean that the practice was invented by Latin American dictators.[7] Rather, the fact that the idea originated in Latin America seems to speak of the need to give a name to a phenomenon that was very widespread in the region during those years. This phenomenon required a word that could convey the suffering of the people, attract national and international attention, and allow the relatives of the disappeared to recognise and help each other. In fact, at the beginning of the 1970s, the relatives of the disappeared in Chile used the category of 'detainees.' This category was later replaced by that of 'unrecovered detainees' until it consolidated in the mid-1970s into the more specific category of the 'detainee-disappeared' (*detenido desaparecido*) or simply 'disappeared' (*desaparecidos*).[8]

It is, of course, quite irrelevant who in the region first came up with the word; perhaps it was Argentina, perhaps it was Chile or Guatemala, or perhaps it is a case of spontaneous convergence, given the similarities that

6 While the UN Declaration on the Protection of All Persons from Enforced Disappearance dates from 1992, a more articulated legal framework was first developed in Latin American in 1996, in the Inter-American Convention on Forced Disappearance of Persons. At a global level, an equivalent legal framework was only adopted in 2010 through the International Convention for the Protection of All Persons from Enforced Disappearance.

7 An earlier well documented case of such a practice comes from the 'night and fog' decree in Nazi Germany as discussed in this volume by Kai Cornelius at. 83-88. There is, however, ongoing discussion as to whether some cases that fall under international regulation are genuine cases of 'enforced disappereance.' One example that has been discussed is the case of El-Masri against USA. In 2012 the European Court of Human Rights considered that his detention was a case of enforced disappearance, even though El-Masri was liberated and could file the legal case directly, see Chwastiak 2015, 4.

8 Díaz 2022, 7.

the phenomenon has had in these and many other countries in the region.[9] What we do know is that the use of the idea of the 'disappeared' emerged to name a particular type of victim of a particular type of political violence, and this type of violence began in this region in the 1960s in Guatemala. It was later practised by every dictatorship in the Southern Cone in the 1970s and 80s, and was officially consolidated as a regional practice in the 'Condor Plan.'[10]

Although the extent of the practice varied greatly, in all the South American dictatorships disappearances were carried out by the repressive agencies of the military regimes in a somewhat similar way: a group of armed men would arrest someone commonly identified as a political opponent, without giving any reason for the arrest or any information as to where they were being taken. Often these arrests were made at night in their homes, but sometimes they were made in public places such as the victim's workplace, in the streets or at universities.[11] The state agents often dressed as civilians and put the detainees in a car without a number plate.[12]

Once abducted, the person would never be found and a 'wall of silence' would be built around their fate. The authorities of these dictatorships systematically denied having made the arrests and refused to provide any information about the whereabouts of the victims. The lack of information also benefited from the complicity of the judiciary, which systematically

9 Compare Zallaquett 2011 referring to Chile and Gatti 2011 referring to Argentina.

10 Frey 2009, 53 et seq. The practice was used paradigmatically in Chile, Argentina, Uruguay, Paraguay, Bolivia and Brasil, all of which were part of Operation Condor. Operation Condor was an agreement among the dictator of many Latin American countries to reinforce their repressive mechanisms by sharing information, cooperating with the clandestine transfer of individuals, and by facilitating the execution of state repression beyond state borders. The meeting where the agreement was reached took place in Chile in 1975 with the concurrence of Argentine, Bolivia, Chile, Paraguay and Uruguay. Later the Operation would be joined by Brasil (1976) and Ecuador and Perú (1978). For more information of Operation Condor see the web page of Plan Condor Project, available at: https://plancondor.org/en/historical-context (accessed 2 July 2025).

11 According to the official report of the Human Rights Division of the Ministry of Justice, most of the Argentinean disappeared were abducted individually from their houses or residences during the night, see the report, available at: https://www.argentina.gob.ar/derechoshumanos/ANM/ruvte/2015 (accessed 2 July 2025). See also Adams 2019, 343 et seq.

12 Adams 2019, 343 et seq.

rejected thousands of *habeas corpus* petitions filed in all these countries and failed to open the corresponding criminal investigations.[13]

Silence and lack of information have long survived the end of these regimes due to a military pact of silence against which amnesty laws, truth commissions and belated judicial prosecutions have been largely powerless. Thus, in addition to the similarities in the modus operandi of Latin American disappearances, our experiences share the devastating fact that we still do not know what happened to most of our *desaparecidos* after their abduction. The lack of information and disclosure is so radical that after four, five or even six decades of searching, we know very little about what happened to them after their abduction, and we are still unable to say exactly how many people have disappeared, as we continue to learn of new victims. In Chile, for example, the number of 'desaparecidos' has risen from around 1,000, as estimated by the Rettig Report in the early 1990s, to almost 1,500, as estimated by the National Search Plan in 2024. After 50 years, we only know the fate of around 300 victims. The figures are even less clear in Argentina, where the official estimate by CONADEP, in the Nunca Más report of 1984, was 8,960 forcibly disappeared people.[14] Some human rights organization, however, speak of 30,000.[15] And the current official figure from the Ministry of Justice, from 2015, speaks of 7,018 forcibly disappeared persons, of whom only 637 have been identified.[16] In any case, the numbers are staggering, and so is the lack of information.[17]

Today, most people believe with relative certainty that the disappeared were eventually executed by state agents who then disposed of their bodies illegally and secretly, throwing them into rivers or the sea or burying them in secret mass graves. But we are also relatively certain that in many cases the disappeared were not immediately executed, but were subjected to prolonged detention, torture and sexual violence.[18] This lack of specific knowledge about what has happened to each of them since the day they

13 See generally, Cárdenas et al., *forthcoming*.

14 *Nunca Mas*, CONADEP 1984, 49.

15 Ibid, 14.

16 See reports of the Human Rights Division of the Ministry of Justice, most of the Argentinean disappeared were abducted individually from their houses or residences during the night, see the report, available at: https://www.argentina.gob.ar/derechos humanos/ANM/ruvte/2015 (accessed 2 July 2025).

17 Regarding the Argentinean debate about the numbers of victims, see Crenzel 2024.

18 In the Argentinean case, for example, 80% of the disappeared were seen during their captivity by other detainees. See report of the Human Rights Division of the Ministry of Justice, most of the Argentinean disappeared were abducted individually from their

were arrested is an agonising common feature of the Latin American *detenido desaparecido.*

These are all characteristics that speak of a specific form of state violence in which the *desaparecido*, more than being illegally detained and then executed, was 'sucked' by the repressive agents of the state into a dark hole from which they have not yet been allowed to return and in which the aim seems to have been to erase a whole group of people in such a way as to ensure that no one remembers them and what they stand for.[19] This explains why, in describing the general phenomenology of this practice, we also need to pay attention to the type of victim being targeted.

The victims of enforced disappearance in Latin American dictatorships had specific characteristics. They were mostly male, young and active workers, mostly peasants or labourers from low-income backgrounds.[20] Importantly, they were also politically active, and although many did not belong to any official organisation, most were members of left-wing political parties or social movements.[21]

What is peculiar about these victims is that they represent the political agent who has always been present in the ideal constructions of Western democracy and yet has often been effectively disenfranchised. In this sense, Gatti argues that the 'modelic disappeared' was not just any person, but the modern citizen-as-individual, consisting of a rational and enlightened agent that emerged in Latin America in those years and an agent that then had a historical existence, but which today is only an abstract or ahistorical entity.[22] Moreover, at that historical moment, these victims were not only

houses or residences during the night, see the report, available at: https://www.argentina.gob.ar/derechoshumanos/ANM/ruvte/2015 (accessed 2 July 2025).

19 Gatti 2014, 1. See also, CONADEP 1984, 12.

20 Adams 2019, 342. In Chile, according to the latest official data, 94.84% of the victims were male, 50, 28% were either farmers or laborers, around two thirds had between 18 and 34 years old, 6% were underaged, and 80% were under 44 years old. See, available at: https://www.plannacionaldebusqueda.cl/victimas/ (accessed 2 July 2025). In Argentina, 73% were male and 60% had between 20 and 29 years old, according to the official reports of the human rights division of the Ministry of Justice, see the statistical report, available at: https://www.argentina.gob.ar/derechoshumanos/ANM/ruvte/2015 (accessed 2 July 2025). Also in Paraguay, most of the victims belonged to this age group, see Mendieta et al. 2024.

21 In Chile around 60% belonged to either the Socialist Party, the Communist Party or the Revolutionary Left Movement (MIR), see, available at: https://www.plannacionaldebusqueda.cl/victimas/ (accessed 2 July 2025). See also Mendieta 2024 for a similar feature in the Paraguayan case.

22 Gatti 2011, 527.

important political agents, but also political opponents of the oligarchies that supported and maintained the Latin American dictatorships, as well as their international allies. Although they were political opponents institutionally organised in social movements and political parties, they were not described as such, but as terrorists, insurgents, subversives or traitors.[23] They were presented as imaginary enemies in an imaginary war.

2. Normative and political significance of enforced disappearances

From a legal perspective, enforced disappearance encompasses many well-known crimes, such as illegal detention, kidnapping, murder, torture, rape, obstruction of justice, judicial misconduct, and so on.[24] But the practice also entails harms that cannot be conveyed by simply adding up all the harms associated with this set of crimes, and certainly not by their legal definition.[25] Therefore, rather than focusing on the harms contained in all of the singular traditional crimes committed in this practice, I would like to consider what additional harms are imposed by enforced disappearance as a form of political violence. To do so, I would like to start by highlighting some of the characteristics of enforced disappearance as a crime.[26]

Firstly, enforced disappearance is a 'concentric' type of crime, in the sense that its target is not only the person who is disappeared by state

23 Unlike the 'transnational disappeared,' the 'modelic disappeared' were often members of political and intellectual groups who had ties with international organizations, creating with time an international awareness that would put pressure against the practice and would later give raise to the broader 'Transnational Disappeared.' In Gatti's view, this practice is an expression of modernity and civilization attempting to weed out that which risk it, in this case, the product of civilization itself: the civilized individual. Gatti 2014, 28 et seq.

24 As defined by the International Convention for the Protection of All Persons against Enforced Disappearance, the practice consists of the 'arrest, detention, abduction or any other form of deprivation of liberty by agents of the State or by persons or groups of persons acting with the authorization, support or acquiescence of the State, followed by a refusal to acknowledge the deprivation of liberty or by concealment of the fate or whereabouts of the disappeared person, which place such a person outside the protection of the law.'

25 According to Bargu 2014, enforced disappearances are 'agglutinative' in the sense that they entail the violation of many different rights and the commission of many different crimes simultaneously. However, as a distinct legal figure, it conveys normative and factual features that go beyond the sum of its parts.

26 Bargu 2014.

agents, but also his or her family and the public at large, who are diminished, intimidated and demobilised by this event. This is now explicitly recognised in the literature, but also in Article 24 of the International Convention for the Protection of All Persons from Enforced Disappearance.[27]

Secondly, beyond the immediate harms of enforced disappearance, this crime also imposes a 'harm without end' through an element of uncertainty and a systematic and institutionalised refusal to acknowledge and redress the harm. As I will argue in more detail later, enforced disappearance profoundly and indefinitely disrupts not only the lives of the disappeared, but also the lives of their relatives and political communities at large. Relatives are unable to mourn or exercise many of their rights and communities are unable to rebuild a genuine form of democratic life.

Thirdly, the aim of enforced disappearance as a state practice is to erase the person, in the sense of completely erasing his or her existence not only from the future but also from the past, as if he or she had never existed: to erase the person as well as the memory of the person and the symbols that signal his or her existence. In this way, existence is taken away from the *desaparecido* and from all those who had valued relationships with them.[28]

Fourthly, as mentioned above, the agent is the state, either directly or through unofficial agents, and the victim is always perceived as a political opponent, who is then presented to the public as an enemy of the state, a traitor or a terrorist. The 'modelic disappeared' is thus essentially a victim of political violence, whose sacrifice is instrumental to the constitution of state or public power.

On the basis of these general characteristics, we can present the practice as having two dimensions of normative significance which I explore in the next sections. On the one hand, it is a practice that destroys someone and something of value, deeply violating many individual rights of the disappeared as well as their families and social circles. On the other hand, it is a strategic practice because it aims at constituting something new that harms the collective by reinterpreting the limits and scope of power and political and civil rights.

---

27 According to article 24(1), the victim of the crime of enforced disappereance is the disappeared as well as 'any individual who has suffered harm as the direct result of an enforced disappearance.' See also Fulton 2014, 774.

28 Bargu 2014, 61-63.

2.1 The destructive dimension of enforced disappearance

As Gabriel Gatti has argued, enforced disappearances sever identities by literally and effectively disembodying the subject: bodies are severed from their identities. This rupture is expressed in the appearance of bodies without identities and identities without bodies. He presents this meaning as a rupture, a catastrophe.[29] The disappearance creates a rupture of meaning that prevents us both from grieving and from living in a world that makes sense; a world that we can explain with the language we know. But what does it mean to say that disappearances create a rupture in understanding the world and how is this a harm?

Gatti's description of the difficulty that disappearances create in understanding and explaining the world is, in my view, part of the explicit purpose of this crime. Law operates through abstract rules, but it regulates a concrete reality, the concrete reality of legal subjects or entities. The person, or the individual, is a legal entity embodied in a material body with an identity; without a body, the law can no longer fully recognize the individual as its subject. Neither alive nor dead, the two modes of existence we know in political life, a disappeared person's existence becomes an interrogation mark. In this way, the abduction creates a vacuum not only around the existence of a person, but also around justice. Because if the person's existence is placed in this nebulous space, impunity is easily secured for state agents and for the civilians who supported these regimes.

So, from a practical point of view, making an event inexplicable or inaccessible to language is a way of making it immune to the reach of the law. Without the body, the victim's legal identity begins to recede, her very existence as a legal subject is placed in limbo, and the more nebulous the victim becomes, the more nebulous her perpetrator and his responsibility also become.

This separation of identity and existence also affects the social relations of the disappeared, those who remain in a seemingly full existence, but

29 'It is not a trauma that interrupts normality, not a lasting trauma that harms the normal but can be overcome because there are institutions for it; neither is it a disruptive, intense, and tremendous but brief event, like an earthquake or a tsunami. These all have in common the separation of meaning from fact, but in a catastrophe that separation is neither overcome – because there is nothing to overcome it with – nor does it end – because it is permanent. It is the disarticulation of words from things, of meanings from facts, a disarticulation turned into structure.' (Gatti 2014, 16).

who can no longer understand the existence that is officially recognised over them. A mother is cut off from her motherhood because her child is suddenly taken from physical existence, but this fact is officially denied. Disappearance thus creates childless mothers and fathers, married women without husbands who are not widows, and children without parents who are not orphans. But while the individual *desaparecido* can be effectively erased as an embodied entity, his or her identity can't be effectively severed to the extent that it affects the identity of others who resist the attempted severance and the new identity offered to them. Mothers and wives are the emblem of this resistance. This resistance is expressed through legal actions as well as through performances that signal the reality of their relationship and the existence of their *desaparecidos*, demanding the truth and also helping to create a collective memory. A notable example is the 'lonely cueca', a couple's dance performed alone by the wives, mothers and daughters of Chilean *desaparecidos*. The white scarf worn by the mothers and grandmothers of the Plaza de Mayo also has this meaning. It is a shawl that was originally made with the old-fashioned cloth used for nappies, which allowed them to recognise each other through their broken but resilient motherhood.

These acts of resistance make visible the violence and the horror they have suffered, but also the rejection of this severed identity, imposed by the dictatorships and maintained by the institutions of transitional and democratic justice. And while the acts of resistance frustrate the completion of the total disappearance, their impotence against the military pact of silence also shows the extent of the damage caused.

In the aftermath of the abduction, the close relatives of the disappeared have not only faced extreme suffering and anxiety, but have also been deprived of the opportunity to grieve. If, under normal circumstances, the passage of time can facilitate the grieving process, this is not the case here. The passage of time seems to have the opposite effect, as lack of information, lack of recognition and systematic impunity keep the disappeared in 'an eternally provisional status.'[30] The status is not only provisional but also unsituated: not only is there no body, but there is no place and no time to consider as a space for mourning. In this lack of certainty, no funeral rites can be performed. Mourning is also problematic for the relatives of the disappeared because it forces them to presume death despite the lack of

30 Bourguignon 2021, 14.

evidence and some argue that this creates feelings of guilt or betrayal. Some even describe this dilemma as placing relatives in the position of being responsible for the death of the disappeared if they declare them dead.[31] If they give up on their search for justice, they may even perceive themselves as abandoning the *desaparecidos*.[32]

The pain of losing their loved ones in this space of uncertainty is later accompanied by the pain and powerlessness of the denial of information and justice by the institutions on which they once relied. This pain also does not diminish with time, but reproduces itself every day in every encounter the victims have with legal and political institutions and in the searches in which they have invested almost all their time and energy for years and even decades.[33]

The relatives of the disappeared suffered many other, perhaps secondary, kinds of harms. Many faced financial problems, as most of the victims were the breadwinners of the family unit. Many relatives of the disappeared suffered rupture with their social and extended family circle, they were shunned away by their communities and in many cases they were seen as 'dangerous.'[34] As a consequence, they had to create a whole new life, with new relationships that could understand and accompany them in their predicament.[35] Many correlate this experience with symptoms of depression and post-traumatic stress disorder.[36]

In sum, as an instance of destructive state violence, enforced disappearance is an erasing violence that questions identity by separating it from the body, from the law and from social relations.[37] The identity of the disappeared and its relations are severed by erasing the symbols that signal the legal existence of an individual: the body, whether alive or dead. The disappeared are neither here with the living nor in the past with the dead. Nothing signals their existence except the persistent resistance of those who remember them and search for them but cannot speak of them in the words that used to make up their world. Therefore, a new status had to be created to signal their existence and to resist the erasing violence, namely the status of the disappeared, which carries with it infinite suffering.

---

31 A review of these experiences can be found in Bourguignon 2021, 18.
32 Bourguignon 2021, 27.
33 Adams 2019, 346 et seq.
34 Bourguignon 2021, 21.
35 Adams 2019, 345, 350–2. Bourguignon 2021, 20.
36 Bourguignon 2021, 20.
37 Bargu 2014, 44.

2.2 Enforced disappearance as a constitutive political ritual

The rationale for this series of behaviours that constitute the practice of enforced disappearance was most obviously the suppression of political opposition by getting rid of political opponents in a way that would ensure impunity. However, beyond the constitution of power through the immediate neutralisation and demobilisation of the political opposition, something else is being conceived here. The practice was also very explicitely aimed at creating fear to demobilise the political community and perhaps forget the political projects and views that the disappeared stand for. This paralysing fear is created by exploiting the tension between visibility and invisibility. Everyone knows or hears that people are 'disappeared', but few know for sure, many doubt, and no one knows exactly 'when, how, who or how many' are disappeared and what happens to them after their abduction.[38]

As I mentioned earlier, in the Southern Cone of Latin America, disappearances were targeted against political opponents who were not presented as such. There was a discourse of internal or even regional war in which the disappeared were presented as an enemy of the nation or nations waging that war: a terrorist, subversive or even a traitor. This discourse is important because it created a context of exceptionality and emergency, with almost no normative standards for state action, and helped to shift responsibility for violence from state agents to the victims. Tortures, executions and disappearances appeared as a kind of sublimation of the victims' own fate, brought about by their own decision to betray the nation. The disappeared had thus chosen to disappear by going against the very existence of the nation, but also against the role that the individuals they represented (young, male, low-income workers) were expected to play in the political life of their community. This discourse and the secrecy in which disappearances were carried out allowed the dictatorships to maintain an alliance with the civilian elites, because in order to present the alliance between the military and the anti-democratic elites as saviours from our enemies they could not appear as ruthless murderers.[39] Enforced disappearances were

38 This idea is taken from Bargu 2014.

39 Zalaquett: 'That was the feeling among the military. In their view, the younger, the more intellectually prepared, and the more militant, the worse. Such opponents were seen as irredeemable. Yet, because society would not accept a 'parade of coffins,' the rulers felt they had to kill those deemed as dangerous opponents and bury them in secrecy, thinking that eventually their relatives would forget'.

thus a method by which dictatorships could impose a new order by force and still present it as a salvation or even a civilising process.

The constitutive dimension of this violence was the imposition of a totalitarian political arrangement between the state and its subjects, especially those represented by the disappeared (low-income workers and leftist political agents). The whole discourse of war and rescue was obviously false and did not stand the test of time, as there was no real struggle in the execution of the arrests. As explained above, the alleged 'enemies' were usually taken from their homes in the middle of the night, or from their workplaces, universities or streets, often by a group of people dressed as civilians, but who were obviously agents of the state secret police. The fact that the detainees were later summarily executed and, in most cases, disappeared, shows that they were not an enemy to be fought in defence of a sovereign power, but rather sacrificial figures to be purged from society in order to give birth to a new kind of sovereign, i.e. an absolute one, as well as a new kind of citizen, i.e. a subject with limited political agency.

Enforced disappearances attempt to reduce fully active political agents to non-existence and in doing so the new sovereign signals that it is its own prerogative to determine who exists and who does not. Where people can be disappeared in this way, sovereignty no longer resides in the individual, the citizen, the people. And this is signaled by the very fact that identity is now something that can only be taken and given by the sovereign, who thus has primary and total power over the individual. This is not exactly the power of life and death that Foucault identified as pre-modern sovereign power.[40] What is taken and given are identities and relations that give historical meaning to our existence because they go beyond life and death. The message is that the militant, the son, the husband, the wife and the daughter existed through the sovereign and because of the sovereign. As a traitor, he or she will no longer exist, not even in the identity he or she once had. Instead, he or she is erased and placed in the temporary limbo discussed in the previous sections.

It is important to note that seeing enforced disappearances as instrumental in the constitution of an authoritarian political arrangement with limited political agency for certain groups explains why the 'return to democracy' was not able to undo this political configuration by itself. In order to fully restore democratic political relations, the state had to recognise the disappeared, search for them and restore the rights of the groups they

40 Foucault 1978 (1990), 135–40.

represented and their families. This has not yet happened properly in many countries in the region.

3. Conclusion

José Zalaquett argued that the normative evolution in Latin America has been a victory for human rights, proving the generals who developed the strategy of disappearances completely wrong. Once they were out of power, their thesis that 'the end justifies the means' did not stand up to the tenacity of the mothers, who pushed for the development of a legal architecture that shattered their expectations of impunity. But how far have we come in repairing the damage caused by enforced disappearances? Thinking about this crime in terms of the two dimensions of meaning considered above, i.e. the destruction of identities and the constitution of a new kind of sovereign and a new kind of citizen, sheds some light on the question of how we should respond to these events and how far we have come in this endeavour.

The destructive dimension, understood as the severing of identities and the profound disruption of the ability to understand the world of the relatives of the disappeared, suggests that a refusal to search and a refusal to provide information should be more central to the regulation of this crime. In this way, we recognise that the victims are not only the disappeared, but also those who remain. It also speaks to the importance of truth and the legal recognition of a specific status of the *desaparecido*, allowing victims to exercise their rights and mourn without feelings of guilt or betrayal.[41]

The constitutive dimension of enforced disappearance explains why an official policy of search is so important. The relevant search is not primarily or exclusively the search for the body. We will probably never find most of them, but we must still search and try to reconstruct the history of the person after his or her abduction. By searching and trying to know more, the state redefines itself and restores the democratic political relationship: it recognises that it cannot do what it has tried to do, i.e. erase or redefine identities. By searching, it restores the right of individuals to be recognised for who they are: mothers as mothers, wives as wives, daughters as daughters. The search is a way, perhaps a new way, of signaling someone's existence when the body, alive or dead, is no longer there. Whether and how

41 See in this sense, Luci 2024, 182–4 and Fulton 2014, 783–6.

national criminal law could or should give a more central role to the duty to search is a question for another day.

It is possible that the political and normative meanings of the practice that I have described by considering the Latin American case will speak to phenomena that have occurred and continue to occur elsewhere.[42] This quest for erasure is not, of course, a phenomenon peculiar to Latin America; many modern authoritarian powers are based on actions and ideologies that seek to erase certain identities, groups, or even entire nations, both spatially and historically.[43] In erasing their political opponents, Latin American dictators also created something, a new political configuration. This new political configuration was not sustainable over time, but it will only be fully undone when the disappeared are brought back into legal existence, both through formal recognition and material efforts to recover their bodies and their post-abduction trajectories.

Bibliography

Adams, Jacqueline. 2019. ''Enforced disappearance: Family members' experiences'. *Human Rights Review*. 20.3. 335–60.

Arendt, Hannah. 2019. *The human condition*. Chicago: University of Chicago Press.

Banu, Bargu. 2014. 'Sovereignty as Erasure: Rethinking Enforced Disappearances.' *Qui Parle*. 23.1. 35–75. URL: https://doi.org/10.5250/quiparle.23.1.0035 (accessed 2 July 2025).

Bianchi, Maria Giovanna and Luci, Monica (eds.). 2024. *Psychoanalytic, Psychosocial, and Human Rights Perspectives on Enforced Disappearance*. New York/Abingdon: Routledge.

Bourguignon, Manon, Dermitzel, Alice and Katz, Muriel. 2021. 'Grief among relatives of disappeared persons in the context of state violence: An impossible process?'. *Torture Journal*. 31.2. 14–33.

Cárdenas, Claudia et al. (eds.). 2025. *Transitional Justice and the Criminal Responsibility of Judges*. New York/Abingdon: Routledge (forthcoming).

Chwastiak, Michele. 2015. 'Commodifying state crime: Accounting and 'extraordinary rendition''. *Critical Perspectives on Accounting*. 28. 1–12.

42 Though a case can be made that the international regulation of enforced disappearances does the best it can to give recognition to the human pains that are entailed by these practices.

43 The attempt to erase Palestine's historical and geographical existence is perhaps the most emblematic example of this desire to erase today. Sadly, however, this is not the only example of this phenomenon that can be found in the present day.

CONADEP. 1984. *Nunca Más*. San Francisco/ Buenos Aires: Edueba. URL: https://www.cultura.gob.ar/media/uploads/lc_nuncamas_digital1.pdf (accessed 2 July 2025).

Crenzel, Emilio. 2024. '¿Cuántos son los desaparecidos y cuantas las víctimas de la desaparición forzada en la Argentina? Debates político-memoriales e investigación académica'. *Latin American Research Review*. 59.4. 948–64.

Diaz, Paola. 2022. 'Love the world, love our loved ones: Personal and public experience of political disappearance in Chile'. *Violence: An International Journal*. 3.2. 199–217.

Duhaime, Bernard. 2023. 'Enforced disappearances in the contemporary world: The recent contributions of the United Nations Working Group on Enforced or Involuntary Disappearances'. In Bianchi, Maria Giovanna and Luci, Monica (eds.). *Psychoanalytic, Psychosocial, and Human Rights Perspectives on Enforced Disappearance*. 19–35. New York/ Abingdon: Routledge.

Dulitzky, Ariel. 2019. 'The Latin-American Flavor of Enforced Disappearances'. *Chicago Journal of International Law*. 19.2. 423–89.

Eghbariah, Rabea. 2024. 'Toward Nakba as a Legal Concept'. *Columbia Law Review*. 124.4. 887–992.

Foucault, Michel. 1990 (1978). *The history of sexuality*. vol. 1. New York: Vintage Books.

Frey, Barbara A. 2009. 'Los Desaparecidos: The Latin American Experience as a Narrative Framework for the International Norm against Enforced Disappearances' *Hispanic Issues On Line*.5. 52–72.

Fulton, Sarah. 2014. 'Redress for Enforced Disappearance: Why Financial Compensation is not Enough'. *Journal of International Criminal Justice*. 12.4. 769–86.

Gatti, Gabriel. 2011. 'De un continente al otro: el desaparecido transnacional, la cultura humanitaria y las víctimas totales en tiempos de guerra global'. *Política y sociedad*. 48.3. 519–36.

Gatti, Gabriel. 2014. Surviving forced disappearances in Argentina and Uruguay. London: Palgrave Macmillan.

Lorca, Rocío. 2024. 'Should Feminists be Worried about Impunity?'. *Harvard Human Rights Journal*. 37. 47–79.

Luci, Monica. 2024. Tortured and disappeared bodies. The problem of knowing. In Bianchi, Maria Giovanna and Luci, Monica (eds.). *Psychoanalytic, Psychosocial, and Human Rights Perspectives on Enforced Disappearance*. New York/ Abingdon: Routledge. 171–87.

Mendieta, Maximiliano, Velaztiquí, Alina and Franco, Shirley (eds.). 2024. 'Desapariciones forzadas y ejecuciones extrajudiciales durante la dictadura de Alfredo Stroessner'. *Revista Internacional de Investigación en Ciencias Sociales*. 20.1. 103–20.

Sikkink, Kathryn and Lutz, Ellen. 2001. 'The justice cascade: The evolution and impact of foreign human rights trials in Latin America'. *Chicago Journal of International Law*. 2.1. 1–33.

Zalaquett, José. 2011. 'The Emergence of 'Disappearances' as a Normative Issue'. In Booth Walling, Carrie and Waltz, Susan (eds.). *Human Rights: From Practice to Policy*. Ann Arbor, Michigan: University of Michigan.

List of Contributors

Claudia Marcela Cárdenas Aravena is Associate Professor at the Law Faculty of the Universidad de Chile.

Javier Contesse is Associate Professor at the Law Faculty of the Universidad de Chile.

Kai Cornelius is Professor at the Law Faculty of the Universität Hamburg (Germany) and Judge at the Higher Regional Court in Hamburg.

Leandro Dias is Postdoctoral Fellow at the Law Faculty of the Julius-Maximilians-Universität Würzburg (Germany).

Aziz Epik is Professor at the Law Faculty of the Universität Hamburg (Germany).

Julia Geneuss is Professor at the Law Faculty of the Universität Potsdam (Germany).

Florian Jeßberger is Professor at the Law Faculty of the Humboldt-Universität zu Berlin (Germany).

Gerhard Kemp is Professor at the Law Department of the University of the West of England Bristol (UK).

Milan Kuhli is Professor at the Law Faculty of the Universität Hamburg (Germany) and Judge at the Higher Regional Court in Hamburg.

Rocío Lorca is Associate Professor at the Law Faculty of the Universidad de Chile.

Juan Pablo Mañalich is Professor in the Department of Criminal Sciences at the Law Faculty of the Universidad de Chile.

Antonio Martins is Professor at the Universidade do Estado do Rio de Janeiro (Brazil) and Professor at Brazil's Universidade Federal do Rio de Janeiro.

Maximilian Murck is Coordinator of the Human Identification Programme at the United Nations Population Fund (UNFPA) Mexico.

Denys Shylin is Associate Professor at the Department of Criminal Procedure, Detective and Search Activities of the Odessa Law Academy (Ukraine).

Burcu Yaşar is Doctoral Candidate at the Universität Hamburg (Germany).

Rocío Yoguez is Adviser to the Human Identification Programme at the United Nations Population Fund (UNFPA) Mexico.